# Lebanese Arabic Voices

Authentic Listening and Reading
Practice in Levantine Colloquial Arabic

lingualism

© 2024 by Matthew Aldrich

The author's moral rights have been asserted.
All rights reserved. No part of this document may be reproduced or transmitted in any form or by any means, electronic, mechanical, photocopying, recording, or otherwise, without prior written permission of the publisher.

ISBN: 978-1-949650-99-0

website: www.lingualism.com

email: contact@lingualism.com

# Table of Contents

**Introduction** ................................................................................................ iv
    How can this book help me? ........................................................................ iv
    Can I benefit from this book at my level of Arabic? .................................... iv

  *How to Use This Book* ................................................................................. v

  *The Texts and Translations* ........................................................................ vii
    Lines .......................................................................................................... vii
    Translations ............................................................................................... vii
    Fillers ........................................................................................................ vii

**Introductions** ............................................................................................. 1
  *Charbel's Introduction* ................................................................................ 1
  *Nisrine's Introduction* ................................................................................. 6
  *Waleed's Introduction* ............................................................................... 10
  *Rita's Introduction* .................................................................................... 14
  *Mohammad's Introduction* ....................................................................... 19
  *Sandy's Introduction* ................................................................................ 23

**Daily Routines** .......................................................................................... 28
  *Charbel's Daily Routine* ............................................................................ 28
  *Rita's Daily Routine* .................................................................................. 32
  *Sandy's Daily Routine* .............................................................................. 37

**Childhood Memories** ............................................................................... 41
  *Charbel's Childhood Memory* ................................................................... 41
  *Nisrine's Childhood Memory* .................................................................... 45
  *Mohammad's Childhood Memory* ............................................................ 50

**Vacations** ................................................................................................. 55
  *Nisrine's Vacation* ..................................................................................... 55
  *Waleed's Vacation* .................................................................................... 59
  *Rita's Vacation* ......................................................................................... 64

## Hobbies ........................................................................................................... 70

*Waleed's Hobbies* .......................................................................................... 70

*Mohammad's Hobbies* ................................................................................... 75

*Sandy's Hobbies* ............................................................................................ 79

## Culture .............................................................................................. 83

*Charbel: Dabke* ............................................................................................. 83

*Nisrine: Festivals* ........................................................................................... 87

*Waleed: The Book Fair* .................................................................................. 91

*Rita: Lebanese Food* ..................................................................................... 95

*Mohammad: The Arabic Language* ............................................................. 100

*Sandy: Lebanese Cinema* ............................................................................ 104

## Social Issues ................................................................................. 109

*Charbel: The Beirut Explosion* .................................................................... 109

*Nisrine: The Economic Crisis* ...................................................................... 113

*Waleed: Electricity in Lebanon* ................................................................... 117

*Rita: Religion in Lebanon* ........................................................................... 122

*Mohammad: Corruption and Favoritism in Lebanon* .................................. 127

*Sandy: Employment in Lebanon* ................................................................. 131

## Free Topics .................................................................................... 136

*Charbel: The Oud* ........................................................................................ 136

*Nisrine: My Job* ........................................................................................... 140

*Waleed: My Military Service* ...................................................................... 144

*Rita: Lebanese Abroad* ............................................................................... 149

*Mohammad: Personal Growth* .................................................................... 154

*Sandy: The Lebanese Music Scene* ............................................................. 158

شَرْبِل
Charbel

| | |
|---|---|
| Introduction | 1 |
| Daily Routine | 28 |
| Childhood Memory | 41 |
| Culture | 83 |
| Social Issue | 109 |
| Free Topic | 136 |

نِسْرين
Nisrine

| | |
|---|---|
| Introduction | 6 |
| Childhood Memory | 45 |
| Vacation | 55 |
| Culture | 87 |
| Social Issue | 113 |
| Free Topic | 140 |

ريتا
Rita

| | |
|---|---|
| Introduction | 14 |
| Daily Routine | 32 |
| Vacation | 64 |
| Culture | 95 |
| Social Issue | 122 |
| Free Topic | 149 |

وَليد
Waleed

| | |
|---|---|
| Introduction | 10 |
| Vacation | 59 |
| Hobby | 70 |
| Culture | 91 |
| Social Issue | 117 |
| Free Topic | 144 |

مْحمَّد
Mohammad

| | |
|---|---|
| Introduction | 19 |
| Childhood Memory | 50 |
| Hobby | 75 |
| Culture | 100 |
| Social Issue | 127 |
| Free Topic | 154 |

ساْندي
Sandy

| | |
|---|---|
| Introduction | 23 |
| Daily Routine | 37 |
| Hobby | 79 |
| Culture | 104 |
| Social Issue | 131 |
| Free Topic | 158 |

# Introduction

**Lebanese Arabic Voices** is designed to help you improve your comprehension of Levantine Colloquial Arabic by using its audio component (available as free, downloadable MP3s from **www.lingualism.com/audio**) alongside the guided exercises in the book.

Six native speakers from around Lebanon and abroad have each contributed six *audio essays* on various topics, which in total make up the 36 segments found in this book. The contributors spoke naturally and spontaneously without reading prepared texts. The audio essays were then transcribed in Arabic script with diacritics (tashkeel) and translated into English. Studying these texts is a unique opportunity to better understand the patterns, usage, and idiosyncrasies of Arabic as spoken by Lebanese today.

## How can this book help me?

You will hear the speakers in Lebanese Arabic Voices occasionally make what you are sure are mistakes; you're likely right. Words may be mispronounced or misused; grammatical rules may not always be followed; sentences may be left unfinished if the speaker decides to rephrase what they are saying. This poses an extra challenge for listening. However, it is also very insightful to hear natural, spoken Arabic at various speeds by several native speakers. Unfortunately, this is something most coursebooks lack, in favor of carefully prepared, unnaturally slow, flawless speech. **It is hoped that Lebanese Arabic Voices fills that gap and provides some refreshingly natural, challenging opportunities for improving listening skills.**

## Can I benefit from this book at my level of Arabic?

This book is best suited for intermediate and more advanced learners who have some knowledge of Levantine Arabic, or at least, Modern Standard Arabic. However, even lower-level students can reap some benefits from listening to and studying the segments. Just keep in mind that the goal is ***not*** to understand 100%. The first time you listen, depending on your level, you may understand, say, 1%, 10%, 50%, or 90% of what you hear in a segment. If, after going through the exercises and studying the text while relistening several times, you are able to increase the percentage you can understand, you've made progress and are successfully developing your skills and pushing your level up. If this mindset is adopted, the materials in Lebanese Arabic Voices can be useful to learners at a wide range of levels.

# How to Use This Book

To get the most out of this book, you need to exercise a bit of **discipline**—discipline to resist reading the texts and their translations before you have thoroughly studied the listenings. This cannot be emphasized enough. Once you have read the texts and translations, the dynamics of what you can obtain from listening to the segments changes fundamentally. You should first listen to a segment *several* times while working your way through the exercises in the book. These have been designed to help you first understand the gist and gradually discover details as you relisten. Only once you have come to understand as much as you can through the exercises should you move on to study the text and translation that follow. This approach will result in maximum efficiency in improving your listening skills. A step-by-step guideline follows.

1. **CHOOSE A SEGMENT TO STUDY:** The segments can be studied in any order. The MP3s that accompany Lebanese Arabic Voices are available as free downloads at **www.lingualism.com/audio**, where you can also stream the audio directly.
2. **TITLE AND KEYWORDS:** *Before you listen the first time, be sure to read the title of the segment and study the keywords.* Going into a listening "blind"—without having any context, without even knowing the topic—makes listening comprehension in a foreign language extremely difficult. Just by knowing the general topic, we are able to improve the amount we can understand, as we are able to draw on knowledge from our past experiences, anticipate what might be said, recognize known words, and guess new words and phrases.
3. **MAIN IDEA:** *Now, determine the "Main Idea" from among the four choices.* If you are not fairly confident that you know the main idea, listen one more time to narrow down your choices by process of elimination. Once you are confident you have determined the main idea of the segment, check your answer. (Answers for the exercises are found at the end of each segment.) If you were incorrect, listen one more time with the main idea in mind.
4. **TRUE OR FALSE:** *Answer the "True or False" questions.* (Do not read ahead to the multiple-choice questions as some of these questions themselves may answer the true-or-false questions.) If you feel unsure of any of your answers, listen to the segment again before checking your answers. You will notice that a small number follows most of the answers in the answer key. These numbers correspond to the line number in the text and translation that reveals the answer. If you do not understand why you got an answer wrong, quickly look at the text and/or translation for that line number. (Here's where you have to use your self-discipline *not* to read beyond the specified line number!) Listen again and place a check next to each true-or-false question as you hear the answer.
5. **MULTIPLE CHOICE:** *Answer the "Multiple Choice" questions.* Follow the same guidelines as for the true-or-false questions. Note that both the true-or-false and multiple-choice questions are based on information found in the segment, according to the information provided by the speaker, regardless of the accuracy of the information. You can think of each question as being preceded by "According to _the speaker_ ..." or "_The speaker_ mentions that...". Assume that the time of speaking is the present. That is, if a question asks, "Is she still in Beirut?" it means as of the time she recorded the segment.
6. **MATCHING:** *Match the Arabic words and phrases to their English translations.* You will learn by spending time playing with the words, so don't look up the answers too quickly. Try

finding matches through educated guesses and by process of elimination. After you have matched the words and checked your answers, listen again while you check off the words as you hear them. The vocabulary in the matching exercises focuses mostly on high-frequency adverbs, connectors, and phrases. Such words are frequently heard in spoken language and are vital for connecting ideas to produce natural speech.

7. **TEXT AND TRANSLATION:** Now that you have worked your way through the exercises and have managed to pick up more of what has been said, you can feel free to move on to study the text and translation for the segment. This part is more *freestyle*. Depending on your level of Arabic and level of comfort with the text, you can approach this in several ways. For instance, you can cover the Arabic side and first read the translation; then, try to translate the English back into Arabic based on what you remember. Also, you can simply try to brainstorm some possible Arabic equivalents for the words or phrases in the English translation; then, check the Arabic side and see how it was actually said. Conversely, you can cover the English side first and relisten while you read along with the Arabic, perhaps pausing the audio to repeat each line aloud. In any case, the side-by-side arrangement of the Arabic text and its English translation allows you to cover one side and test yourself in various ways. You should be able to match up most words and phrases with their equivalents in English. You may want to highlight useful and interesting vocabulary and phrases you want to learn.

8. **VOCABULARY:** Vocabulary exercises follow the text and translation in the first half of the book. These exercises focus on content words—mostly nouns, verbs, and adjectives. The vocabulary that an intermediate learner already knows and that which they need to learn will vary greatly from person to person. Each exercise draws your attention to some interesting vocabulary items found in the text. Each item is followed by a reference to the line number where the answer can be found. You are also encouraged to continue to discover additional useful vocabulary—both words and phrases—which you can write in your own notebook.)

9. **LISTEN AGAIN:** Try listening again later to the segments you have already studied. You will find that you can understand more and with more ease the following day. (Studies have shown that material learned is consolidated and organized in the brain during sleep.)

Visit **www.lingualism.com/audio**, **where you can find the free accompanying audio to download or stream (at variable playback rates).**

# The Texts and Translations

## Lines
The text and translation for each segment have been divided into numbered "lines," which are not necessarily complete sentences or even clauses but are manageable chunks that can be studied.

## Translations
Good style has, at times, been sacrificed in favor of direct translations so that Arabic words and phrases can easily be matched up to their English equivalents. You are encouraged to think of alternative ways lines could be translated into English.

## Fillers
Fillers, which are used to signal that the speaker is thinking of what to say next, are a common and natural part of spoken language. To avoid cluttering the text, uh… (الله...) and um… (امم...) are not written. Words that function as fillers are always written but are often left untranslated, as they do not add substantial meaning to the sentence. يَعْني is the most common filler in Levantine Arabic and could translate as *that is* or *you know*.

Another trait of spoken discourse is that the speaker may misspeak, then back up to correct himself or herself. Also, a speaker may decide to rephrase a sentence, or simply not finish it. These are all marked with ellipses (...) so that you can easily see that the *word* you didn't catch is, in fact, not a complete word at all or is an unfinished thought. These ellipses are meant to aid you in deciphering the listening. However, when you are reading for meaning, anything before an ellipsis can be ignored.

# Introductions

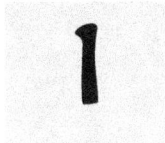

## Charbel's Introduction

### Keywords

مْجوّز married    ضَيْعة village    مسيحي Christian

### Main Idea

a. Charbel is a 32-year-old married man who works in a company and loves music.
b. Charbel is a 43-year-old single man who lives with his dog, Dora, and works as a professor in Beirut.
c. Charbel is a divorced man who loves sports and lives with his parents in a small village.
d. Charbel is a Marionite Christian monk who loves traveling and lives in Qannoubine Valley.

### True or False

1. Charbel is from a large city in Lebanon.
2. Charbel is from a large city in Lebanon.
3. Charbel completed his Masters in MBA at a university outside Lebanon.
4. Charbel has a deep interest in music and plays the oud.
5. Charbel pursued a degree in Business Computing and also completed a Masters in MBA at USEK.

### Multiple Choice

1. Regarding his family, Charbel mentioned that:
   a. his parents are from different villages
   b. both his brother and sister are married with children
   c. he has no siblings
   d. none of the above

2. In his free time, Charbel likes to ____.
   a. play music   b. travel   c. go to the village   d. all of the above

3. Why is the Qannoubine Valley significant according to Charbel?
   a. It is famous for its natural beauty and wildlife.
   b. The valley is known for its historical significance to Lebanese culture.
   c. The valley is a popular tourist destination for its hot springs.
   d. It was a hiding place for Maronite Christian monks during times of persecution.

# Matching

| | |
|---|---|
| حدّ | at the same time |
| بسّ | because |
| بسّ | before |
| قبِل ما | besides that |
| هلّأ | both of them |
| غيْر هيْك | but |
| عَ | even if |
| بِذات الوَقِت | generally |
| هوْل | long ago |
| مبْدأيّاً | near |
| تْنيْناتُن | not only |
| هِنّي | now |
| لأِنّو | that's all |
| هاي هِيِّ | that's why |
| مِن زمان | there is/are |
| مِشان هيْك | they |
| في | those |
| مِش بسّ | to |
| حتّى إذا | when |

# Text

| | | |
|---|---|---|
| هاي، كيفْكُن؟ إسْمي شرْبِل. | 1 | Hi, how are you? My name is Charbel. |
| عُمْري تْنيْن وتْلاتين سِنة. | 2 | I am thirty-two years old. |
| مْجوّز، وعِنْدي صَبي. | 3 | Married, and I have a son. |
| خِلْقان بِضَيْعة صْغيْرة بِشْمال لِبْنان، إسْما مَزْرعِة النّهر. | 4 | Born in a small village in North Lebanon called Mazraat Al Nahr. |
| هيِّ ضَيْعة مِن قضاء زْغرْتا. | 5 | It's a village in the Zgharta District. |
| أنا مْواليد الواحْدة وتِسْعين. | 6 | I was born in 1991. |
| أنا مسيحي مارونِي. | 7 | I am a Maronite Christian. |
| رْبيت مِش بِالضَّيْعة، رْبيت مع أهْلي بِالدّوْرة، هيِّ مِنْطِقة بِبيْروت. | 8 | I didn't grow up in the village; I was raised with my family in Dora, an area of Beirut. |
| عِشِت كِلّ حَياتْنا هوْنيك. | 9 | I lived all our lives there. |
| تقْريباً الدّوْرة، هيِّ حدّ البحر، | 10 | Dora is near the sea, |
| وبسّ تْجوّزِت، نقلِت عَ مِنْطِقة تانْية إسْما بْصاليم. | 11 | but when I got married, I moved to another area called Bsalim. |
| درسِت بِمدْرسِةْ Sacré-Cœur (القلْب الأقْدس) بِالجِمَّيْزي بِبيْروت حدّ الدّاوْن تاوْن. | 12 | I studied at the Sacre-Coeur (the Sacred Heart) School in Gemmayze, Beirut, near downtown. |
| وبسّ خلّصِت مدْرسِة عْمِلِت بِالجّامْعة Business Computing. | 13 | After finishing school, I majored in Business Computing at university. |
| جامعْتي كان هيِّ الـ USEK بِالكسْليك، كسْليك جونْية. | 14 | My university was USEK in Kaslik, Kaslik Jounieh. |
| وشْتغلِت بسّ يَعْني... بسّ تقْريباً قبل ما إتْجوّز، عْمِلِت Masters بِالـ MBA كمان بِالـ USEK. | 15 | I worked, but before getting married, I did my Masters in MBA also at USEK. |
| أخدِت Masters بِالـ Management وأخدِت شهادِة من HEC Montréal كندا. | 16 | I got a master's in management and a certificate from HEC Montreal, Canada. |
| هلّأ بِشْتغِل بِشِرْكِة FMCG بِالـ Stock Control. | 17 | Now, I work in an FMCG company in stock (inventory) control. |
| كْتير بْحِبّ الموسيقى، بْحِبّ السْبور وبعْزُف على آلةْ العود. | 18 | I really love music; I love sports; and I play the oud. |
| غيْر هيْك، بْحِبّ كْتير أطْلع عَ الضَّيْعة وبْحِبّ لِبْنان. | 19 | Besides that, I really like to go to the village, and I love Lebanon. |

| | | |
|---|---|---|
| وبَذات الوَقِت بْحِبّ شوف بِلْدان تانْيِة ونْسافِر وإكْتِشِف بِلْدان تانْيِة وحضارات جْديدِة ودوق أكِل طيِّب غيْر بلد. | 20 | And at the same time, I like to see other countries, travel, discover other countries and new cultures, and taste delicious food from other countries. |
| كِنّا نْسافِر أنا ومرْتي تِقْريباً كِلّ سِنِة، | 21 | My wife and I used to travel almost every year, |
| بسّ هلّأ بِالْوَضِع بِلِبْنان مع الأزْمِة وخْبار كوروْنا وكِلّ القِصص اللي عم بِتْصير شْوَيِّة صارِت الأمور أصْعب. | 22 | but now, with the situation in Lebanon, the crisis, and the news about COVID and everything that's happening, things have become a bit harder. |
| انْشاالله الصّيْفية الجايِة تْكون أحْسن على لِبْنان. | 23 | God willing, next summer will be better for Lebanon. |
| وهوْل هِنّي مبْدأيّاً عنّي. | 24 | Those were some things about me in general. |
| و... أيْه، أنا عِنْدي خيّ وإخِت وتْنيْناتُن مْجوّزين وعِنْدُن وْلاد. | 25 | And yeah, I have a brother and a sister; both are married and have children. |
| وبِدّي... كِنِت بدّي قول إنّو بيّي وإمّي هِنّي كمان مِن نفْس الضّيْعة مِن مزْرعِة النّهِر. | 26 | And I want... I wanted to say that my father and mother are also from the same village, Mazraat Al Nahr. |
| سوْ usually بلِبْنان بيكون... إنّو ما ضروري يكونوا مِن نفْس الضّيْعة لَيِتْجوّزوا، | 27 | So usually, in Lebanon, it's not necessary for people to be from the same village to get married, |
| بسّ ساقِبِت ضَيْعِتْنا صْغيرِة وساقبوا أهْلي مِن ذات الضّيْعة. | 28 | but it happened that our village is small, and my parents are from the same village. |
| سوْ ما عِنْدي ضَيْعة تانْيِة عِنْدي ضَيْعة واحْدِة. | 29 | So, I only have one village. |
| لأنّو أنا مثلاً عِنْدي رْفِقات بيروحوا مثلاً عَ ضَيْعِة بيّن أوْ ضَيْعِة إمّن. | 30 | Because, for example, I have friends who go to their father's or mother's village. |
| سوْ هاي هيِّ. ضَيْعِتْنا كْتير حِلْوِة هيِّ على أوّل وادي المْقدّس بيقولولو وادي قنّوبين. | 31 | So, that's it. Our village is very beautiful. It's at the edge of the Holy Valley, which they call Qannoubine Valley. |
| هوّ... مِن زمان كان في كْتير رِهْبان الموارْنِة المسيحية كانوا يِتْخبّوا بِهَيْدا الوادي، مِشان هيْك سمّوه. | 32 | Long ago, many Maronite Christian monks used to hide in this valley. That's why it was named so. |
| وَقِت كانوا يِضْطهْدوا المسيحية قديماً كانوا هوْل الرِّهْبان يِتْخبّوا بِهَيْدا الوادي فيو كْتير مغاوِر ومِشان هيْك سمّوه الوادي المْقدّس. | 33 | In ancient times, when Christianity was persecuted, these monks used to hide in this valley, which has many caves, and that's why they named it the Holy Valley. |
| وبِالْمنْطِقة فوْق بِالشّمال في كْتير كنايِس وأديرة. | 34 | And in the area above, in the north, there are many churches and monasteries. |

|  |  |  |
|---|---|---|
| 35 | هلّأ مِش بسّ فوْق بِكِلّ لِبْنان هُوِّ يُعْتبر السِّياحة الدِّينية في كتير قَوية إنّ كان مسيحيّاً وَلّا إسْلاميّاً، | Well, not only in the north but all over Lebanon, religious tourism is very strong, whether for Christians or Muslims, |
| 36 | بسّ الأكْتر كان إنّو في بِالشُّمال الكنايِس والمعالِم الدِّينية. | but most of the religious landmarks and churches are in the north. |
| 37 | وحتّى إذا بدّك بِتْشوفوا القُصص الأثارية اللي كانِت مَوْجودِة مِن قبِل. | And even if you want, you can see the archaeological sites that have been there since then. |
| 38 | و... هوْل هِنّي. | And that's it. |

## Vocabulary

1. I was born in...[6] _____
2. to grow up[8] _____
3. to play [an instrument][18] _____
4. delicious[20] _____
5. crisis[22] _____

6. to happen that...[28] _____
7. valley[31] _____
8. monks[32] _____
9. caves[33] _____
10. north[34] _____

## Answers

**Main Idea:** a **True or False:** 1. F[4] 2. T[11] 3. F[16] 4. T[18] 5. T[13-15] **Multiple Choice:** 1. b[25] 2. c[18-20] 3. d[32-33] **Matching:** ع / to / بِذات besides that / غيْر هيْك now / هلّأ before / قبِل ما when / بسّ but / بسّ near / حدّ because / لِأنّو they / هِنّي both of them / تْنَيْناتُن generally / مبْدأيّاً those / هوْل at the same time / الوَقت not only / مِش بسّ there is/are / في that's why / مِشان هيْك long ago / مِن زمان that's all / هاي هيِّ even if / حتّى إذا **Vocabulary:** 1. أنا مْواليد 2. رِبي 3. عزف على 4. طيِّب 5. أزْمِة 6. ساقب 7. وادي 8. رِهْبان 9. مغاوِر 10. شْمال

# 2 Nisrine's Introduction

## Keywords

مُعَلِّمة teacher     هَنْدَسِة دِيكُور interior design

## Main Idea

a. The daily life and dynamics within Nisrine's family.
b. Nisrine's hobbies and leisure activities.
c. Nisrine's career and her aspirations in the field of interior design.
d. The characteristics and culture of Nisrine's hometown in northern Lebanon.

## True or False

1. Nisrine lives alone in a small apartment in Tikrit.
2. Nisrine's sister is studying mechanical engineering.
3. Nisrine teaches higher education subjects at a university.
4. Nisrine has always wanted to be a teacher since she was young.
5. Nisrine has expressed a desire to further her education in interior design by taking more courses.

## Multiple Choice

1. What does Nisrine aspire to do in the future regarding her career?

    a. Open her own school
    b. Work abroad in interior design
    c. Start a family business
    d. Become a full-time artist

2. Why is Nisrine not working in her field of interior design?

    a. There are very limited work opportunities in interior design in Lebanon.
    b. She prefers teaching over interior design.
    c. She has lost interest in interior design.
    d. She is furthering her studies in interior design.

3. Which of the following does Nisrine **not** mention?

    a. Her educational background in interior design
    b. Participating in local community events
    c. When she graduated from university
    d. Her current profession as a teacher

# Matching

| | |
|---|---|
| حاليّاً | but |
| بعْدو | considering that... |
| كْتير | currently |
| بسّ | especially |
| مع إنّو | even |
| بسّ | even though |
| خْصوصي | over time |
| بِحِكِم إنّو | really |
| مع الوَقِت | so |
| حتّى | still |
| فا | when |

# Text

1. مرْحبا، أنا نِسْرين.

   Hello! I am Nisrine.

2. أنا عمْري خمْسة وعِشْرين سِنة، أنا مِن لبْنان، مِن ضَيْعة إسْما تِكْريت عكّار، مَوْجودِة بشْمال لبْنان.

   I am twenty-five years old, from Lebanon, from a village called Tikrit in Akkar, located in northern Lebanon.

3. أنا حاليّاً ساكْنِة فيا.

   I am currently living there.

4. أنا درست interior design وتْخرّجِت مِن الجامْعة بِسِنةْ الألْفين وتِسِعْطعْش.

   I studied interior design and graduated from university in 2018.

5. أنا حاليّاً عزْبا وعايْشِة مع أهْلي بالبيْت.

   I am currently single and living with my family at home.

6. نحْنا بالبيْت عايْشين سبع أشْخاص:

   There are seven of us living in the house:

7. أنا وبيّي وإمّي، وإخْواتي التْلاتِة، وعمْتي عايْشِة معْنا، عمْتي كْبيرة بالعِمْر.

   Myself, my father, my mother, my three siblings, and my aunt, who is elderly.

8. عِنْدي إخِت بِنِت وخيّان صبـ... خيّان شباب.

   I have a sister and two... two brothers.

9. إخْتي بْتِدْرُس أوّل سِنة جامْعة برمْجةْ كومْبْيوتِر، خيّي مْهنْدِس ميكانيك وخيّي الصِّغير بعْدو بالمدْرسِة.

   My sister is studying computer programming in her first year of university; one of my brothers is a mechanical engineer, and the younger brother is still in school.

10. إمّي بْتِشْتِغِل مْعلّمِة وبيّي بْيِشْتِغِل تاكْسي.

    My mother works as a teacher, and my father works as a taxi driver.

| | | |
|---|---|---|
| و... أنا حالِيّاً عم بِشْتِغِل مْعَلّمِة كَمان عِنّا بِالمَدْرَسِة... عِنّا بِالضَّيْعَة في مَدْرَسِة قَريبِة مِنّا. | 11 | And... I am currently working as a teacher too, in the school... here in our village at a school nearby. |
| بْعَلِّم مات وسْيانْس. | 12 | I teach math and science. |
| بْعَلِّم صْفوف أوّل وتاني وتالِت يَعْني الصِّغار. | 13 | I teach first, second, and third grades, meaning the younger ones. |
| وكْتير بْحِبّ شِغْلي، كْتير بْحِبّ التَّعْليم ومجال التَّعْليم. | 14 | And I really love my job; I really love teaching and the field of education. |
| بْحِبّ إنّي عم عَلِّم أعْمار صْغيرِة لِأنّو أنا بْحِبّ الوْلاد كْتير. | 15 | I love teaching young ages because I really like children |
| وكان حِلْمي وَقِت كِنِت صْغيرِة إنّي بسّ أكْبَر صير مْعَلّمِة مع إنّو أنا تْخَصّصِت interior design. | 16 | And it was my dream when I was young that when I grew up, I would become a teacher, even though I specialized in interior design. |
| هَنْدَسِة ديكور كْتير بْعيدِة عن مجال التَّعْليم. | 17 | Interior design is quite different from the field of education. |
| بسّ نِحْنا هوْن عِنّا بِالمَنْطِقة وبِلِبْنان كْتير قَليل الشِّغِل بْهَيْدا الإخْتِصاص. | 18 | But here in our region and in Lebanon, there's very little work in this specialty. |
| كْتير بْحِبّ إنّي قَريبِة من الوْلاد والتّلاميذ اللي بْعَلِّمُن الوْلاد كْتير بيحِبّوني. | 19 | I really love being close to the children and the students I teach; the children really like me. |
| و... ومِن هِواياتي الرَّسِم والتَّلْوين. | 20 | And... among my hobbies are drawing and coloring. |
| كْتير بْحِبّ الرَّسِم والتَّلْوين. | 21 | I really love to draw and color. |
| خْصوصي البورْتْري، كْتير بْحِبّ إنّي إرْسُم لَوْحات ولَوِّنُن. | 22 | Especially portraits. I really love to draw and color them. |
| بِحِكم إنّي أنا كِنِت عم بِدْرُس interior design ويأوّل سِنِة كِنِت آخُد كورْسات drawing و painting، | 23 | Considering I was studying interior design, in the first year, I took courses in drawing and painting. |
| فا كْتير حَبّيْت هَيْدا المجال. | 24 | I really loved this field. |
| بْحِبّ إنّي طَوِّر حالي في أكْتَر وأكْتَر مع الوَقِت. | 25 | I love to develop myself more and more over time. |
| بْحِبّ كَمان القِراءة وبْحِبّ السّباحة. | 26 | I also love reading and swimming. |
| وبِالنِّسْبِة لـ future plans بِالنِّسْبِة لإلي، أنا لِأنّي دِرِسِت interior design، بْحِبّ إنّي طَوِّر حالي أكْتَر بْهَيْدا المجال. | 27 | Regarding future plans for me, since I studied interior design, I want to develop myself further in this field. |
| بْحِبّ إنّي أعْمِل كورْسات أكْتَر وأكْتَر. | 28 | I want to take more courses. |

| | |
|---|---|
| 29 | حتّى إنّو أنا بحْلم إنّي انْشاالله بكْرا ومع الإيّام قدّم، حتّى سافِر لبرّاةْ لبْنان وإشْتغِل بمجالي لأنّو أنا كْتير بْحِبّ مجال الهنْدسةْ الدّيكوْر. |
| 30 | كْتير كِنِت شاطْرة فيه وكْتير بْحِبّ إنّي كفّي وإنّي إشْتغِل فيه، بسّ نِحْنا عنّا هوْن بلِبْنان كْتير قليل الشّغِل فيه. |
| 31 | فا أنا عم خطّط إنّي قوّي حالي أكْتر بهيْدا المجال، كورْسات ودوْرات، |
| 32 | وانْشاالله بقْدر حقّق حِلْمي وصير مع الوَقِت مهنْدِسةْ ديكوْر كْتير مشْهورة وكْتير ناجْحة، انْشاالله. |

I even dream that, God willing, one day, I will travel abroad from Lebanon and work in my field because I really love the field of interior design.

I was very good at it and really wanted to be independent and work in it, but here in Lebanon, there's very little work in it.

So, I am planning to strengthen myself more in this field with courses and training,

and God willing, I will be able to achieve my dream and become a very famous and successful interior designer over time, God willing.

## Vocabulary

1. to graduate from[4] _____
2. to work as[10] _____
3. field[14] _____
4. to major in[16] _____
5. to color[22] _____

6. course[23] _____
7. to develop oneself[27] _____
8. good at[30] _____
9. to plan[31] _____
10. to achieve[32] _____

---

## Answers

**Main Idea:** c **True or False:** 1. F[6-7] 2. F[9] 3. F[12-13] 4. T[16] 5. T[27-28] **Multiple Choice:** 1. b[29-30] 2. a[18-19] 3. b **Matching:** حاليّاً currently / بعْدو still / كْتير really / بسّ when / إنّو even though / مع بسّ but / خْصوصي especially / إنّو بحِكِم considering that.. / مع الوَقِت over time / حتّى even / فا so **Vocabulary:** 1. تخْرّج مِن / 2. شْتغِل / 3. مجال / 4. تْخصّص / 5. لوّن / 6. كورْس / 7. طوّر حالو / 8. شاطِر في / 9. خطّط / 10. حقّق

# 3 Waleed's Introduction

## Keywords

تْجوّز to get married   مجال field   عُلوم science

## Main Idea

a. Waleed's life is centered around his love for literature and his career as a literary writer.
b. Waleed discusses his journey as a chemistry graduate who combined his passion for science and writing into a career.
c. Waleed primarily tells us about his family background and his role as a father.
d. Waleed's main focus is on his future ambitions in the field of educational training for teachers across the Arab region.

## True or False

1. Waleed currently lives with his wife and son in Beirut.
2. Waleed's professional career began in a field that was widely popular in Lebanon in 2002.
3. Waleed's current work involves educational technology, and he has ambitions to work internationally in this field.
4. Waleed's work in science journalism primarily involves editing scientific texts and simplifying complex concepts for children.
5. Waleed has ambitions to remain solely a local trainer in Lebanon.

## Multiple Choice

1. What degree did Waleed graduate with from university?

    a. Literature   b. Journalism   c. Chemistry   d. *None of the above*

2. How does Waleed describe his family background?

    a. As part of a large family, being the second-to-last son

    b. As an only child in a small family

    c. As the eldest of several siblings

    d. As an orphan who never knew his parents

3. Which of the following activities does Waleed mention as his hobbies?

    a. Cooking and gardening   c. Creative writing and poetry

    b. Playing sports   d. Reading literature and watching documentary programs

# Matching

| | |
|---|---|
| هَلّأ | among which |
| هَيْدا | as I mentioned |
| فا | I mean |
| لَيْش | in addition to |
| حَتّى | now |
| بِالإِضافِة إلى | so |
| يَعْني | so that |
| مِنّا | specifically |
| اللي | that |
| مِتِل ما قِلِت | that, which, who |
| تحْديداً | this |
| إنّو | why |

# Text

1. مَرْحَبا، أَنا إِسْمي وَليد.
   Hello, my name is Waleed.

2. عُمْري أَرْبَعة وأَرْبَعين سِنة، يَعْني بِحِسْبِة بَسيطة، خْلِقِت سِنِة أَلْف وتِسْعْميّة وتِسْعة وسَبْعين.
   I am 44 years old, which means, by simple calculation, I was born in 1979.

3. أَنا لِبْناني، بْعيش بِمَدينِة بَيْروت، فْيا خْلِقِت، كْبِرِت، تْعَلَّمِت، شْتَغَلِت، وتْجَوَّزِت،
   I am Lebanese and live in the city of Beirut, where I was born, grew up, educated, worked, and got married,

4. وهَلَّأ عَم بْعيش بِبَيْروت أَنا ومَرْتي وبَناتي لْتْنَيْن اللي أَعْمارُن تِسْعة سْنين وعَشْر سْنين.
   and now I live in Beirut with my wife and my two daughters, aged nine and ten.

5. سِنة أَلْفَيْن وواحد تْخَرَّجِت مِن الجامْعة بِإِخْتِصاص الكيميا وشْتَغَلِت بِمَجال كان يُعْتَبَر سِنِة الأَلْفَيْن وتْنَيْن مَجال جْديد،
   In 2001, I graduated from university with a degree in Chemistry and worked in a field that was considered new in 2002,

6. يَعْني مِهْنة ما كانِت مَوْجودة بِكِتْرة بِلِبْنان، وهِيِّ بِالصَّحافة العِلْمية.
   a profession not very common in Lebanon at that time, which is science journalism.

7. هَلَّأ كيف أَنا شْتَغَلِت بِهَيْدا المَجال؟ أَنا خِرّيج عُلوم وكان عِنْدي مَيْل إلى الأداب.
   Now, how did I get into this field? I am a science graduate with a leaning towards literature.

|  |  |  |
|---|---|---|
| 8 | وكِنْت هاوي قِراءة، وكان عِنْدي يَعْني الْقُدْرة إنّو إكْتُب أشْياء خَواطِر أوْ نُصوص أدبية قصيرة. | And I enjoyed reading and had the ability to write thoughts or short literary texts. |
| 9 | فا هوْن جْتمعِت الهوِاية مع الإخْتِصاص الجامِعي ونْطلقِت بِمجال الْكِتابة العِلْمية. | So here, I combined my hobby with my university major and embarked on the field of scientific writing. |
| 10 | شْتغلِت على تحْرير نُصوص عِلْمية، الإجابة على أسْئِلة عِلْمية مِتِل ليْش السّما زرْقا، ليْش سُمِّيت الأنْهار... البحْر الأحْمر بِهالْإسْم، | I worked on editing scientific texts, answering scientific questions like why the sky is blue and why the rivers... the Red Sea is named as such, |
| 11 | بِالْإضافة إلى تبْسيط الْعُلوم حتّى يِقْدروا الأوْلاد الصُّغار تْلاميذ الْمدارِس يِفْهموا هالْعُلوم... المفاهيم العِلْمية الْمعقّدة الكِبيرة. | in addition to simplifying science so that young children and school students can understand these sciences... these complex scientific concepts. |
| 12 | أنا رْبيت أنا وصْغير بِعايْلة كْبيرة، هيِّ مْكوّنة كانِت مِن البيّ والإمّ، تْلات أخْوة بنات وشبّان، | I grew up, as a child, in a large family that consisted of my father and mother, three brothers and sisters, |
| 13 | وأنا كِنِت التّالِت وكان ترْتيبي بِهيْدي العايْلة الخامِس أوْ قبِل آخِر ولد. | and I was the third child, the fifth in the family lineup, or the second-to-last son. |
| 14 | يَعْني ما كِنِت الطِّفْل المُدلّل بِالْعايْلة وما كِنِت الأخّ الكِبير. | I mean, I wasn't the baby of the family, nor was I the eldest sibling. |
| 15 | عِنْدي هِوايات مُخْتلِفة وكْتيرة يَعْني مِنّا، مِتِل ما قِلِت قبل شْويّ، مْحبِّة الْعُلوم، الإطِّلاع، الكِتابة، الْقِراءة الأدبية، النُّصوص، الرّوايات، أحْضر الوِث... البرامج الوَثائِقية اللي... | I have various hobbies, well, many, as I mentioned earlier, like a love for science, research, literary writing, reading literature, texts, novels, and watching docu... documentary programs which... |
| 16 | يَعْني مثلاً، كان في برْنامج صْغير كِنِت حِبّ أحْضرو أنا وصْغير اللي هوّ يِرْبُط بيْن الإخْتِراعات يْبلِّش مثلاً مِن إخْتِراع الدّولاب | Well, for example, there was this little program I loved watching as a child, which made connections between inventions, starting from the invention of the wheel, |
| 17 | وكيف إخْتِراع الدّولاب اللي هوّ صار بِالْعُصور القديمة أدّى مثلاً بِالْعصْر الحديث لإخْتِراع كْتير كْبير وبْتجي بِتْطلّع إنّو شو كيف البشرية... العقْل البشري قدِر يِرْبُط بيْن الدّولاب وهيْدا الإخْتِراع. | and how the invention of the wheel in ancient times led to significant inventions in modern times, showing how humankind... the human mind could connect the wheel to this invention. |
| 18 | حاليّاً عم بِشْتِغِل بِقِطاع التّعْليم، مِتِل ما قِلِت، وتِحْديداً عِنْدي خِبْرة كْتير طويلة بِمجال التّكْنولوجيا التّعْليمية. | Currently, I am working in the education sector, as I mentioned, and specifically, I have extensive experience in educational technology. |

| | | |
|---|---|---|
| وواحد مِن أهْدافي المُسْتقْبَليّة إنّو طوِّر حالي بِمَجال التّدْريب، لَأُطْلَع لَصير مِن مُدرِّب مَحلّي فَقَط بِلِبْنان إلى مُدرِّب لكافّةّ مُعَلِّمي المَنْطِقة العَربية وساعِدُن على وُصول لدَمْج التِّكْنولوجْيا بِالعَمَليّة التّعْليمية بِشَكِل أفْضل. | 19 | One of my future goals is to develop myself in the training field, to go from being just a local trainer in Lebanon to a trainer for all teachers in the Arab region, helping them to better integrate technology into the educational process. |
| فا دْعولي إتْوَفَّق. | 20 | So, pray for my success. |

## Vocabulary

1. calculation[2] _____
2. my wife[4] _____
3. journalism[6] _____
4. to embark on[9] _____
5. second-to-last[13] _____

6. documentaries[15] _____
7. wheel[16] _____
8. invention[16] _____
9. to lead to[17] _____
10. education[18] _____

---

## Answers

**Main Idea:** b **True or False:** 1. F[4] 2. F[6] 3. T[18-19] 4. T[10] 5. F[19] **Multiple Choice:** 1. c[5] 2. a[13] 3. d[15-16] **Matching:** هلّأ now / هَيْدا this / فا so / لَيْش why / حتّى so that / بِالإضافة إلى in addition to / يَعْني I mean / إنّو that / تحْديداً specifically / مِتِل ما قِلت as I mentioned / اللي that, which, who / مِنّا among which / إخْتِراع 8. / دولاب 7. / برامِج وَثائْقية 6. / قَبِل آخِر 5. / نْطلَق بـ 4. / صحافة 3. / مرْتي 2. / حِسْبة 1. :**Vocabulary** / أدّى لـ 9. / تعْليم 10.

13 | Lebanese Arabic Voices

# 4 Rita's Introduction

## Keywords

بْحِبّ I like   قْرايْبِين relatives   سِنة (سْنين) year

## Main Idea

a. Rita, a 33-year-old living permanently in Lebanon with her immediate family, works as a teacher in Jbeil, sharing her passion for education and local traditions.

b. At 33, Rita has spent her adult life abroad, having lived in both America and the UAE, and returns to Lebanon annually to visit her family. She has pursued education and a career in International Relations and politics, cherishing her times with her niece and nephew during visits.

c. Rita, a recent graduate from the University of Beirut, has embarked on a new journey in America to explore her interests in music and arts, away from her extensive family in Lebanon.

d. A lifelong resident of Washington, Rita occasionally visits relatives in Lebanon, pursuing a career in healthcare while nurturing a hobby in culinary arts.

## True or False

1. Rita has been living in Lebanon continuously since she was a teenager.
2. Rita returns to Lebanon frequently, normally once a year.
3. Rita's parents live in the UAE.
4. Rita has a nephew and a niece.
5. Rita mentions her husband's nationality.

## Multiple Choice

1. What aspect of living abroad does Rita find most difficult?

    a. Adjusting to different cultures
    b. Finding suitable employment
    c. Seeing loved ones age and change during her absences
    d. Learning the local language

2. What did Rita complete her master's degree in?

    a. Media Studies
    b. International Relations
    c. English literature
    d. *None of the above*

3. In which order does Rita talk about the following topics?

   a. Family, career, hobbies
   c. Family, hobbies, career
   b. Hobbies, education, family
   d. Education, family, hobbies

## Matching

|  |  |
|---|---|
| مِن وَقْتا ما | a little bit |
| مرّة بِالسِّنة | as |
| إلّا | at least |
| عَ القليلة | because |
| هِنّي | except |
| مِتِل ما | gradually |
| هوْنيكي | maybe |
| فجْأة | my |
| لإنّو | once a year |
| كِلّ ما... كِلّ ما | regarding, as for |
| وَقِت | since |
| شوْيّ شوْيّ | suddenly |
| إنْ... أوْ | the more... the more |
| شوْيّ | there |
| يِمْكِن | they |
| الـ___تبعي | when |
| بِالنِّسْبِة لَـ | whether... or |

# Text

|  | | |
|---|---|---|
| 1 | إِسْمي ريتا، عُمْري تْلاتة وتْلاتين سِنِة. | My name is Rita, I'm 33 years old. |
| 2 | خْلِقِت بِجْبيل بِلِبْنان. | I was born in Jbeil, Lebanon. |
| 3 | بسّ صرْلي برّاةْ لِبْنان مِن وَقْتا ما كان عُمْري خمسْطعْشر سِنِة، عِشِت بينْ أميرْكا والإمارات. | But I've been outside Lebanon since I was 15 years old, living between America and the UAE. |
| 4 | بِرْجع عَ لِبْنان عَ القليلِة مرّة بالسِّنِة، | I return to Lebanon at least once a year, |
| 5 | إلّا وَقِت كورْونا، ما قْدِرِت إجي | except during the Corona times, when I couldn't go, |
| 6 | بسّ بْقيت ما بقى عَ القليلِة بِجي على لِبْنان مرّة بالسِّنِة. | but I've made sure to at least visit Lebanon once a year. |
| 7 | كِلّ عايْلْتي عايْشة بِلِبْنان، يَعْني إمّي وبيّي وكِلّ قْرايبيني وإخْتي وعايْلِتا. | My entire family lives in Lebanon, meaning my mom, dad, all my relatives, and my sister and her family. |
| 8 | إخْتي مْجوّزة عِنْدا صبي وبِنت، كْتير بْحِبّن وكْتير مهْضومين. | My sister is married and has a son and a daughter. I love them a lot, and they are very adorable. |
| 9 | الصّبي عُمْرو أرْبعة سْنين والبِنت عُمْرا سِنة ونُصّ. | The boy is four years old, and the girl is one and a half years old. |
| 10 | مِن أكْتر الإشْيا اللي بْحِبّا بِحَياتي هنّي وْلاد إخْتي. | One of the things I love most in my life is my niece and nephew. |
| 11 | أنا عايْشة، مِتِل ما ذكرِت بأميرْكا، مع جوْزي، عايْشين بواشِنْطِن. | I live, as I mentioned, in America with my husband. We live in Washington. |
| 12 | بْحِبّ أميرْكا كْتير، أميرْكا بَيْتي التّاني بِكِلّ مَعْنى الكِلْمة. | I really like America. It's my second home in every sense of the word. |
| 13 | صرْلي هوْنيكي كذا سِنِة. | I've been there for several years. |
| 14 | يمكِن شغْلِة مِن الإشْيا اللي بِتْزعِّل بِالْغُرْبِة هيِّ بسّ إرْجع عَ لِبْنان وشوف النّاس اللي بْحِبّن كِبْروا فجْأة. | Maybe one of the things that saddens me about being abroad is returning to Lebanon and seeing people I love have grown up suddenly. |
| 15 | هَيْدا مِن أكْتر الإشْيا اللي عم لاقْيا صعْبِة كِلّ ما بِكْبر، | This is one of the things I find most difficult as I grow older, |
| 16 | لأنّو كِلّ ما أنا عم بِكْبر، كِلّ ما النّاس اللي حوْلاييّ عم تِكْبر. | because the older I get, the older the people around me are getting too. |
| 17 | وَقِت اللي يْكون الواحد عايِش قريب مِن عالم وعم بيْشوفُن عم يِكْبروا شْوَيّ شْوَيّ هايْنِة. | When one lives close to people and sees them growing up gradually, it's easier. |

| | |
|---|---|
| 18 | بسّ وَقِت الواحد بيسافِر وبيرْجع بيشوفُن كِبْروا فجْأة، كْتير هالشّي صعِب. |
| 19 | إن كِنِت عم بِحْكي عن وْلاد إخْتي أوْ إذا عم بِحْكي عن قرايْبيني اللي أكْبر شْوَيّ بالْعُمُر. |
| 20 | يمْكِن هَيْدي شِغْلِة مِن أصْعب الإشْيا اللي عم بْحِسّا بالْعيشِة بالْغُرْبة. |
| 21 | بسّ بذات الوَقِت عيشْتي برّاةْ لِبْنان وغُرْبْتي خلِّتْني إتْخرّج مِن أميرْكا. |
| 22 | عْمِلت اللّيسانْس تبعي أوْ bachelor's بالْعلاقات الدُّوَلية مِن جامْعةْ واشِنْطن بواشِنْطن ستايْت وعْمِلت الماسْتيرْز تبعي كمان بالْعلاقات الدُّوَلية من جورْج تاوْن بواشِنْطن دي سي. |
| 23 | بالنِّسْبة لشِغْلي شاغْلِة بأميرْكا بالسِّياسة، إنّ كان البحْث السِّياسي أوْ التّحْليل السِّياسي وبسّ كِنت ساكْنِة بالإمارات كِنت إشْتِغِل بالْعلاقات العامّة. |
| 24 | بالنِّسْبة للْوظيفِة المُسْتقْبلية يمْكِن يلّي بطْمحْلا هِيّ وظيفِة بْتجمع بين العلاقات العامّة والسِّياسة يلّي هنّي قِطاعين أنا كْتير بْحِبُّن، بْحِبّ كْتير إشْتِغل فيُن. |
| 25 | بِالنِّسْبة لهواياتي بْحِبّ كْتير الكتيبة، يَعْني بِكْتُب بِوَقْتي الخاص حتّى إذا ما خصّوا بالشِّغل أوْ الجامْعة. |
| 26 | بْحِبّ كْتير غنّي، بْحِبّ كْتير أحْضر أفْلام، ومُسلْسلات. |
| 27 | بْحِبّ كْتير سافِر، هَوْدي مِن أكْتر الإشْيا يلّي بْحِبُّن. |
| 28 | هَيْدي هيْك مُلخّص صْغير عن أنا مين وشو بْحِبّ وشو بْحِبّ أعْمُل وانْشاالله يْكون عطاكُن فِكْرة صْغيرِة عنّي. |

| | |
|---|---|
| 18 | But when one moves abroad and returns to find them suddenly grown up, it's very hard. |
| 19 | Whether I'm talking about my niece and nephew or my relatives who are a bit older. |
| 20 | Maybe this is one of the hardest things I feel about living abroad. |
| 21 | But at the same time, my life outside Lebanon and my expatriation led me to graduate in America. |
| 22 | I got my bachelor's (or 'bachelor's) in International Relations from the University of Washington in Washington State and my master's in International Relations from Georgetown in Washington DC. |
| 23 | Regarding my job, I work in politics in America, be it political research or political analysis, and when I lived in the UAE, I worked in public relations. |
| 24 | As for my future job, maybe what I aspire to is a job that combines public relations and politics, two fields I really love and enjoy working in. |
| 25 | Regarding my hobbies, I really love writing, meaning I write in my free time, even if it's not related to work or university. |
| 26 | I love singing. I really enjoy watching movies and TV series. |
| 27 | I really like to travel. It's one of the things I love most. |
| 28 | This is a brief summary about who I am, what I love, and what I like to do, and I hope it has given you a small idea about me. |

## Vocabulary

1. boy[8] _____
2. cute, adorable[8] _____
3. to upset[14] _____
4. to grow[17] _____
5. thing[20] _____

6. bachelor's degree[22] _____
7. international relations[23] _____
8. to aspire to[24] _____
9. to be related to[25] _____
10. summary[28] _____

_____

## Answers

**Main Idea:** b **True or False:** 1. F[3] 2. T[4-6] 3. F[7] 4. T[8-10] 5. F[11] **Multiple Choice:** 1. c[14-20] 2. b[22] 3. a[7, 23, 25] **Matching:** as / مِتِل ما they / هِنّي at least / عَ القليلة except / إلّا once a year / مرّة بالسّنة since / مِن وَقْتا ما when / وَقْت shway shway / شْوَيّ شْوَيّ gradually, there / هوْنيكي suddenly / فجْأة because / لإنّو the more... the more / كِلّ ما... كِلّ ما regarding, as for / بالنِّسْبة لَـ my / الـ___ـي tabaʿi / تبعي maybe / يمْكِن a little bit / شْوَيّ whether... or / إن... أوْ **Vocabulary:** 1. صبي / 2. مهْضوم / 3. زعّل / 4. كِبِر / 5. شغْلة / 6. ليسانْس / 7. العلاقات الدوَّلية / 8. طمح لَـ / 9. خصّ بِـ / 10. مُلخَّص

# 5 Mohammad's Introduction

## Keywords

عاش to live    ساكِن living

## Main Idea

a. Mohammad lives with his family in Beirut, works in a local school, and enjoys playing video games.
b. Mohammad lives alone near Sidon, studies Translation at university, and works as a freelancer translating games.
c. Mohammad, a recent graduate in Engineering, resides in Jezzine with his wife and children and works in a technology firm.
d. Mohammad currently lives in Saudi Arabia with his parents and sister, works as a teacher, and enjoys playing sports.

## True or False

1. Mohammad currently lives with his family in Sidon.
2. Mohammad is currently studying Translation at LIU University in Sidon.
3. Mohammad's work involves translating games for consoles and computers as a freelancer.
4. One of Mohammad's favorite activities is to read in natural, quiet settings.
5. Mohammad tells us how he envisions his future.

## Multiple Choice

1. Where did Mohammad complete his studies up to the terminal level?

    a. Al-Baha    b. Garden City School    c. LIU University    d. *None of the above*

2. What is Mohammad's current occupation?

    a. An employee at a gaming studio          c. A teacher at a local school
    b. A freelancer working with a Turkish company    d. *None of the above*

3. In which type of environment does Mohammad wish to live in the future?

    a. In a bustling city center    c. A quiet and peaceful setting with a garden
    b. Near the sea                 d. *None of the above*

## Matching

| | |
|---|---|
| مِنّا | (in the capacity) as |
| مِن بعْدا | after that |
| بعْدْني | everything |
| مِن لمّا | I still... |
| بدّا | in order to, so that |
| عِنْدا | okay |
| كَـ | she has |
| كِلّو | she wants |
| ماشي الحال | she/it is not |
| حتّى | since |

## Text

| |  |  |
|---|---|---|
| 1 | إسْمي مْحمّد، عُمْري تْلاتة وعِشْرين سِنة. | My name is Mohammad. I'm 23 years old. |
| 2 | خِلْقان بِمدينةْ صَيْدا بالجْنوب، هَيْدي مدينة ساحْلية قديمة كْتير تُعْتبر مِن أقْدم المُدُن بالْعالم. | I was born in the city of Sidon in the south, an ancient coastal city considered one of the oldest in the world. |
| 3 | بسيطة مِنّا مِتطوّرة قدّ بيروت، بسّ بِتْضلّا كْتير حِلْوة يَعْني. | It's simple, not as developed as Beirut, but it remains very beautiful. |
| 4 | خْلِقِت فيا وحاليّاً ساكِن بِشرق هَيْدي المدينة بِمِنْطقة إسْما كْفرجرّة. | I was born there and currently live in the eastern part of this city, in an area called Kfar Jarra. |
| 5 | هَيْدي المِنْطقة بين جِزّين وبين صَيْدا قريبة عَ التْنين. | This area is located between Jezzine and Sidon, close to both. |
| 6 | درسِت بِالْبهاء مِن الصّفّ الأوّل للصّفّ السّابِع. | I studied at Al-Baha from first to seventh grade. |
| 7 | مِن بعْدا رِحِت على مدْرسة إسْما مدْرسةْ الغارْدِن سيتي، كمّلِت فيا دِراسْتي للتّرْمينال. | After that, I went to a school called Garden City School, where I completed my studies up to the terminal level. |
| 8 | مِن بعْد التّرْمينال، سجّلِت بِجامْعةْ الـ LIU هوْن بِصَيْدا. | After the terminal level, I enrolled at LIU University here in Sidon. |
| 9 | سجّلِت ترْجمة وبعْدْني لهلّأ عم كمِّل بِإخْتِصاصي، يَعْني بعْدِلّي تْلات موادّ وبْخلِّص. | I registered for Translation, and I am still continuing my specialization. I mean, I have three more courses to complete, and then I will be done. |

| | | |
|---|---|---|
| 10 | I'm single and live alone. | أنا عِزّابي، عايِش لحالي. |
| 11 | My father has been abroad, living in Riyadh since I was two years old. | بَيِّي صِرْلو مِن لمّا كان عُمْري سِنْتين مْسافِر وساكِن بالرِّياض. |
| 12 | And about three years ago, my mom moved to him; I mean, she decided to live with him. | وإمّي مِن تْلات سْنين تقْريباً نقلِت لعِنْدو، يَعْني صار بدّا تْعيش معو. |
| 13 | I have a sister who is married with a young daughter named Nour, who is also living in Saudi Arabia with my parents. | عِنْدي إخْت مْجوْزِة وعِنْدا بِنْت صْغيرِة، إسْما نور، كَمان ساكْنِة بالسَّعودية مع أهْلي. |
| 14 | I have a brother named Ali, with two sons, living close to me. I see him often, thank God. | وعِنْدي خيّ إسْمو علي، عِنْدو صِبْيانان ساكِن قْريب مِنّي، دايْماً بْشوفو، الحَمْدلله. |
| 15 | Currently, I'm working from home as a freelancer with a Turkish company. | حاليّاً عم بِشْتِغِل مِن البيْت كـfreelancer مع شِرْكِة تِرْكية. |
| 16 | I work in translation, translating games for phones, PlayStation, and PC from English to Arabic. | عم بِشْتِغِل بالتّرْجمِة بإخْتِصاصي، بْترْجِم ألْعاب على التِّليفوْن، ألْعاب على الـPlayStation، ألْعاب على الـPC |
| 17 | Everything is translated from English to Arabic. | كِلّو بْترْجِم مِن الإنْكْليزي للعْربي. |
| 18 | It's going okay with them, even though I'm slaving away, and they pay me very little, I'm gaining experience, thank God. | ماشي الحال معُن مع إنّو عم بِشْتِغِل بالسُّخْرة وعم بيقبْضوني كْتير قليل، بسّ إنّو عم بِكْسب خِبْرة، الحَمْدلله. |
| 19 | My hobbies include writing and reading. | مِن هِواياتي الكِتابِة والقِراءة. |
| 20 | I really love to read; I take books with me and go by car to a place with a beautiful natural view. | بْحِبّ كْتير إقْرأ، يَعْني باخُد معي كُتُب وبْروح بالسَّيارة على مِنْطقة هيْك فيا منْظر طبيعي وحِلو، |
| 21 | and just sit there, reading and enjoying. | وبِسْردا هوْنيك، يَعْني بْضلّني عم بِقْرأ. |
| 22 | I like to write in two languages, in English and in Arabic. | وبْحِبّ كْتير إكْتُب باللغْتين بالإنْكْليزي وبالعْربي. |
| 23 | I keep learning new vocabulary and grammar to improve myself and write more. | بْضلّني بِتْعلّم vocab جْديد، كلِمات جْديدة وقْواعِد، يَعْني لحتّى حسِّن مِن حالي وإكْتُب أكْتر. |
| 24 | My future plan is to get married and have children, living with my wife and kids in a house away from the hassle, away from the world, and away from the hubbub, | خِطّتي المُسْتقْبلية هيّ أنّي إتْجوّز ويْكون عِنْدي وْلاد، عايِش أنا ومرتي ووْلادي بْبيْت هيْك بْعيد عن القرف وبْعيد عن العالم وبْعيد عن الطَوْشة، |
| 25 | in a house with a garden, so I can watch my kids play and provide them with toys. | بيْت هيْك يْكون فيّو جْنيْنِة لحتّى شوف الوْلاد عم يِلْعبوا، وجِبلُن ألْعاب. |

26 يَعْني كَمِّل حَياتي بْبَساطة، هَيْدي هِيِّ أهْدافي المُسْتَقْبَلية.

In short, I want to lead a simple life; these are my future goals.

## Vocabulary

1. born[2] _____
2. beautiful[3] _____
3. single[10] _____
4. alone[10] _____
5. my father[11] _____
6. my mother[12] _____
7. my parents[13] _____
8. I keep [doing][23] _____
9. to improve oneself[23] _____
10. hubbub, clamor[24] _____

## Answers

**Main Idea:** b **True or False:** 1. F[10] 2. T[8-9] 3. T[16] 4. T[20-21] 5. T[24-26] **Multiple Choice:** 1. b[7] 2. b[15] 3. c[24-26] **Matching:** مِنّا she/it is not / مِن بَعْدا after that / بَعْدْني I still... / مِن لمّا since / بدّا she wants / عِنْدا she has / كَـ (in the capacity) as / كِلّو everything / ماشي الحال okay / حتّى in order to, so that **Vocabulary:** 1. خِلْقان / 2. حِلو / 3. عِزّابي / 4. لحالي / 5. بَيِّي / 6. إمّي / 7. أهْلي / 8. بْضَلّني / 9. حسّن مِن حالو / 10. طَوْشِة

# 6 Sandy's Introduction

## Keywords

| طبيعة nature | غنّى to sing |

## Main Idea

a. Sandy is a single mom, a passionate lover of nature and sports, and has a diverse career in cinema and music.
b. Sandy is a professional oud player who has dedicated her life solely to music.
c. Sandy's primary focus is on her academic achievements and language skills.
d. Sandy is a dedicated CrossFit athlete who trains competitively.

## True or False

1. Sandy was born and currently lives in the same area in Beirut.
2. Sandy has a son in kindergarten named Mario.
3. Sandy has a contract with a music production company and is actively producing new songs.
4. Sandy's son, Ian, shares her enthusiasm for nature and outdoor activities.
5. Sandy's career in TV is diverse, working in production and directing segments in news programs, reality TV, and commercials.

## Multiple Choice

1. How does Sandy describe her relationship with her family?

    a. Sandy is very close to her family and sees them almost every day.

    b. She has a distant relationship with them.

    c. She only meets her family on special occasions.

    d. She has lost contact with her family.

2. What does Sandy say about her experience with the oud?

    a. She is a professional oud player.

    b. She has never tried playing the oud.

    c. She teaches oud at the National Conservatory.

    d. She learned it for a short period and enjoys playing.

3. What is Sandy's sentiment regarding living in Lebanon?

    a. She plans to move abroad soon.

    b. She is indifferent about her country.

    c. She dislikes Lebanon and criticizes it heavily.

    d. She loves Lebanon deeply and prefers to stay despite ongoing conflicts.

## Matching

| | |
|---|---|
| هلّأ | (not) at all |
| عِنْدي | actually; by the way |
| كْتير | as much as |
| كِلّ شي | because |
| عِنّا | everything |
| تبعي | here |
| عَ فِكْرة | I can't |
| هوْن | I have |
| منّي | I'm not |
| ما فيني | mine |
| أبداً | never |
| فا | now |
| قدّ ما | so |
| لَأنّو | very, really; a lot, much, many |
| بِالأحْرى | we have |

## Text

| | | |
|---|---|---|
| مرْحَبا، أنا إسْمي سانْدي. | 1 | Hello, my name is Sandy. |
| عُمْري أرْبَعة وتْلاتين سِنة، مَواليد تْلاتة وعِشْرين تْنين ألْف وتِسِعْميّة وتِسْعة وتْمانين. | 2 | I am 34 years old, born on the 23rd of January 1989. |
| خِلْقانة بالأشْرَفية بْبَيْروت، بسّ الأصْل مِن دير القمر مِن الشّوف. | 3 | I was born in Achrafieh, Beirut, but originally from Deir el Qamar in the Chouf district. |
| وهلّأ سكّان بْعَبْدا الحدد. | 4 | Currently, we reside in Hadath, Baabda. |
| عِنْدي إبْني إسْمو إيان، عُمْرو خمْس سْنين. | 5 | I have a son named Ian; he's five years old. |
| بالمَدْرسة بْصفّ الـ كيْ جي ٣، بُرْجو العقْرب، بْحِبّو كْتير. | 6 | He's in KG3 at school, a Scorpio, and I love him very much. |
| أنا إمّ عزْبا منْفِصْلة عن بيّو لإبْني، بسّ عايْشة أنا وإبْني وشْريك حَياتي إسْمو ماريو. | 7 | I'm a single mom, separated from my son's father, but I live with my son and my partner, Mario. |
| إلي أرْبع سْنين أنا وياه، كْتير مِنْحِبّ بَعْضنا. | 8 | We've been together for four years, and we love each other very much. |
| مِن هِواياتي كلّ شي خصّو بِالطّبيعة، السْبور وتحْديداً الـ CrossFit. | 9 | My hobbies involve anything related to nature, sports, and specifically CrossFit. |
| كْتير بْحِبّ أعْمل هيْدي الرِّياضة لأنّو بِتْشغِّل الجِسِم كِلّو وبْوَقْت كْتير قَصير وبِـ intensity كْتير عالْية. | 10 | I really love this sport because it involves the whole body, takes a short amount of time, and has a very high intensity. |
| بْحِبّ كْتير السْباحة. | 11 | I really enjoy swimming. |
| بْحِبّ كلّ شي خصّو بِالطّبيعة: المشي، الرّكِض، التّخْييم، البيكْنيكْس. | 12 | I love everything related to nature: walking, running, camping, picnics. |
| دايْماً بْروح أنا وإبْني عَ هيْك محلّات. | 13 | My son and I always go to such places. |
| كمان بْحِبّ إنّو يْحِبّ الطّبيعة ويْحِبّ الحَيَوانات. | 14 | I also want him to love nature and animals. |
| عِنّا بسَيْنة صْغيرة بالبيْت إسْمو نيو. | 15 | We have a small cat at home named Neo. |
| بْحِبّ أحْضر كْتير فْلومة، طبْعاً. | 16 | I enjoy watching a lot of movies, of course. |
| بحْضر كْتير مْسلْسلات مِن كلّ البلْدان ومِن كلّ الجِنْسيات ومِن كلّ اللّغات. | 17 | I watch a lot of TV series from all countries, of all nationalities, and in all languages. |
| بحْكي تْلات لغّات. | 18 | I speak three languages. |
| عِنْدي إخِت أكْبر مِنّي إسْما سالي، أكْبر مِنّي بْسِنة. | 19 | I have an older sister named Sally. She's a year older than me. |
| والبابا والماما، بْحِبّن كْتير. | 20 | My dad and mom, I love them a lot. |

| | | |
|---|---|---|
| صُحْبِة كْتير أنا ويّاهُن، كِلّ يوْم بْشوفُن تَقْريباً. | 21 | We have a very close relationship, and I see them almost every day. |
| شْتِغِلْت بِالسّينِما أوْ بِالمجال تَبعي حتّى قَبِل ما خلِّص جامْعة. | 22 | I started working in cinema or in my field even before I graduated from university. |
| درِسْت أكيد إخْراج سينِما بِجامْعِةْ الرّوح القُدُس بِالْكَسْليك، بلِّشْت بِالْألْفيْن وسَبْعة وتْخَرَّجْت بِالْألْفيْن وعَشْرة. | 23 | I studied cinema directing at the Holy Spirit University of Kaslik, starting in 2007 and graduating in 2010. |
| بَسّ بلِّشْت شِغِل بِالْألْفيْن وتْمانْية، عَ فِكْرة. | 24 | But I actually started working in 2008. |
| بِالدّومان بلِّشِت صوِّر ما وَرا الكَواليس، بِتْصْوير لِدِعايات لِمْسَلْسلات. | 25 | In this domain, I began by filming behind the scenes, shooting commercials for TV series. |
| وبَعْديْن تْنَقَلِت، صِرِت إشْتِغِل كـ... بِالْإنْتاج. إشْتِغِل كمُخْرِجِة فَقَرات بِبَرامِج تِليفِزْيونية إخْبارية. | 26 | And then I transitioned to production. I worked as a director of segments in news television programs. |
| شْتِغِلِت شْوَيّ بِالرِّياليتي تيفي مِتِل ما بْيْقولوا، شْتِغِلِت كْتير بِالدِّعايات وبَعْدْني مْثابْرة بِهَيْدا الدّومان. | 27 | I've worked a bit in reality TV, as they call it, and a lot in commercials, and I'm still persevering in this domain. |
| أنا بْغَنّي، بِكْتُب وبْلَحِّن. | 28 | I sing, write, and compose music. |
| كمان ماضْية كونْترا مع شِرْكِةْ إنْتاج موسيقي وشِرْكِةْ توْزيع كمان هوْن بِالْعالم العربي بِالشّرْق الْأوْسَط. | 29 | I also have a contract with a music production company and a distribution company here in the Arab world, in the Middle East. |
| وهَلّأ عم بِنْتُج أغاني جْديدة لإلي. | 30 | And now, I am producing new songs for myself. |
| عِنْدي كذا غِنية already نازْلة على السّوق. | 31 | I already have several songs released on the market. |
| مِن هِواياتي كمان إنّي إعْزُف على العود، شْوَيّ مِش كْتير. | 32 | Another one of my hobbies is playing the oud, just a little. |
| مِنّي مِثالية بِالْعَزِف بَسّ إنّو تْعَلِّمِت لِفتْرة صْغيرة كمان بِالْكونْسيرْفاتْوار الوَطَني غْناء شَرْقي وعوْد. | 33 | I'm not perfect at playing, but I learned for a short period at the National Conservatory, including Arabic singing and oud. |
| بْغَنّي شَرْقي وبْغَنّي غَرْبي. لحَياتي أوْ لِمُسْتَقْبَلي ما فيني كْتير خَطِّط. | 34 | I sing both oriental and Western songs. As for my life or future, I can't plan much. |
| كَوْني عايْشة بِلِبْنان في صِراعات مِنْقَطِع فيّا نِحْنا اللِّبْنانية اللي عايْشين هوْن، | 35 | Since I live in Lebanon, there are ongoing conflicts that we Lebanese that live here are going through, |
| بَسّ بْحِبّ بَلَدي كْتير وما بِتْرِكو أبَداً. | 36 | but I love my country very much and would never leave it. |
| جرَّبِت عيش برّا، ما قْدِرْت، فا عَم نْجَرِّب نْضَلّ بِوَطَنّا وبِأرْضْنا قدّ ما مْنِقْدِر، | 37 | I tried living abroad but couldn't, so I'm trying to stay in our country and on our land as much as I can, |

| | |
|---|---|
| 38 | because Lebanon is very beautiful and irreplaceable. There's really nothing like it at all. | لِأنّو لِبْنان حِلو كْتير وما في مِنّو كْتير، ما في مِنّو أبداً بِالْأخْرى. |

## Vocabulary

1. sign of the zodiac[6] _____
2. in a very short time[10] _____
3. cat[15] _____
4. movie, film[16] _____
5. older than[19] _____
6. domain, field[25] _____
7. behind the scenes[25] _____
8. commercial[25] _____
9. to compose[28] _____
10. abroad[37] _____

---

## Answers

**Main Idea:** a **True or False:** 1. F[3-4] 2. F[5-6] 3. T[29-31] 4. T[13] 5. T[25-27] **Multiple Choice:** 1. a[19-21] 2. d[32-33] 3. d[35-38] **Matching:** هلّأ now / عِنْدي I have / كْتير very, really; a lot, much, many / كِلّ شي everything / عِنّا we have / قدّ ما so / فا never / أبداً I can't / ما فيني I'm not / مِنّي here / هوْن actually; by the way / عَ فِكْرة mine / تبعي as much as / فيلِم 4. بْسَيْنة 3. بِوَقْت كْتير قصير 2. بِرج .1 :**Vocabulary** at all (not) بِالْأخْرى / because لَأنّو / 5. أكْبَر مِن / (فْلومة) 6. دوْمان / 7. وَرا الكَواليس / 8. دِعاية / 9. لحِّن / 10. برّا

# Daily Routines

## 7 Charbel's Daily Routine

### Keywords

روتين routine    شِغِل work

### Main Idea

a. Charbel and his wife have a flexible daily schedule with lots of personal time.
b. Their routine revolves around their baby, work, and completing household chores.
c. The couple spends their weekdays working and their weekends traveling.
d. They frequently go out for dinner and entertainment during the week.

### True or False

1. Charbel's parents always take care of the baby while he and his wife are at work.
2. Charbel and his wife work very different hours.
3. The couple spends their evenings relaxing and watching TV after putting the baby to bed.
4. On weekends, Charbel and his wife prioritize spending time outside, especially for meals.
5. Charbel and his wife try to take the baby out as much as possible on weekdays.

### Multiple Choice

1. When do Charbel and his wife usually wake up in the morning?
    a. At five in the morning
    b. Around seven or seven-thirty
    c. Around six or six-thirty
    d. None of the above

2. How does Charbel describe the feeling of time passing in their daily routine?
    a. Exciting and fulfilling
    b. Slow and monotonous
    c. Pressuring and fast-moving
    d. Relaxing and enjoyable

3. According to Charbel, what happens almost every day?
    a. They go out for dinner
    b. They visit their parents
    c. They argue about money
    d. They follow the same daily routine

## Matching

| | |
|---|---|
| كِرْمال | almost every |
| صراحة | around |
| سوْ | as much as we can |
| سَوى | for |
| لإلْنا | for us |
| عنّا | honestly |
| شي | how |
| ذات الشّي | so |
| صوْب | something |
| تقريباً كِلّ | somewhere |
| شي محلّ | that's why |
| قدّ ما فينا | the same thing |
| كيف | together |
| مِشان هيْك | we have |

## Text

1. هاي. كِرْمال شو مْنعْمُل يَوْمِيّاً؟
   Hi. As for what we are doing daily?

2. صراحة هلّأ مع بايْبي صار هيْك شْوَيّ الرّوتين اليَوْمي تبعْنا عنْجدّ روتين.
   Honestly, now, with the baby, our daily routine has really become a routine.

3. يَعْني مْنوعى الصُّبح أنا ومرْتي.
   We wake up in the morning, my wife and I.

4. منْحضِّر غْراض البايْبي ومنْغيِّرْلو... منْطعْميه، منْلبْسو.
   We prepare the baby's stuff, we change him, feed him, dress him.

5. ومنْكون جاهْزين نحْنا إنّو نْروح على الشِّغِل وبْذات الوَقِت بدّنا نْوَصِّل البايْبي عنْد أهْلي أوْ أهْلا.
   And we get ready to go to work, and at the same time, we need to drop the baby off at my parents' or her parents'.

6. سوْ منِنْطُلِق نحْنا على الطّريق، منْوَصِّل البايْبي عنْد مطْرح ما رايح.
   So, we set off, drop the baby where he's going.

7. ومنْرْجع كِلّ واحد بْيِتْكِّل بيروح على شِغْلو.
   And then each of us goes to work.

| | | |
|---|---|---|
| مِنْخلِّص شِغِل تقْريبًا سَوى بالسّاعة خمْسِة، خمْسِة ونُصّ، مِنرْجع مِنْروح ناخُد البايْبي. | 8 | We finish work around the same time, usually around five or five-thirty, and go pick up the baby. |
| مْنطْلع على البيْت، مْنحمّمو، مِنْطعْميه، مِنْغيّرْلو، مْنِلْعب شْوَيّ معو. | 9 | We get home, bathe him, feed him, change him, play with him for a while. |
| مِنْقضّي وَقْت سَوى، ومْنِنيْمو. | 10 | We spend time together and then put him to bed. |
| وبسّ يْنام بيكون هوْن نحْنا بلّش نْهار جْديد لإلْنا، لنْخلِّص شو في عنّا خْبار بالْبيْت لنْخلّصا. | 11 | Once he is asleep, our new day starts for us to finish whatever chores we have at home. |
| مْنعْمُل أكِل، مْنِتعشّى، مْنحْضِر شي على التّيفي، أوْ كِلّ واحد إذا عِنْدو شي يَعمْلو بْيَعملْو. | 12 | We make dinner, eat, watch something on TV, or if each of us has something to do, they do it. |
| ومْنِرْجع مْنِتحمّم ومِنْنام، ومْنوعى تاني نْهار ذات الشّيّ. | 13 | Then we shower, go to bed, and wake up the next day to the same thing. |
| بْيبلّش نْهارْنا تقْريباً صوْب السّاعة سِتّة، سِتّة ونُصّ الصُّبْح. | 14 | Our day starts around six or six-thirty in the morning. |
| ولنْنام عشية تقْريباً صوْب السّاعة طْنعْش. | 15 | And we go to bed around twelve at night. |
| وهيْك تِقْريبًا كِلّ يوْم مْنعْمُل هيْك. | 16 | And almost every day, we do this. |
| بالويك أنْد، مْنِضْهر مْناخُد البايْبي مِنْضهْرو. | 17 | On weekends, we go out and take the baby out with us. |
| بدّنا نْروح شي محلّ عَ الموْل. | 18 | We might go to a mall. |
| عشية عنّا دينر، بدّنا نِتعشّى شي محلّ. | 19 | And in the evening, we have dinner; we like to eat dinner somewhere. |
| بدّنا نِسْهر شي محلّ. | 20 | We like to spend the evening somewhere. |
| الأحد مِنْروح الصُّبْح نِتروّوّق شي محلّ. | 21 | And on Sundays, we go out for breakfast somewhere. |
| يَعْني مِنْجرِّب نِضْهر قدّ ما فينا ونْضهِّر البايْبي قدّ ما فينا بالْويك أنْد كْرمال نْموّه عَ حالْنا على الـ... على الويك اللي كان كْتير طَويل. | 22 | We try to go out as much as we can and take the baby out as much as we can on weekends to make up for the long week we had. |
| وهيْك بْتحِسّ بْضغِط وبِسِرْعِة الحَياةْ كيف بْتصير عمّ تِرْكُض والوَقِت عمّ بْيِرْكُض. | 23 | And so, you feel the pressure and how fast life goes by, running, and time running. |
| وإنْتَ بْتِطلّع بْتْلاقي حالك خُلْصِت السّنِة وما عْمِلْت شي، ما قضّيْت وَقِت لنفْسك. | 24 | And when you look back, you find the year has ended, and you haven't done anything, haven't spent time for yourself. |
| مِشان هيْك يَعْني مِنْجرِّب قدّ ما فينا نِسْتفيد مِن الوَقِت ونْكون مبْسوطين. | 25 | So, that's why we try as much as we can to make the most of the time and be happy. |

## Vocabulary

1. to feed[4] _____
2. my parents[5] _____
3. to finish[8] _____
4. to put to bed[10] _____
5. to begin[11] _____
6. to do[12] _____
7. twelve[15] _____
8. to go out[22] _____
9. to end[24] _____
10. to benefit from[25] _____

_____

## Answers

**Main Idea:** b **True or False:** 1. F[5] 2. F[8] 3. T[12] 4. T[17-21] 5. F[22] **Multiple Choice:** 1. c[14] 2. c[23] 3. d[16] **Matching:** كِرْمال / for / صراحة honestly / سوْ so / سَوى together / لإلْنا for us / عِنّا we have / شي something as / قدّ ما فينا much as we can / كيف how / هيْك مِشان that's why **Vocabulary:** 1. طعْمى 2. أهْلي 3. خلّص 4. نيّم / ذات الشّي the same thing / صوْب around / تِقْريباً كِلّ almost every / شي محلّ somewhere / 5. بلّش 6. عِمِل 7. طْنعْش 8. ضهر 9. خُلِص 10. سْتفاد مِن

31 | Lebanese Arabic Voices

# 8 Rita's Daily Routine

## Keywords

نْهار day     مطّلِع informed, up-to-date

## Main Idea

a. Rita focuses on her professional routine related to her new job.
b. Rita tells us primarily about her fitness routine and gym activities.
c. Rita describes her routine as a student, emphasizing her study habits.
d. *None of the above*

## True or False

1. Rita currently has a full-time job, which heavily influences her daily routine.
2. Rita takes her coffee black.
3. One of Rita's daily activities is going for a walk, which she considers her preferred form of physical exercise.
4. Cooking is a newly discovered hobby for Rita since she had more time after moving.
5. Listening to audiobooks or podcasts is a part of Rita's cooking routine.

## Multiple Choice

1. What does Rita like to do first thing in the morning?

   a. Go for a walk    b. Drink coffee    c. Read the news    d. Make breakfast

2. How does Rita keep herself informed about current events?

   a. By attending local community meetings

   b. Through social media

   c. Watching the news and reading about politics

   d. Consulting with friends and family

3. In the evening, what activity do Rita and her husband often enjoy together?

   a. Cooking dinner    c. Reading books

   b. Gardening    d. Going to the gym

## Matching

| | |
|---|---|
| مِش مِن زَمان | (not) at all |
| مِنّي | after __ing |
| تَـ | after that |
| أَبَداً | but |
| مِن بَعْد هيْك | depending on |
| مِن بَعْد ما | either... or |
| بِما إِنّو | I am not |
| أَمّا... أَمّا | I mean |
| شي | recently |
| قَصْدي | since, because |
| حَسَب | so that, in order to |
| بَسّ | some, a(n) |
| إِيّام | sometimes |

## Text

1. بَدّي خَبِّرْكُن شْوَيّ عَن نْهار بِحَياتي، شو بَعْمُل كِلّ يوْم.
   I want to tell you a bit about a day in my life, what I do every day.

2. أَنا مِش مِن زَمان نَقَلِت مِن وِلاية لَوِلاية بْأَميرْكا، وهَلّأ عَم نْبِّش عَ شُغْل جْديد لِأَنّو ضْطَرّيْت إِتْرُك شِغْلي بِالْوِلاية يَلّي فَلّيْنا مِنّا.
   I recently moved from one state to another in America, and now I am looking for a new job as I had to leave my job in the state we moved from.

3. بَقى هَلّأ، بِما إِنّو مِنّي عَم بِشْتِغِل، نْهاري أَكيد ما بْيِشْبِه الإِيّام اللي كانِت عيشا بَسّ كِنِت إِشْتِغِل.
   So now, since I am not working, my days definitely don't resemble the days when I was working.

4. بَسّ رَح إِشْرِحِلْكُن عَن نْهاري هَلّأ.
   But I'll explain to you about my day now.

5. بوعى الصِّبِح بَكّير لِأَنّو جَوْزي شُغْلو بَكّير، بَقى مْنوعى إِجْمالاً سَوا بْذات الوَقِت أَوْ إِيّام بوعى شْوَيّ مِن بَعْدو تَنام شْوَيّ زْيادِة.
   I wake up early in the morning because my husband starts work early, so we usually wake up together around that time, or on some days, I wake up a little later, so I can sleep in a bit more.

6. بوعى بْفَرْشي سْناني وبِرْجَع أَوّل شي بَعْمْلو بِشْرَب قَهْوِة.
   I brush my teeth, and the first thing I do is drink coffee.

|  |  |  |
|---|---|---|
| 7 | ما في حكي ما في شُغِل ما في شي إلّا ما تِنْشرب القَهْوِة. | No talking, no work, nothing happens until coffee is consumed. |
| 8 | ما بْحِبّ القَهْوِة السّوْدا أبداً، لازِم يْكون في حليب مع القَهْوِة تفيِّي إشْربا. | I don't like black coffee at all; it must have milk for me to drink it. |
| 9 | ومِن بَعْد هيْك، بْحِبّ روح إمْشي. | And after that, I like to go for a walk. |
| 10 | إيّام بِمْشي ساعة، إيّام أكْتر. | Some days, I walk for an hour, and some days, more. |
| 11 | هَيْدا أكْتر تمْرين رِياضي بْحِبّو، وأكْتر تمْرين رِياضي بْحِسّ بيناسِب وبيفيد جِسْمي. | This is the physical exercise I like the most and the one I feel suits and benefits my body. |
| 12 | مِن بَعْد ما إمْشي، بِرْجع عَ البيْت. | After walking, I return home. |
| 13 | إيّام بْقْرا الأخْبار، بِحْضُر الأخْبار أوْ هيْك تضلّني مطلّعة خْصوصيّة عَ السّياسيّة اللي هوّ مَوْضوع كْتير بيهمّني. | Some days, I read the news and watch the news to keep myself informed, especially about politics, which is a subject that interests me a lot. |
| 14 | حتّى إنّو... منّي عم بِشْتِغل هلاّ، بدّي ضلّني مطّلعة وبدّي ضلّني مطّلعة ومْتابعة كِلّ الإشْيا اللي عم بْتصير دوَليّاً وإقْليميّاً وحتّى بِقلْب بأميرْكا. | Even though I'm not working right now, I want to stay informed and keep up with everything that's happening internationally, regionally, and even inside the US. |
| 15 | مِن بَعْد هيْك، بْروح على سوبِرْماركِت وبْجيب غْراض تكرْمال بلّش أعْمُل غدا. | After that, I go to the supermarket to get groceries, then start making lunch. |
| 16 | الطّبْخ هوّ شي أنا كْتير بْحِبّو. | Cooking is something I really love. |
| 17 | بسّ ما كان يْكون عِنْدي وَقِت إلو كْتير قبل بسّ كِنِت إشْتِغِل، | I didn't used to have much time for it before when I was working, |
| 18 | وهلاّ بما إنّو عِنْدي بْريْك صْغيرة مِن الشّغِل تكِنِت لقيت شُغِل تاني، عم لاقي وَقِت أكْتر إنّو أُطْبُخ. | but now that I have a small break from work until I find another job, I find more time to cook. |
| 19 | وهَيْدا شي كْتير حابّتو. | And I really enjoy that. |
| 20 | بْحِبّ هيْك إتْفنّن بأكْلات وأعْمُل شي جْديد ويِطْلع طيِّب. | I like to get creative with dishes, try something new, and make it delicious. |
| 21 | أنا وعم بْطبُّخ، بْحِبّ كمان إتْسمّع أمّا podcast، أمّا عَ شي كْتاب بِسمعو سمع مِتِل يَعْني قصْدي audiobook. | While I'm cooking, I also like to listen to either a podcast or I listen to a book, like, I mean, an audiobook. |
| 22 | كْتير بْحِبّ أعْمُل هيْك أنا وعم بْطبُخ. | I really enjoy doing this while cooking. |
| 23 | بْيِقْطع الوَقِت كْتير بْسِرْعة وبِذات الوَقِت بْكون إتْعلّم شي جْديد أوْ إقْرا كْتاب جْديد أوْ اللي هيِّ. | It makes time pass quickly, and at the same time, I learn something new or "read" a new book. |

| | |
|---|---|
| 24 | After I finish cooking, I clean up, tidy up, and make the bed. |
| 25 | Maybe I'll go for a walk if I have time, depending on the weather, depending on the climate, depending on my mood. |
| 26 | When my husband comes home, some days we go to the gym together, and after getting back from the gym, we have dinner. |
| 27 | Some days, he cleans up after dinner and does the dishes, or I do, depending. |
| 28 | But he likes to take over these tasks sometimes because I would have been the one cooking. |
| 29 | And after we finish, we like to sit down and watch a series, a movie, or a documentary about a topic we want to learn more about. |
| 30 | And we sit sometimes, like, for an hour or two, depending on how interested we are in what we're watching. |
| 31 | And when that's over, we go brush our teeth and go to sleep. |
| 32 | And that's a day in my life now. |
| 33 | If I were to explain to you what my day was like when I was working, it would have been very different. |

مِن بَعْد ما خَلَّص طبخ، بْنضِّف وبْضبْضِب وبعْمُل بْساوي التّخِت.

يمْكِن إرْجع روح إمْشي إذا كان عِنْدي وَقِت، حسب كيف الجوّ، حسب كيف الطّقس، حسب كيف مزاجي.

بسّ يِجي جَوْزي عَ البيْت إيّام مِنْروح عَ الجّيم مع بعْضْنا وبسّ نِرْجع مِن الجّيم، مْنقْعُد مْنِتْعشّى.

إيّام هُوّ بِيْرَتِّب مِن بَعْد العشا وبْيِجْلي أَوْ أنا حسب،

بسّ بيحِبّ إيّام ياخُد هُوّ عنّي الإشيا لأنّو أنا بْكون طابْخة.

ومِن بَعْد ما نْخلِّص مِنْحِبّ نقْعُد نحضر شي مُسلْسل أوّ فيلْم أوْ فيلْم وَثائِقي عن مَوْضوع حابّين نِتْعلّم عنّو أكْتر.

ومْنُقْعد إيّام، يَعْني ساعة ساعْتيْن حسب ما نْكون مِهْتمّين باللّي عم نِحْضرو.

وبسّ يِخْلصوا، مِنْفوت مِنْفَرْشي سْنانْنا ومِنْنام.

وهَيْدا نْهار بحَياتي هلّأ.

لَوْ كِنت عم بِشْرحِلْكُن كيف نْهاري وَقت كِنت عم بِشْتِغِل كان بيكون كْتير مِخْتِلِف.

## Vocabulary

1. to look for[2] _____
2. early[5] _____
3. to work[3] _____
4. to brush one's teeth[6] _____
5. physical exercise[11] _____
6. groceries[15] _____
7. delicious[20] _____
8. to listen to[21] _____
9. to tidy up[24] _____
10. series[29] _____

## Answers

**Main Idea:** d **True or False:** 1. F[2] 2. F[8] 3. T[9-11] 4. T[17-18] 5. T[21-23] **Multiple Choice:** 1. b[6-8] 2. c[13-14] 3. d[26] **Matching:** مِن بعْد هيْك after / مِش مِن زمان recently / منّي I am not / تَـ so that, in order to / أبداً (not) at all / قصْدي I mean / شي some, a(n) / أمّا... أمّا either... or / بما إنّو since, because / مِن بعْد ما after ___ing / that / إيّام sometimes / بسّ but / حسب depending on / **Vocabulary:** 1. عَ بشّ / 2. بكّير / 3. شْتغِل / 4. فرْشى سْنانو / 5. تمْرين رِياضي / 6. غْراض / 7. طيِّب / 8. تسْمع / 9. ضبْضب / 10. مُسلْسل

# 9 Sandy's Daily Routine

## Keywords

روتين يَوْمي daily routine      وعي (يوعى) to wake up

## Main Idea

a. Sandy spends most of her day outside the house, attending various social events and meetings.
b. Sandy's day is primarily focused on her music career, with most of her time spent in the studio.
c. Sandy's routine revolves around managing household chores, taking care of her son, working from home, and spending time with family.
d. Sandy dedicates the majority of her day to fitness activities and sports.

## True or False

1. Sandy's son takes a bus to school every morning.
2. Sandy works exclusively from an office outside her home.
3. Sandy and her son have lunch with her parents every day.
4. In the evenings, Sandy usually goes out to social events or meetings.
5. Sandy ensures she is back home before her son returns from school, even when she has work outside.

## Multiple Choice

1. What is one of Sandy's key responsibilities in the morning?

    a. Going to the gym for a workout
    b. Attending early morning business meetings
    c. Recording music at the studio
    d. Preparing food and getting her son ready for school

2. How does Sandy typically spend her time after her son leaves for school?

    a. Immediately starting her household chores
    b. Going for a morning run
    c. Having coffee and a chat with her partner, Mario
    d. Working on her music

3. Where does Sandy go to meet people for work or meetings?

    a. At her home office
    b. At a café or coffee shop
    c. In a studio
    d. At her partner's workplace

## Matching

|  |  |
|---|---|
| عادي | depending on |
| كَوْني | generally |
| إلّا أذا | here |
| سَوى | of course |
| بَعْدين | since/as I... |
| أَكيد | some, a(n) |
| إن كان | sometimes |
| هوْني | that, which, who |
| هِنّي | then |
| مرّات | they |
| حسب | together |
| شي | typical, usual |
| يَلّي | unless |
| مبْدَأيّاً | whether |

## Text

| |  |  |
|---|---|---|
| 1 | مرْحبا، إذا بدّي خبِّركُن عن روتيني اليَوْمي أوْ كيف نْهار عادي مِن حَياتي كيف بيكون شكْلو، | Hello, if I were to tell you about my daily routine or what a typical day in my life looks like, |
| 2 | فيّي خبِّركُن إنّو بوعى تقْريباً السّاعة سِتّة الصُّبح كِلّ يوْم، بْفوت، بْحضِّرلو أكْلو لإبْني لَياخِدُن معوع المدْرسِة. | I can tell you that I usually wake up around six in the morning every day, get up, and prepare food for my son to take to school. |
| 3 | بْحضِّرلو شنْتو وغْراضو، بْوَعّي بْلْبِّسو. | I get his bag and things ready, wake him up, and get him dressed. |
| 4 | بْيجي الباص بْياخدو على المدْرسِة. | Then the bus comes to take him to school. |
| 5 | وكَوْني أنا بِشْتِغِل أوْنْلايْن، غالِباً ما يْكون شِغْلي مِن قلْب البيْت. | Since I work online, most of my work is done from home. |
| 6 | ما بِضْطرّ إضْهر كْتير لبرّا، إلّا إذا كان عِنْدي تُصْوير أوْ تِسْجيل أوْ أيّ شي بيطلّب مِنّي إنّي إضْهر. | I don't have to go out much unless I have a shoot or recording session or something that requires me to go out. |

| | |
|---|---|
| 7 | After my son leaves for school, I spend some time with my "roommate," Mario. |
| 8 | We have coffee together, chat for a while, watch some TV, catch up on the news, and then each of us starts our work. |
| 9 | He goes to his job, and I start my work at home, if my work is at home. |
| 10 | Of course, being at home, I have to do some household chores. |
| 11 | Whether it's laundry, dishwashing, cleaning, ironing, all those things that a homemaker needs to do. |
| 12 | From here until around two-thirty or three in the afternoon, it's time for my son to come back from school. |
| 13 | He arrives, and I greet him with a big kiss and a hug, and then we go to visit grandma and grandpa. |
| 14 | Their house is not too far from ours, just a ten-minute drive. |
| 15 | We go out to have lunch together every day, so they get to see him, and we also eat healthy food because I don't cook much, haha! |
| 16 | After eating, we sit for a while and have a cup of coffee. |
| 17 | Then my son and I return to Hadath. |
| 18 | I go to my sports class, and by then, my partner has returned home and takes care of Ian until I come back. |
| 19 | He has... we have dinner together, all of us for sure. Then he takes a bath and goes to bed. |
| 20 | We spend the evening together. If we have guests, we entertain them. |
| 21 | If we have some work at home, we do it together. |
| 22 | If not, we watch a movie or series. |

مِن بَعْد ما يْفِلّ إبْني عَلى المَدْرَسِة، بِقْعُد شْوَيّ أنا وشْريكي بالسَّكَن ماريو.

مِنِشْرَب قَهْوِة سَوى، مْنِتْحدّث شْوَيّ، مْنِحْضَر شْوَيِّة تِليفِزْيون، مْنِحْضَر أخْبار، وبَعْدَين كِلّ واحد بيبَلِّش شِغْلو.

هُوِّ بيروح عَلى شِغْلو وأنا بَلِّش شِغْلي بالْبَيْت، إذا كان شِغْلي بالْبَيْت.

أكيد كَوْني بالْبَيْت بْكون مِضْطَرّة أعْمِل شْوَيِّة أشْغال بِقَلْب البَيْت.

إن كان غَسيل، جَلي، تَنْضيف، كَوي، كِلّ هَولي القُصَص يَلّي حيّلا ربِّة مَنْزِل بِدّا تَعْمِلُن.

مِن هَوْني للسّاعة تَقْريباً تِنْتَين ونُصّ تْلاتة بَعْد الضُّهُر بيكون صار وَقِت يوصل إبْني مِن المَدْرَسة.

بْيوصَل، بِسْتِقْبِلُو بوسُو بَوْسِة كْتير كْبيرة وعَبْوطة، ومْنِرْجَع مْنِطْلَع عِنْد التّيْتا وجِدّو.

بَيْتُن مِش كْتير بْعيد عَن بَيْتْنا، عَشَر دْقايِق بالسِّيّارة.

مْنِطْلَع مْنِتْغَدّى سَوى كِلّ يَوْم، هَيْك هِنِّي بيْشوفوا ونِحْنا كَمان مِنِتْغَدّى أكِل صُحّي لأنّو أنا ما بِطْبُخ كْتير، ههه!

مْناكُل، مِنْخَلِّص، مِنِقْعُد شْوَيّ مِنِشْرَب فِنْجان قَهْوِة.

وبِرْجَع بِنْزَل أنا وإبْني عَلى الحَدَد.

أنا بْروح عَلى صَفّ السْبور وهَوْن بيكون رِجَع شْريكي بالْبَيْت بْيِقْعُد وبْيِهْتَمّ بإيان لكِنِت أنا رْجِعِت.

بْيِتْعَشّى... مْنِتْعَشّى سَوى، كِلّنا أكيد بْيِتْحَمَّم بيفوت بْنام.

مْنِقْعُد بالسَّهْرة. إذا عِنّا عالَم نِسْتِقْبِلُن مْنِسْتِقْبِلُن.

إذا عِنّا شْوَيِّة شِغِل بالبَيْت مِنِشْتِغِل سَوى.

إذا ما عِنّا شي، مْنِقْعُد مِنِحْضَر فْلومة أوْ مُسَلْسَلات.

| | | |
|---|---|---|
| و... مرّات مْنِشْرب كاس ومرّات مْنِشْرب كاسِة شاي ومرّات مْنِشْرب سحْلب، حسب شو عَ بالْنا وحسب الطّقْس كيف بيكون. | 23 | And... sometimes we drink a glass [of wine], sometimes tea, and sometimes sahlab, depending on our mood and the weather. |
| وتِقْريباً عَ السّاعة طْنَعْش، حْدَعْش ونُصّ عشية أوْ طْنَعْش، بْفوت بْنام وبِرْجع بوعى تاني نْهار بعْمِل نفْس الشّي. | 24 | Usually, around 12... or 11:30 or 12 at night, I go to sleep and then wake up the next day to do the same routine. |
| أكيد مرّات بيكون عِنْدي شِغِل برّاة البيْت. | 25 | Of course, sometimes I have work outside the house. |
| بِهيْدي الحالة أكيد بْرتّب حالي وبِضْهر بْخلّص الشّغِل يلّي عِنْدي ياه. | 26 | In those cases, I organize myself and go out to finish the work I have. |
| وأكيد بِتْأكّد إنّي إرْجع قبل ما يْصير وَقْت إنّو إبْني يوصل مِن المدْرسِة. | 27 | And I always make sure to return before it's time for my son to come back from school. |
| مرّات بْروح عَ السْتوديو بْسجّل موسيقى. | 28 | Sometimes, I go to the studio to record music. |
| إذا عِنْدي شِغِل عِنْدي إِجْتِماع بْروح عَ شي مقْهى أوْ عَ شي كافيه بجْتِمع مع الأشخاص يلّي عِنْدي إجْتِماع معن. | 29 | If I have work or a meeting, I go to a coffee shop or café to meet with the people I have appointments with. |
| بْخلّص يلّي عِنْدي وبِرْجع على البيْت. | 30 | I finish what I have to do and then return home. |
| مبْدأيّاً هيْك بيكونوا نْهاراتي بأرْضية الجِّمْعة. | 31 | Generally, that's how my days go on weekdays. |

## Vocabulary

1. to wake [someone] up[3] _____
2. to require[6] _____
3. to leave[7] _____
4. housewife[11] _____
5. kiss[13] _____
6. partner[18] _____
7. to take a bath[19] _____
8. at night[24] _____
9. the next day[24] _____
10. on weekdays[31] _____

## Answers

**Main Idea:** c **True or False:** 1. T[4] 2. F[5] 3. T[13-15] 4. F[20-22] 5. T[27] **Multiple Choice:** 1. d[2-3] 2. c[8] 3. b[29] **Matching:** أكيد of / then بَعْدين / together سَوى / unless إلّا أذا / since/as I... كَوْني / typical, usual عادي / شي some, a(n) / depending on حسب / sometimes مرّات / they هِنّي / here هوْني / whether إن كان / of course / يلّي that, which, who / مبْدأيّاً generally **Vocabulary:** 1. وَعّى (يْوَعّي) 2. طلّب 3. فلّ 4. ربّة بيْت 5. بَوْسِة 6. شريك 7. تْحمّم 8. عشية 9. تاني يوْم 10. بأرْضية الجِّمْعة

# Childhood Memories

## 10 Charbel's Childhood Memory

### Keywords

تْذَكّر to remember    مدينِةْ ملاهي amusement park    غوْلر goalie

### Main Idea

a. Charbel's childhood was predominantly spent indoors, engaged in solitary activities.
b. Charbel's childhood memories are a mix of outdoor activities with his father and playing creative games with friends.
c. Most of Charbel's childhood memories involve traveling to different cities with his family.
d. Charbel remembers his childhood as a time of technological advancements and modern entertainment.

### True or False

1. Charbel's father would often take a nap before taking him to the amusement park.
2. Swimming was a regular activity Charbel did with his father on Sundays.
3. Charbel believes that life was simpler and more enjoyable in his childhood compared to now.
4. Television was the primary form of entertainment in Charbel's childhood.
5. Charbel mentions playing a variety of games, including soccer, during his childhood.

### Multiple Choice

1. According to Charbel, what has changed significantly from his childhood to the present?

   a. The prevalence of technology and social media
   b. The availability of public transportation
   c. The way people communicate with each other
   d. The types of games children play

2. How did Charbel and his friends adapt their games when they didn't have enough players for a game of soccer?

   a. They would play a different game entirely.
   b. They created the 'Blind Goalie' game.
   c. They would call more friends to join.
   d. *None of the above*

3. What does Charbel think about the pace of life in his childhood compared to now?

    a. It was simpler and more leisurely.

    b. It was more hectic and stressful.

    c. There was more emphasis on outdoor activities.

    d. Life was more focused on family gatherings.

## Matching

|  |  |
|---|---|
| حدّ | after |
| بعْد | also |
| كِرْمال | each other |
| سوْ | everyone |
| بعْض | near |
| كمان | so |
| أنا وصْغير | so that; in order to |
| وَقْتا | then, at that time |
| ما كان في | there wasn't/weren't |
| هال | this, these |
| فيك | we were |
| كِنّا | when I was little |
| كِلّ العالم | you can |

## Text

|  |  |
|---|---|
| مِن القُصص اللي بِتْذكّرا أنا وصْغير وخاصّةً هلّأ هيْك مع عِنْدي بايْبي وهيْكي، سوْ بِتْذكّر إنّو كِلّ نْهار أحد كِنت نِقّ على بيّي ياخِدْني على مدينةْ الملاهي. | One of the stories I remember from when I was young, especially now that I have a baby, is that every Sunday, I used to nag my father to take me to the amusement park. |
| كان في حدّ بَيْتْنا على الدّوْرة مدينةْ الملاهي صْغيرة. | There was a small amusement park near our house in Dora. |

| | |
|---|---|
| 3 | After lunch, I used to start nagging my dad, saying: "Don't sleep, don't sleep! Let's go play at the amusement park." |
| 3 | كِنِت بَعْد الغَدا نِتْغدّى هيْك سوْ صير نِقّ على بيّي إنّو: "ما تْنام ما تْنام خلّينا نْروح نِلْعب بمدينِةْ الملاهي." |
| 4 | He would sleep for an hour, and I would eagerly wait for him to wake up so I could then say, "Please, let's go!" |
| 4 | كان هوّ يْنام شي ساعة وأنا إبْقى مْحرْقس ناطِر لَيوعى كِرْمال إرْجع قِلّو: "بْليز خلّينا نْروح". |
| 5 | So, he would take me to the amusement park, and we would play on the... what we call bumper cars, the electric cars that bump into each other. |
| 5 | سوْ كان ياخِدْني على مدينِةْ الملاهي ونِلْعب بالـ... نْقِلّا أوْتوْ توِمْبوْنوز اللي هيِّ السّيارات اللي عَ الكَهْربا يْخبْطوا بَعْض. |
| 6 | That was the game/ride I played the most. |
| 6 | كانت هَيْدي اللِّعْبة الأكْتَر شي إلْعبا. |
| 7 | Another memory I have from when I was young is when my dad and I used to go, also on Sundays... get on the bus and go swim in the swimming pool. |
| 7 | وكمان مِن الـ memories اللي بْتذكّرْن كمان وأنا وصْغير اللي هيِّ وَقْتا كِنّا نْروح كمان نهار الأحد نِطْلع بالْباص ونْروح أنا وبيّي عَ الـ... نِتْسبّح عَ المَسْبح. |
| 8 | So, these are the things I remember, and I recall how things used to be easier and life was simpler. |
| 8 | سوْ هوْلي هيْك بِتْذكّرْن وبِتْذكّر إنّو كيف كانت الأمور أسْهل وأمور الحَياةْ كانت أهْيَن. |
| 9 | There weren't these problems, no social media, no phones. |
| 9 | ما في هالْمَشاكِل، وما كان في هالـ... ما كان في هالسّوْشِيل ميدْيا، ما كان في تِليفوْنات. |
| 10 | The most we would do was watch TV, and the rest was all activities. |
| 10 | كان إنّو مَكْسيموم اللي بدّنا نعمْلو هوِّ نِحْضر تيفي والباقي كان كِلّو activities. |
| 11 | We would play with bicycles and play ball, and there was a game called 'Blind Goalie.' |
| 11 | كِنّا نِلْعب بالْبيسِكْلات، نِلْعب بالطّابة وفي لِعْبة كان إسْما غوْلْر أعْمى. |
| 12 | It was because we didn't have enough players [to play soccer]. |
| 12 | هوِّ بيكون لأنّو إنتَ ما بيكون عِنْدك عدد كْفايِة مِن اللّعّيبة، |
| 13 | So let's say if there were four of us, you could play two-on-two, |
| 13 | سوْ let's say كِنّا أرْبع أشْخاص فيك تِلْعب تْنيْن عَ تْنيْن، |
| 14 | but if there were five of us, someone had to be the goalie. |
| 14 | بسّ إذا كِنّا مثلاً خمْسِة مجْبور حدا يوقف غوْلْر. |
| 15 | So, one would stand as a goalie at the goal, turn his back to the players, and throw the ball far away. |
| 15 | سوْ كان يوقف غوْلْر واحد على كِنّا عم نِلْعب فوتبوْل، يوقف غوْلْر واحد على المرْمى ويبرِّم ضهْرو للّعّيبة ويْكِب الطّابة بْعيد. |
| 16 | The first one to get the ball would be the one to attack the goal. |
| 16 | وأوّل حدا بْياخُد البوْزيشِن هوِّ بيصير إنّو بدّو يهْجُم على الغوْل. |

**43** | Lebanese Arabic Voices

| | | |
|---|---|---|
| سوْ كان نْلاقي ألْعاب وخْبار وحْكايات . | 17 | So we would find games and stories. |
| كانِت الأُمور أحْلى. | 18 | Things were nicer. |
| إذا بتْشوف هلّأ كِلّ العالم على الآيْباد وعلى التِّيكْتوك وعلى الإنْسْتا. | 19 | If you look now, everyone is on the iPad, TikTok, and Instagram. |
| أيْه بِعْتِقِد كانِت الحَياةْ أهْيَن قبِل. | 20 | Yeah, I think life used to be simpler. |

## Vocabulary

1. to nag[1] _____
2. to wake up[2] _____
3. bumper cars[5] _____
4. [amusement park] ride[6] _____
5. simpler[8] _____

6. ball[11] _____
7. there were four of us[13] _____
8. have to, must[14] _____
9. soccer[15] _____
10. I believe[20] _____

_____

## Answers

**Main Idea:** b **True or False:** 1. T[4] 2. T[7] 3. T[8, 18, 20] 4. F[10] 5. T[11-17] **Multiple Choice:** 1. a[9] 2. b[12-16] 3. a[20] **Matching:** حدّ near / بعْد after / كرْمال so that; in order to / سوْ so / بعْض each other / كمان also / أنا فيك this, these / هالـ there wasn't/weren't / ما كان في then, at that time / وَقْتا when I was little / وصْغير you can / كِنّا we were / كِلّ العالم everyone **Vocabulary:** 1. نقّ على 2. وعي 3. أوْتوْ توـمْبوْنوز 4. لِعْبِة 5. أهْيَن 6. طابِة 7. كِنّا أرْبع أشْخاص 8. مجْبور 9. فوتْبوْل 10. بِعْتِقِد

# 11  Nisrine's Childhood Memory

## Keywords

تْذَكَّر to remember    ذِكْرى memory

## Main Idea

a. Nisrine talks about when her father taught her to ride a bicycle.
b. Nisrine shares the special memories she has visiting her grandparents in their village.
c. Nisrine discusses her academic achievements during her school years.
d. Nisrine tells us about a special school trip that she remembers fondly.

## True or False

1. Nisrine's childhood was mostly spent indoors due to the lack of outdoor spaces in her village.
2. Nisrine's special school trip was her first time visiting Beirut.
3. Nisrine saw a lot of animals at Dream Park.
4. Nisrine has unfortunately lost all the photos and souvenirs from her childhood trip.
5. Nisrine ends on a note of regret about her childhood experiences.

## Multiple Choice

1. What was a significant part of Nisrine's playtime in her village?

    a. Watching television with her family
    b. Attending local community events
    c. Practicing indoor games
    d. Playing with her first bicycle and exploring the village

2. Where did Nisrine's memorable school trip take her?

    a. Dream Park   b. Byblos   c. Rabbit Island   d. All of he above

3. Which of the following is true?

    a. It was her first time going to a zoo.

    b. It was her first trip without her family.

    c. It was her first time returning home at night.

    d. It was her first time on an airplane.

## Matching

| | |
|---|---|
| بِحِكِم إنّو | all kinds (of) |
| أيْمتا | also |
| كِرْمال | as soon as |
| اللي | considering that... |
| كمان | never |
| أوّل ما | so that, in order to |
| مع بعْض | still |
| كِلّ أنْواع | that, who, which |
| كْتير | to |
| بعْدو لهلّأ | very |
| ويّاه | when |
| على | with (one) |
| أبداً | with each other |

## Text

| | | |
|---|---|---|
| أحْلى إيّام حَياتي بِتْذكّرُن عِشْتُن وَقْتا كِنِت صْغيرة. | 1 | The best days of my life, I remember living them when I was young. |
| أحْلى إيّام هِنّي، إيّام الطُفولةِ، ودايْماً بِتْذكّرُن وبِنْبُسِط مِن قلْبي. | 2 | The best days are those of childhood, always remembered, and they bring joy to my heart. |
| إنّو أنا عِشِت إيّام حِلْوة وَقْتا كِنِت صْغيرة. | 3 | Indeed, I lived beautiful days when I was young. |
| كْتير عِنْدي ذِكْرايات حِلْوة وَقْتا كِنِت صْغيرة. | 4 | I have many sweet memories from that time. |
| وأحْلى ذِكْرايات بِتْذكّرا وَقْتا كِنّا نِلْعب، أنا ووْلاد عمّي وإخْواتي. | 5 | And the best memories I recall are when we used to play, me, my cousins, and my siblings. |
| نِحْنا بِحِكِم إنّو عايْشين بِضَيْعة، كِنّا دايْماً كِلّ يوْم ما نْصدِّق أيْمتا يِطْلع الضَوْ كِرْمال نِنْزل نِلْعب مع بعْض. | 6 | Living in a village, we could never wait for the sun to rise every day, so we could go out and play together. |
| كِنّا نِلْعب كْتير ألْعاب حِلْوة. | 7 | We used to play a lot of great games. |
| بِتْذكّر أوّل بيسِكْلات جبْلي ياها بيّي. | 8 | I remember the first bicycle my father got me. |

| | |
|---|---|
| 9 | We used to play with it, me, my cousins, siblings, and we roamed and explored the whole village. |
| 10 | And I remember the days we used to play in the garden, with flowers, in the dirt, running around and having fun. |
| 11 | We always invented the most wonderful games to entertain ourselves. |
| 12 | I also remember a very special day from my childhood, which was my first trip I went on with my school friends and teachers. |
| 13 | It was a very special day for me, a really beautiful day. |
| 14 | I get happy when I remember that day. |
| 15 | I remember, on that trip, we went from Akkar to Beirut. |
| 16 | As soon as we arrived, we went to Dream Park, to the amusement park. |
| 17 | My friends and I played a lot, had a lot of fun, laughed, and enjoyed ourselves. |
| 18 | Then we went to a forest, to the zoo. |
| 19 | We saw all kinds of animals and took photos with each other and with the animals. |
| 20 | I remember those were the first photos I took with my friends. |
| 21 | I still have those photos. And they are very precious to me, these photos. |
| 22 | After the zoo, I went... we went together... all of us went to Byblos. |
| 23 | We strolled in the markets of Byblos, bought souvenirs, and exchanged gifts with my friends. |
| 24 | I still have those gifts. |

صِرِت إلْعَب فِيا، نِحْنا وبِيْت عمّي وإخْواتي ونْروح نْكَزْدِر ونِبْرُم كِلّ الضِّيْعة.

وبِتْذكّر إيّام الكِنّا نِلْعَب بِالبِسْتان وبِالوَرِد ونِلْعَب بِالتْراب، ونْضِلّنا نِرْكُض ونِنْبْسِط.

ودايْماً نِخْتِرِع أحْلى... أحْلى الألْعاب اللي كِنّا نِتْسلّى فِيْن.

وكَمان بِتْذكّر يوْم كْتير مُميّز عِنْدي وَقْتا كِنِت صْغيرة، وهُوّ... هِيّ أوّل رِحْلِة رِحِت فِيا مع رِفْقاتي بِالمَدْرسِة ومع المْعلّمات.

كان يوْم كْتير مُميّز عِنْدي، وكان يوْم كْتير حِلو.

بِنْبِسِط وَقْتا بِتْذكّر هَيْدا النْهار.

بِتْذكّر رِحْنا بِهَيْدي الرِّحْلِة من عكّار على بِيْروت.

أوّل... أوّل ما وْصِلْنا، رِحْنا على Dream Park، على مدينِة المَلاهي.

لعِبِت أنا ورِفْقاتي، كْتير نْبسطْنا، كْتير ضْحِكْنا، كْتير تْسلّينا.

ورْجِعْنا رِحْنا... رِحْنا على غابِة الـ... على حديقِة الحَيَوانات.

شِفْنا كِلّ أنْواع الحَيَوانات وتْصوّرْنا مع بعْض، وتْصوّرْنا نِحْنا والحَيَوانات.

بِتْذكّر بِهَيْدي الرِّحْلِة كانِت أوّل صُوَر باخِدُن مع رِفْقاتي.

وبِعْدُن هَيْدول الصُّوَر معي، وكْتير غالْيين بِالنِّسْبة لإلي هَيْدول الصُّوَر.

وبعْد حديقِة الحَيَوانات رِحِت... رِحْنا مع بعْض... كِلِّياتْنا رِحْنا على جْبيْل.

كَزْدَرْنا بِأسْواق جْبيْل وشْتريْنا تِذْكار من هوْنيك، وهديْت رِفْقاتي وهِنّي هدوني.

وبعْدُن الهدايا معي.

| | | |
|---|---|---|
| 25 | كْتير بْحِبّ إنّي قضّيْت أحْلى إيّام حَياتي، أنا ورِفْقاتي. | I really love that I spent the best days of my life with my friends. |
| 26 | رِفْقاتي بعْدُن لهلّأ، أنا ويّاهُن مْنِحْكي دايْماً ومِنْشوف بعْض ومْنِتْقابل. | My friends are still around. They and I always talk and meet up. |
| 27 | وبعْد جْبيْل خلّصْنا، ورْجِعْنا جينا على المينا بطْرابْلُس. | After Byblos, we finished and returned to the port of Tripoli. |
| 28 | وطْلِعْنا بالْبحِر، كزْدرْنا بالسّفينة. | We went out on the sea and cruised around on a ship. |
| 29 | رحْنا على جزيرِةْ الأرانِب، ورْجِعنا وقعدْنا بالْمينا أكلْنا بوظة. | We visited Rabbit Island, then returned and sat at the port and had ice cream. |
| 30 | وخلّصْنا ورْجِعنا على الضّيْعة. | We finished our trip and returned to the village. |
| 31 | كان وَقِت مِتْأخّر، كان أوّل مرّة بِحَياتي أنا بِتْأخّر عن البيْت وبِرْجع عَ البيْت والدِّني... الدِّني باللّيْل يَعْني. | It was late. For the first time in my life, I stayed out late and returned home at night. |
| 32 | فا هَيْدا نْهار كمان كْتير بْحِبّو، كْتير بْتذكّرو. | So, I also love and always remember that day. |
| 33 | ودايْماً بْذكِّر رِفْقاتي فيْن، وكْتير بْحِبّ إنّو أنا عِشِت إيّام حِلْوِة، وإيّام بِتْذكّرا، وبِتْضلّا بِذاكِرْتي وما بْنْساها أبداً. | I always remind my friends about them, and I really love that I lived beautiful days, days that I remember, that stay in my memory, and I never forget them. |
| 34 | وبْحِبّ إنّو بعِدْني لهلّأ أنا ورِفْقاتي أصْحاب. | I love that, to this day, my friends and I are still close. |
| 35 | وبِتْمنّى دايْماً نْضلّنا هيْك ودايْماً نِلْتقي. | And I hope we always stay this way and continue to meet. |

## Vocabulary

1. cousins[5] _____
2. to hardly be able to wait[6] for _____
3. to roam, wander[9] _____
4. friends[12] _____
5. amusement park[16] _____
6. to have fun[17] _____
7. precious[21] _____
8. to give as a gift[23] _____
9. ice cream[29] _____
10. to stay out[31] _____

## Answers

**Main Idea:** d **True or False:** 1. F[6] 2. F[15] 3. F[16-29] 4. F[20-24] 5. F[33-35] **Multiple Choice:** 1. d[8-9] 2. d[16, 22, 29] 3. c[31] **Matching:** إنّو بِحِكِم considering that... / أيْمتا when / كِرْمال so that, in order to / اللي that, who, which / لهلّأ بعْدو still / كْتير very / أنْواع كِلّ all kinds (of) / بعْض مع with each other / أوّل ما as soon as / كمان ما also / **Vocabulary:** 1. مدينِةْ ملاهي 5. / رِفْقاة 4. / كْزدر 3. / ما صدّق 2. / وْلاد عمّ / ويّاه with (one) / على to / أبداً never 6. نْبسط / 7. غالي / 8. هدى / 9. بوظة / 10. تأخّر عن البيْت

# 12 Mohammad's Childhood Memory

## Keywords

| قِصّة story | خَيّي my brother | مُخَيّم (refugee) camp |
| عِصابة gang | بَواريد خرز pellet guns | |

## Main Idea

a. Mohammad shares how he and his brother got involved with street gangs in the Ain El-Hilweh refugee camp.
b. Mohammad tells us how his family ended up living in the Ain El-Hilweh refugee camp.
c. Mohammad describes his early fascination with the vastness and layout of the Ain El-Hilweh refugee camp.
d. Mohammad recounts the experience of escaping armed clashes near Ain El-Hilweh refugee camp.

## True or False

1. Mohammad lived close to Ain El-Hilweh, the largest refugee camp in Lebanon.
2. Mohammad's visit to Ain El-Hilweh was his first experience seeing the camp.
3. The armed clashes in Ain El-Hilweh started while Mohammad and his brother were still inside the camp buying pellet guns.
4. During the incident, Mohammad's family was able to quickly find a car and leave the area safely.
5. Mohammad's experience during the Eid al-Fitr incident left a lasting impact on him, which he still remembers vividly.

## Multiple Choice

1. Why did Mohammad and his brother buy pellet guns at Ain El-Hilweh camp?

    a. For protection against the gangs
    b. To participate in the fighting
    c. To play with other kids
    d. As a gift for their cousin

2. What did Mohammad's mother keep ready for emergencies?

    a. A first-aid kit
    b. Food and water supplies
    c. A bag with clothes and passports
    d. *None of the above*

3. Where did Mohammad's family flee to after escaping the area near Ain El-Hilweh camp?

   a. They fled to a neighboring country.

   b. They stayed nearby until they found transportation.

   c. They moved permanently to another city.

   d. They returned home immediately after the incident.

## Matching

| | |
|---|---|
| بعْدْني | about, approximately |
| مع إنّو | and whatnot |
| لمّا | even though |
| فا | I still... |
| مرّة | immediately, directly |
| يَعْني | in it |
| وهيْك | obviously |
| بِقلْبو | once, one time |
| فجْأة | so |
| دِغْري | suddenly |
| مْرَيْئاً | that is; I mean |
| شي | until |
| لبيْن ما | when |

# Text

| | | |
|---|---|---|
| حإحْكيلْكُن اليوْم قِصّة عَن طُفولْتي. | 1 | Today, I'm going to tell you a story from my childhood. |
| بَعِدْني لهلّأ بْتِذكّرا، مَع إنّو صِرْلا القِصّة أكْتَر مِن عِشْرين سِنة أوْ تِسِعْطَعْشَر سِنة. | 2 | I still remember it, even though it happened more than twenty—or nineteen—years ago. |
| لمّا كان عُمْري أرْبَعة سْنين، كِنّا ساكْنين أنا وإمّي وإخْتي وخيّي بمِنْطِقة إسْما الفيلّات. | 3 | When I was four years old, my mother, sister, brother, and I lived in an area called The Villas. |
| هَيْدي المِنْطِقة قريبة على مُخيّم عَيْن الحِلْوة بِكْتير. | 4 | This area is very close to the Ain El-Hilweh refugee camp. |
| يَعْني نِصّ بْنايِتْنا كانِت بمُخيّم عَيْن الحِلْوة. | 5 | Half of our building was actually inside Ain El-Hilweh. |
| اللّي ما بْيَعْرِف مُخيّم عَيْن الحِلْوة، مُخيّم عَيْن الحِلْوة هُوّ أكْبَر مُخيّم بلِبْنان، | 6 | For those who don't know Ain El-Hilweh: Ain El-Hilweh is the largest refugee camp in Lebanon, |
| وكان مَشْهور بـ... يَعْني إشْتِباكات بيْن العِصابات اللّي جُوّا، عِصابات مْسَلّحة ومْنَظّمة، عِنْدُن أسْلِحة كْبيرة وتْقيلة. | 7 | and it was known for... well, clashes between gangs inside it, armed and organized gangs with heavy weaponry. |
| كانوا دايْماً يِتْخانقوا مَع بَعْضُن. | 8 | They would constantly fight with each other. |
| فا مرّة كانِت بعيد الفِطِر، هوْن عيد الفِطِر نِحْنا مْنِنْطرو مْناطرة، | 9 | So, once, during Eid al-Fitr... which we eagerly anticipate here... |
| يَعْني كـ...الوْلاد مْنِنْطرو لحتّى نِلْبِس تْياب جْديدة وناخُد عيديّة، | 10 | that is, as children, we look forward to it so that we can wear new clothes and receive 'eidiyah,' |
| يَعْني ناخُد مَصاري مِن قرايْبينّا ونْروح نِشْتِري فْيا أشْيا ونِنْبِسِط، يَعْني وهيْك. | 11 | which means getting money from our relatives to go buy things and enjoy ourselves and whatnot. |
| فا فِتْنا أنا وخيّي مرّة. | 12 | So, my brother and I went out one time. |
| خيّي أكْبَر مِنّي بْخَمْس سْنين، فا هُوّ اللّي كان يْدِلّني عَ كِلّ شي، عْرِفْتوا؟ | 13 | My brother is five years older than me, so he was the one who showed me everything, you know? |
| خيّي أخدْني على المْخيّم لجُوّا نْفوت وبدّْنا نِشْتِري بَواريد خَرَز، يَعْني لنِلْعَب مَع الوْلاد التّانْيين. | 14 | My brother took me into the camp to buy pellet guns to play with other kids. |
| فِتْنا شْترَيْنا برودْتيْن وهيْك. | 15 | We went in, bought two guns, and so on. |
| وكِنِت أوّل مرّة بْشوف المْخيّم، يَعْني أنا كِنِت صْغير وما بعْرِف شي. | 16 | It was my first time seeing the camp, being young and not knowing much. |
| شِفِت المْخيّم قدّي كْبير وقدّي يَعْني واسِع... | 17 | I saw how big and, I mean, spacious the camp is... |

| | |
|---|---|
| 18 | One might think that it is narrow and such, or that it's actually a camp, but it turned out to be very wide and very arge. |
| 19 | After buying what we needed, we left the camp and went back home. |
| 20 | My mom always had a bag ready with clothes, changes [of clothes], and passports, everything needed for emergency situations, in anticipation of these matters. |
| 21 | You know, she understood the whole situation. |
| 22 | So, suddenly... our building was three stories high, and we were on the third floor, I mean, at the top. |
| 23 | So, suddenly, the armed gangs decided to clash, and shooting started with bullets popping and rockets exploding, and... |
| 24 | I mean, they had heavy, not light at all, weapons. |
| 25 | So, my mother quickly took me, my brother, and my sister, grabbed our bags, and ran with us, fleeing the area. |
| 26 | As we were escaping, bullets were firing over us. |
| 27 | I was obviously very scared, as it was my first time feeling something like this or experiencing something like this. |
| 28 | I mean, never before had bullets been flying over my head. |
| 29 | So, we fled on foot for a distance, I mean not as far as you would by car or anything. |
| 30 | We ran outside, to an area away from the camp, but we were still close. |
| 31 | We waited about four hours while the noises continued, and people were shouting. |
| 32 | We were completely exhausted in the end. |
| 33 | We kept waiting about five hours until we found a car that could take us out of Sidon to a safe area, |
| 34 | until all these issues were resolved, |

الواحد بيكون مْفكّر إنّو هُوّ ضيّق وهيْك وإنّو مُخيّم، بسّ هُوّ طِلع كْتير واسِع وكْتير كْبير.

خلّصْنا شْترَيْنا الْغراض وطْلِعْنا لبرّا المُخيّم، رْجِعْنا عَ البيْت.

كانِت دايْماً إمّي تْكون حاطّة شنْطة بقلْبا تْياب وغْيارات وباسْبورات، يَعْني كِلّ شي بيْنعاز بالحالات الطّارْئة تحسُّباً لهَيْدي المَواضيع.

يَعْني هيّ كانِت فِهْمانة القُصّة كُلّا.

فا فجْأة نحْنا بِنايِتْنا تْلاتة طْوابِق ونِحْنا عَ التّالِت يَعْني عالْيين.

فا فجْأة قرّروا العِصاباتِ المُسلّحة إنّو يِشْتِبِكوا وبلّش رْصاص يِفِقّع والصّواريخ تِنْفْجِر و...

يَعْني عِنْدُن أسْلِحة تْقيلة مِش خْفيفة أبداً.

فا إمّي دِغْري أخدِتْنا أنا وخيّي وإخْتي وركضِت فينا مع الشُّنط وهرِبْنا مِن المنْطِقة.

ونِحْنا عم نهْرُب رْصاص عم بيفقّع فوْقْنا.

وأنا طبْعاً مرَيْناً خَيْفان كْتير، لأنّو أوّل مرّة بْحسّ بهيْك شي أوْ إنّو بيمْرُق معي هيْك شي.

يَعْني ولا مرّة تْقوّص فوْقي.

فا هرِبْنا مسافِة مشي، يَعْني مِش إنّو بْعيد بِسيّارة أوْ شي.

هرِبْنا لجُوّا عَ المِنْطِقة أبْعد مِن المُخيّم، بسّ بعِدْنا قْراب.

نطرْنا شي أرْبع ساعات والأصْوات بعْدا عم بِتْلعْلِع والعالم عم بِتْصوِّت يَعْني.

وخلِص خارْبيْنّا عَ الآخِر.

رْجِعْنا نطرْنا شي خمس ساعات لحتّى لاقَيْنا سيّارة تاخِدْنا برّاة صَيْدا على منْطِقة آمْنة، لبينْ ما خْلْصِت هالأمور يَعْني.

| | | |
|---|---|---|
| 35 | This problem went on for something like a month, maybe. | ضلِّتْلا شي شهر يِمْكِن هَيْدي المِشْكِلِة. |
| 36 | It's been a long time since it happened, but I still remember it well and recall the scenes. | وصرْلا كْتير القِصّة مارْقة وبعْدْني لهلّأ بِتْذكَّرا مْنيح ويتْذكَّر المشاهِد. |
| 37 | They never leave my mind. The scenes were so intense. | ما بِتْفارِق بالي. قدّ ما كانِت مشاهِد قَوية يَعْني. |

## Vocabulary

1. known for[7] _____
2. armed[7] _____
3. weapons[7] _____
4. to fight[8] _____
5. to enter[12] _____

6. rockets[23] _____
7. to pop, burst[26] _____
8. to shoot, fire[28] _____
9. to wait[31] _____
10. well[36] _____

---

**Answers**
**Main Idea:** d **True or False:** 1. T[4-5] 2. T[16] 3. F[19-23] 4. F[33] 5. T[36-37] **Multiple Choice:** 1. c[14] 2. c[20] 3. b[30-33] **Matching:** يَعْني that is; I mean / مرّة once, one time / فا so / لمّا when / مع إنّو even though / بعْدْني I still... / شي obviously / مْرَيْثاً immediately, directly / دغْري suddenly / فجْأة in it / بِقلْبو and whatnot / وهيْك / لبيْن ما until **Vocabulary:** 1. مشْهور لـ 2. مْسلّح 3. أسْلِحة 4. تْخانق 5. فات / about, approximately / مْنيح 10. نظر 9. قوّص 8. فقّع 7. صَواريخ 6.

# Vacations

## 13 Nisrine's Vacation

## Keywords

عُطل = أعْطال vacations

## Main Idea

a. Nisrine tells us about her shopping experiences in Beirut malls.
b. Nisrine focuses on a special vacation in Beirut with her family.
c. Nisrine discusses the culinary experiences she had in Beirut.
d. Nisrine shares with us how her fiancé proposed to her while on vacation in Beirut.

## True or False

1. Nisirine mentions that her trip to Beirut was in August of 2018.
2. Nisrine's grandparents live in the Chouf area of Beirut.
3. Nisrine's vacation in Beirut included a trip to the beach.
4. Nisrine and her family stayed indoors most of the time during their vacation in Beirut.
5. During the vacation, Nisrine's uncle proposed to his fiancée, and they planned their wedding.

## Multiple Choice

1. What was the weather like during Nisrine's visit to Chouf?

   a. Warm and sunny
   b. Rainy and windy
   c. Extremely hot
   d. Very cold and snowy

2. Which activities did Nisrine and her family enjoy during their vacation?

   a. Skiing in the mountains
   b. Visiting malls
   c. Camping outdoors
   d. Attending a cultural festival

3. How did Nisrine describe the setting for her uncle's marriage proposal?

   a. In a restaurant
   b. At the beach
   c. On snow with flowers and candles
   d. In a traditional Lebanese house in a village

## Matching

| | |
|---|---|
| مِتِل ما | a few days |
| بِـ | always |
| وَقِت | as |
| كَم يوْم | at that time |
| عنْجَدّ | first |
| فوْق | in |
| أوّل شي | in order to |
| تاني نْهار | that day |
| كان في | the next day |
| عَ طول | there was/were |
| كِرْمال | truly, really |
| بِهَيْدا النْهار | up there |
| بِوَقْتا | when (2x) |
| وَقْتا يَلّي | |

## Text

| | | |
|---|---|---|
| مِتِل ما بْتعِرْفوا، أنا مِن عكّار وأنا ساكْنة بِعكّار. | 1 | As you know, I'm from Akkar, and I live in Akkar. |
| وعِنْدي بيْت جِدّي أهْلا لإمّي ساكْنين بْبيروت. | 2 | And my maternal grandparents live in Beirut. |
| وأحْلى عُطل وأحْلى vacation أنا بْقضّيُن وَقِت بِنْزل عَ بيْروت عِنْد بيْت جِدّي لحتّى نْقضّي إيّام تحِت. | 3 | The best holidays and the best vacations I have are when I go down to Beirut to my grandfather's house to spend days there. |
| بِتْذكّر أحْلى vacation قضّيْتا وَقِت نْزِلْنا بِسِنة الألْفيْن وتمنْطعْش على بيْروت، أنا وإمّي وإخْواتي. | 4 | I remember the best vacation I had was when we went down to Beirut in 2018, me, my mother, and my siblings. |
| كان بِكريسْمِس ونْزِلْنا كمان نْقضّي كَم يوْم تحِت، ونْروح نْكَزْدِر بِبيْروت ونْشوف مناطِق مِنّا زايْرينا قبِل. | 5 | It was Christmas, and we also went down to spend a few days there, exploring Beirut and visiting places we had never seen before. |
| عنْجَدّ كانِت مِن أحْلى أحْلى إيّام حَياتي وأحْلى vacation أنا قضّيْنا. | 6 | Truly, it was one of the best times of my life and the best vacation I had. |

| | |
|---|---|
| 7 | I really love my grandparents, and I love spending a lot of time with them because they love us and take us out. |
| 8 | And we saw many beautiful places. |
| 9 | I remember we went to the mall first, took pictures with the Christmas tree, and my grandparents live in Dora. |
| 10 | We went up to Chouf; I remember at that time, it was very cold, and it was snowy up there. |
| 11 | We also took photos there, went to the food market and to Broumana, visited places we hadn't seen before, and had a lot of fun. |
| 12 | Also, my grandparents celebrated Christmas, and then we made dinner, stayed up late, and had a lot of fun. |
| 13 | The next day, there was also lunch. |
| 14 | I remember during this holiday, this vacation, my uncle proposed... proposed to his fiancée, |
| 15 | and during this... this time, they decided on their wedding date. |
| 16 | I remember it was August 18. |
| 17 | We had a lot of fun at that time, spent many lovely days, and had very, very beautiful moments that I will never forget. |
| 18 | We were always exploring and visiting new places, and we also went to Jezzine in South Lebanon, |
| 19 | in order to get to know the bride's family and formally ask for her hand in marriage. |
| 20 | And I remember, at that time, my uncle made the proposal in Jezzine. It was very, very beautiful. |
| 21 | We planned and executed it, and it turned out really nice; we had a lot of fun that day. |
| 22 | I remember there was snow at that time, and we set up the decor on the snow outside. |

بْحِبُّن لبيْت جدّي كْتير، وبْحِبّ قضّي كْتير وَقِت معُن، لأنّو هِنّي بِيْحِبّونا وبْياخدونا بِكزْدْرونا.

وشِفْنا كْتير مناطِق حِلْوة.

بِتْذكّر إنّو رِحْنا على المول أوّل شي وتْصَوَّرْنا مع شجَرِة الكْريسْمِس، ونِحْنا بيْت جدّي ساكْنين بالدّوْرة.

طْلِعْنا على الشّوف، كان هوْنيك بِتْذكّر بْوَقْتا كانِت... كان برد كْتير وكانِت الدّني مْتلّجة فوْق.

كمان تْصوَّرْنا فوْق، ورِحْنا على سوق الأكِل هوْنيك، ورِحْنا على برْمّانا، زِرْنا مناطِق أوّل مرّة مِنْشوفا وكْتير نْبسطْنا.

كمان بيْت جدّي حْتفلوا بالكْريسْمِس، ورْجِعْنا عِمِلْنا عشا وتْعشّيْنا وسْهِرْنا وكْتير نْبسطْنا.

وتاني نْهار كان كمان في غدا.

وبِتْذكّر بِهيْدي العُطْلة بِهيْدي vacation، خالي عرض... عرض الزّواج عَ خْطيبْتو،

وبِهيْدي... بِهيْدا الوَقِت قرّروا أيْما تاريخ عِرْسُن.

بِتْذكّر كان بِتمنْطعْش تْمانة.

كْتير نْبسطْنا بْوَقْتا وقضّيْنا إيّام كْتير حِلْوة وقضّيْنا لحظات كْتير كْتير حِلْوة ما بِنْساها.

وكِنّا عَ طول نْضلّنا عم نْكزْدِر ونْروح ونْشوف مناطِق جْديدة، وكمان رِحْنا على جِزّين على جْنوب لِبْنان.

كِرْمال نِتْعرّف على أهْلا للْعَروس ونُطْلُبا مِن أهْلا بِشكِل رسْمي،

وبِتْذكّر بْوَقْتا خالي عِمِلّا proposal هوْنيك بِجِزّين كْتير كْتير كان طالِع حِلو.

نِحْنا خطّطْنا ونفّذْنا وطْلِع كْتير حِلو وكْتير نْبسطْنا بِهيْدا النّهار.

وبِتْذكّر إنّو كانِت بْوَقْتا كان في تلج، وبْوَقْتا عِمِلْنا الدّيْكور على التّلج برّا.

| | 23 | We placed flowers and candles, and at night for the proposal, we lit the candles and lights. | حطّيْنا الوِرود والشُموع، وكان باللّيْل الـ proposal وشعّلْنا الشُموع والأضوية. |
| --- | --- | --- | --- |
| | 24 | When the bride entered, the scene was very beautiful, and we were very happy. | وَوَقْتا لـ.. يَلّي فاتِت العروس، كان المنْظر كْتير حِلو وكْتير كْتير نْبسَطْنا. |
| | 25 | I hope that such moments can be repeated or that we spend such holidays again, hopefully soon, with our family and friends. | وبِتْمنّى إنّو هَيْدا الشّي يرْجع يِنْعاد أوْ إنّو قضّي هيْك... هيْك أعْطال انْشاالله عن قريب نِحْنا والعايْلي والرِّفْقا دايماً. |

## Vocabulary

1. to spend³ _____
2. to descend, go down⁴ _____
3. the best days of my life⁶ _____
4. to ascend, go up¹⁰ _____
5. to propose to¹⁴ _____

6. wedding¹⁵ _____
7. bride¹⁹ _____
8. to turn out (to be)²¹ _____
9. snow²² _____
10. to light candles²³ _____

---

**Answers**

**Main Idea:** b **True or False:** 1. F⁵, ¹⁵⁻¹⁶ 2. F⁹ 3. F⁹⁻¹¹, ¹⁸⁻²⁰ 4. F⁸⁻¹¹, ¹⁸⁻¹⁹ 5. T¹⁴⁻¹⁶ **Multiple Choice:** 1. d¹⁰ 2. b⁹⁻¹¹, ¹⁸ 3. c²²⁻²³ **Matching:** مِتِل / as مِتِل / in بـ / وَقْت when / كم يوْم a few days / عنْجدّ truly, really / فوْق up there / بهَيْدا / in order to كرْمال / always ع طول / there was/were كان في / the next day تاني نْهار / first أوّل شي / at that time وَقْتا يَلّي when / بوَقْتا at that time / النّهار that day **Vocabulary:** 1. قضّى / 2. نِزِل / 3. أحْلى إيّام حَياتي / 4. طْلِع / 5. عرض الزّواج ع / 6. عِرِس / 7. عَروس / 8. طْلِع / 9. تلج / 10. شعّل شْموع

**58** | Lebanese Arabic Voices

# 14 Waleed's Vacation

## Keywords

قطر Qatar   زِيارة visit   تجْرُبة experience   حادِث accident, incident

## Main Idea

a. Waleed and his family experienced a thrilling adventure in Qatar, including skydiving and desert safaris.
b. The vacation was a cultural exploration, focusing solely on historical sites and museums in Qatar.
c. It was a surprise family trip that included their children's first flight, visiting various attractions, and an unexpected incident.
d. The trip was a relaxing beach holiday in Qatar, with most of their time spent at seaside resorts and golf courses.

## True or False

1. Waleed and his family visited Qatar during the Qatar World Cup in 2022.
2. This was the first time Waleed's daughters had traveled on a plane.
3. One of the highlights of their trip was visiting the sports museum and learning about soccer history.
4. Waleed's foot was run over and injured.
5. The trip to Qatar was a first-time visit for Waleed and his family.

## Multiple Choice

1. What was the surprise element of Waleed's trip with his daughters?
    a. They were going to meet a famous celebrity in Qatar.
    b. They were told they were moving to Qatar.
    c. They were going to visit their grandparents in Qatar
    d. They didn't know they were traveling until they reached the airport.

2. What was one of the incidents that happened during Waleed's vacation in Qatar?
    a. Losing their luggage at the airport
    b. Experiencing a golf cart accident
    c. Missing a scheduled museum visit
    d. *All of the above*

3. Which of the following did Waleed's family do in Qatar?
   a. Visited Waleed's brother
   b. Visited museums
   c. Explored new cities like Lusail and The Pearl
   d. *All of the above*

## Matching

|  |  |
|---|---|
| عن جْديد | again |
| بحِت | at that time |
| بوَقْتا | first of all |
| أوّل شي | for the first time |
| وينْ | for them |
| أوّل مرّة | however |
| لإنُ | I want |
| نِحْنا | not... until |
| ما... إلّا | only |
| ولكِن | purely |
| ما... إلّا لمّا | we |
| بدّي | whenever, every time |
| كِلّ ما | where |

## Text

|  |  |  |
|---|---|---|
| 1 | Hello, it's Waleed again. | مرْحبا، أنا وَليد عنْ جْديد. |
| 2 | Now, I would like to tell you about one of the best family vacations we had last year. | هلّا، حابِب خبّرِكُن عن واحْدِة من أحْلى الإجازات العائِلية اللي قضّيْنا سِنة الماضْية. |
| 3 | Last year, during the holiday season, specifically in December, my family, consisting of my wife and our two young daughters, aged between nine and ten, and I traveled to Qatar. | السِّنة الماضْية، بِفترْةِ الأعْياد تحْديداً بِشهْر كانون الأوّل، سافرْت أنا وعايْلْتي، المْكوّنة مِن مرْتي وبناتي التْنيْن، الصْغار اللي أعْمارْن بيْن التِّسْعة وعشْر سْنين، على دَوْلةِ قطر. |
| 4 | This trip was after the end of the Qatar World Cup in 2022. | هَيْدي الرِحْلة كانِت بعْد إنْتِهاء المونْديال بِقطر سِنةِ الألْفينْ وتْنينْ وعِشْرينْ. |
| 5 | This was my second visit to Qatar. | وهَيْدي كانِت زْيارْتي التّانْية لِقطر. |

| | | |
|---|---|---|
| 6 | My first visit, which was in 2019, before the coronavirus pandemic, was purely business, so I couldn't explore much. | زْيارة الأولى اللي كانِت سِنِةْ الألْفِين وتِسِعْطَعْش، قَبِل مَوْجِةْ الكورونا، كانِت زْيارة بْحِت مِهنية، يَعْني ما قْدِرِت إضْهر فيها على أيّ مكان. |
| 7 | At that time, Qatar was a huge workshop preparing for the World Cup... for the World Cup activities. | وكانِت قطر بْوَقْتا عِبارة عن وَرْشِة كْبيرِة تحْضير للْمونْديال... لفعليّات المونْديال. |
| 8 | Why did I love this visit more than others? | هَيْدي الزْيارة أنا ليْش حبّيْتا أكْتر من غَيْرا؟ |
| 9 | First, because it was my first trip with my daughters, and at that time, we wanted to give them a surprise. | أوّل شي لأنّو كانِت أوّل سفْرة لإلي مع بناتي ووَقْتا كنّا حابّين نعْملُّن مُفاجئة. |
| 10 | We didn't tell them that we were traveling, keeping it a secret until we reached the airplane gate. | ما خبرْناهُن إنّو نِحْنا مْسافْرين، ترَكْناها لآخِر لحْظة لوْصِلْنا على باب الطّيّارة. |
| 11 | They were surprised, wandering around the airport with all the security, luggage, and checks, not knowing what... what was happening or where we were going. | هنّي مِتفاجْئين عم يبرْموا بالمطار بالأَمْن العام، بالشْنط، بالتِّفْتيش، ما عِرْفانين هنّي شو... شو هَيْدا ووِيْن رايْحين وشو عم بيصير. |
| 12 | When we got to the airplane gate, we told them that we were going to Qatar to visit their uncle, my younger brother, and his family. | لوْصِلْنا لبوّابِةْ الطّيّارة قِلْنالُن بابا نِحْنا رايْحين على قطر هلّأ نْزور عمّو اللي هوّ خيّي الصْغير وعايْلْتو. |
| 13 | Their joy was indescribable, like the happiness of a little child aged two to ten years old, very delighted and content. | فا كانِت فرْحتُن لا توصف، فرْحِت وَلد صْغير عُمْرو سِنتيْن وعشْر سْنين ومبسوطين. |
| 14 | It was their first time on a plane, a new experience for them, | أوّل مرّة رايْحين على الطّيّارة، يَعْني تجْربِة لإلُن جْديدة عْليَن، |
| 15 | and they enjoyed and made the most of their time on the plane. | ونْبسطوا كْتير فيها وحبّوا يِسْتغلّوا وْجودُن بالطّيّارة. |
| 16 | So, our trip was at night, at a late hour, and they didn't sleep during the whole flight. | يَعْني نِحْنا سفرْتِنا كانِت باللّيْل وَقِت مأخّر ما ناموا طول فترِةْ الطّياران. |
| 17 | They only fell asleep when we exited the airplane door and were inside Qatar's airport. | ما ناموا إلّا وَقِت طْلِعْنا مِن باب الطّيّارة وصِرْنا بْقلب المطار بدَوْلِةْ قطر. |
| 18 | When we arrived in Qatar, we did a lot of sightseeing. | بْقطر لمّا وْصِلْنا، قِمْنا بعدد كْبير مِن الزْيارات. |
| 19 | We went to the sports museum. It was a really nice experience. | رِحْنا على المتحف الرّياضي. تجْربِة كانِت كْتير حِلْوة. |

|  |  |  |
|---|---|---|
| 20 | We learned about the history of soccer, saw old and new balls, referees' uniforms, the outfits worn by players, saw a Formula One car, and viewed the Olympic torches. | تْعرَّفْنا على تاريخ الفوتْبول، شِفْنا طابات القديمة والطّابة الجْديدة، شِفْنا تْياب الحُكّام، الأحْزية اللي كانوا يِلْبِسوها اللّعيبة، شِفْنا سيّارة الفورْمولا وان، شِفْنا المشاعِل تعيت الأولومْبْياد. |
| 21 | It was a rich and wonderful visit. | زْيارة كْتير غنية كانت وكْتير حِلْوة. |
| 22 | We also visited the Islamic Museum, the Qatar National Museum, and the new Qatari cities that were opened specifically for the World Cup. | وزِرْنا المتحف الإسلامي، وزِرْنا المتحف القطري، وزِرْنا المُدُن القطرية الجْديدة اللي تمّ إفْتتاحا تحْديداً للموندْيال. |
| 23 | Places like Lusail and The Pearl showed how much Qatar had changed since my first visit. | مِتل لوسيْل مِتل البورْل يَعْني فرقِت كْتير عْلَيّ قطر بين أوّل زْيارة وتاني زْيارة. |
| 24 | We rode the metro, which was a new experience for my kids, as we don't have a metro system in Lebanon. So, we also took the metr. | وطْلِعْنا بالمِتْرو وكانِت تجْرِبة كمان جْديدة لَوْلادي، لأنّو بلِبْنان نحْنا ما عِنّا المِتْرو فا طْلِعْنا بكمان بالمِتْرو. |
| 25 | However, during our visit to Qatar, I was involved in an accident. | ولكِن خِلال زْيارِتْنا لقطر صار تْعرَّضِت لحادث. |
| 26 | The accident happened due to the... the carelessness of the person supposed to transport us from the parking lot to the museum in Qatar– | صار معي هَيْدا الحادث نتيجة عدم الـ... عدم إهْتِمام الشَّخْص لكان مطْلوب إنّو يِنْقِلْنا مثلاً من المَوْقف السِّيارات للمتحف بقطر، |
| 27 | because he didn't... didn't make sure that when he got off the golf cart, he turned off the vehicle so it wouldn't move. | لأنّو ما أخد... ما تْأكّد إنّو لمّا نِزِل من الغولْف كارْت إنّو طفّى العربية لحتّى ما تِمْشي. |
| 28 | He got off and asked me to put the bags in front of the driver's seat, and I did. | نِزِل هوّ مِنّا وطلب مِنّي إنّو حطّ الغْراض قِدّام حدّ السّائِق فا حطّيْت الغْراض. |
| 29 | So, it seems I pressed on the gas pedal, or the accelerator, and it took off. | فا شكْلا ضغطِت على البنْزين أوْ عَ دعْسة الإنْطِلاق ومْشِيت. |
| 30 | It took off, and there was no one around, and out of fear that it might hit someone or hurt someone, I chased it down out of sheer reflex, I chased it and wanted to pull the items from it, | ومْشِيت وما فيا حدا وأنا من خوفي إنّو تِخْبط بحدا أوْ تْعوِّر حدا، لْحِقْتا من بْساطة التِّفْكير لْحِقْتا وبدّي إسْحب مِنّا الغْراض، |
| 31 | but in the end, the golf cart didn't stop until it crashed into a metal pole in the middle of the parking lot. | ما وَقِّفِت بالأخير الغولْف كارْت إلّا لمّا خبطِت بعمود حديد بنُصّ الباركينْغ. |
| 32 | So, at that time, I injured my hand, and the mark of the wound remained for a year, and the scar is still visible to this day. | فا وَقْتا عوّرت إيدي وضلّ أثر الجِرح بعْد سِنِة وبعْدو أثر الجِرح ظاهِر لهلّأ. |

| | | |
|---|---|---|
| 33 | What I want to say is that when you are in any place, any tourist site, during a long or short visit, pay attention to safety | الشّي يَلّي بدّي قولو إنّو نْتِبْهوا لمّا تْكونوا بِأيّ مكان بِأَيّ مكان سِياحي، زْيارة طَويلِة زْيارة قصيرِة لعامِل السّلامة |
| 34 | because I spent five days with my hand wrapped up and in pain every time I moved it. | لِأنّو أنا ضلّيْت لفترِة خمْسْة إيّام وأنا إيدي مِلْفوفِة وفي وَجع أنا وكِلّ ما حرّكا. |
| 35 | So, be careful and stay safe. | فا نْتِبْهوا وبِأمان الله. |

## Vocabulary

1. December[3] _____
2. consisting of[3] _____
3. to tell[10] _____
4. to roam, wander[11] _____
5. indescribable[13] _____
6. ball[20] _____
7. carelessness[26] _____
8. to turn off[27] _____
9. injury, scar[32] _____
10. pain[34] _____

_____

## Answers

**Main Idea:** c **True or False:** 1. F[4] 2. T[14] 3. T[19-20] 4. T[25-34] 5. F[5] **Multiple Choice:** 1. d[10] 2. b[25-32] 3. d[12, 22-23] **Matching:** for the first time / أوّل مرّة / where / ويْن / first of all / أوّل شي / at that time / بوَقْتا / purely / بحِت / again / عن جْديد / I want / بدّي / not... until / ما... إلّا لمّا / however / ولكِن / only / ما... إلّا / we / نحْنا / for them / لإلْن / whenever, every time / كِلّ ما **Vocabulary:** 1. كانون الأوّل / 2. مْكوّن مِن / 3. خبّر / 4. برم / 5. لا توصف / 6. طابِة / 7. عدم إهْتِمام / 8. طفّى / 9. جِرح / 10. وَجع

# 15  Rita's Vacation

## Keywords

خاتِم ring     شارَع to haggle

## Main Idea

a. Rita describes a family trip to Istanbul during her childhood, focusing on the historical sites and family bonding experiences.
b. Rita recounts her solo adventure in Istanbul, appreciating the city's beauty and and sharing memorable experiences.
c. The narrative details her honeymoon in Istanbul, where she enjoyed luxurious stays and romantic dinners.
d. Rita talks about a business trip to Istanbul, where she attended several conferences and had little time for sightseeing.

## True or False

1. Rita's trip to Istanbul was her first experience traveling abroad.
2. Rita's trip to Istanbul was part of a group tour package.
3. A significant aspect of Rita's trip was the sense of independence she felt from funding it herself.
4. Rita bought a silver ring at the Grand Bazaar.
5. Rita stayed in Istanbul during her entire trip.

## Multiple Choice

1. What aspect of her Istanbul trip does Rita emphasize as particularly enjoyable?

    a. Exploring the city on her own
    b. Traveling with a large group of friends
    c. Attending cultural shows and concerts
    d. Shopping for luxury goods

2. Which experience in Istanbul had a lasting impact on Rita?

    a. Taking a guided historical tour of the city
    b. Visiting famous landmarks and museums
    c. Participating in a local cooking class
    d. Negotiating a lower price for a ring at the Grand Bazaar

3. How did Rita find her way back to Istanbul when she got lost?

   a. She used a map and navigated on her own.

   b. A taxi driver offered to help her.

   c. An older woman and her daughter helped her.

   d. She asked for directions at a local café.

## Matching

| | |
|---|---|
| عنْجدّ | as |
| تَـ | even though |
| كَـ | exactly |
| هوْنيك | how |
| بعْدو | I can |
| فيّي | I mean; that is |
| هالْقدّ | I will |
| ويّاه | not |
| شو | so |
| مع إنّو | so that, in order to |
| مِش | still |
| بقِى | that much |
| عَ المظْبوط | there |
| يَعْني | truly, really |
| قدّيْش | what |
| ما رح | with him/it |

# Text

| | | |
|---|---|---|
| 1 | I really love to travel. | أنا كْتير بْحِبّ سافِر. |
| 2 | Traveling is one of the things I love doing the most in the world. | مِن أكتَر الإشيا اللي بْحِبّ أَعْمِلا بِالدِّني هِيِّ السَّفَر. |
| 3 | I feel that traveling truly enriches me, my personality, and my view of the world. | بْحِسّ إنّو عَنجَدّ السَّفَر بْيِغْنيني وبْيِغْني شَخْصيتي وبْيِغْني نَظِرْتي لِلدِّني. |
| 4 | That's why I really love to do it. | مِن هيْك هَيْدا الشّي عَنجَدّ كْتير بْحِبّ أَعْمْلو. |
| 5 | And I feel very fortunate that I've been able to travel to different countries and experience various cultures. | وكْتير بْحِسّ إنّي مَحْظوظة إنّو قْدِرت سافِر عَ بِلْدان مخْتِلْفة وإتْعَرَّف عَ حَضارات مِخْتِلْفة. |
| 6 | One of the best trips I've had and one of the best places I've been to is Istanbul, Turkey. | مِن أَحْلى السَّفْرات يَلّي أَخَدْتُن ومِن أَحْلى المحَلّات يَلّي رِحِت عْلَيْن هِيِّ إسطنْبول بِتِرْكيا. |
| 7 | I remember one of the reasons I really loved this trip was because I went alone, | بِفْتِكِر واحِد مِن الأسْباب يَلّي عَنجَدّ حَبّيْت هَيْدي السَّفْرة هِيِّ إنّو رِحِت وَحْدي، |
| 8 | and it was one of the first times I went by myself on such an adventure, if you will. | وكان مِن أوّل المرّات يَلّي بْروح فيا وَحْدي عَ هيْك مُغامَرة إذا بِدكُّن. |
| 9 | It was also the first time I was paying for my own trip with money I earned from a full-time job, a real job I was holding. | وكان كَمان أوّل مَرّة بِقْبِض يَعْني بْروح عَ سَفْرة دافْعة عْلَيّا مِن مَصاري عم بِقْبِضا مِن شُغِل دَوام كامِل عم بِشْتِغْلو وَظيفة حَقيقية شاغْلِتا. |
| 10 | I was young, and it was the first time that I was traveling with my own earnings, wanting to use my own money for travel, that is. | كِنِت صْغيرة وكان أوّل مَرّة هيْك، إنّو أنا رايْحة مْسافِرة وأنا قابْضة وأنا بَدّي روح إسْتَعْمُل المُصَريّات تْسافِر يَعْني. |
| 11 | This in itself was a wonderful feeling, but also Istanbul as a destination is truly beautiful. | هَيْدا بِحَدّ ذاتو كان شُعور حِلو بَسّ كَمان هِيِّ إسطنْبول كَمحَلّ الواحِد يْسافِر عَليْه عَنجَدّ كْتير حِلْوة. |
| 12 | I feel it's one of those places in the world where you don't necessarily need to take a tourist guide with you, | وبْحِسّ مِن الأماكِن بالْعالَم يَلّي مِنّو الواحِد مِضْطَرّ ياخُد مَعو مَثَلاً دَليل سياحي، |
| 13 | to guide you where to go, what to see, where the beautiful things are. | يَاخْدو ويْدِلّو وين يْروح وين يْشوف وين في إشيا حِلْوة. |
| 14 | Because in Istanbul, wherever you go, wherever you look, whichever direction you turn, there are many beautiful things. | لِأنّو إسْطنْبول وين ما رِحْتوا وين ما طِلِعْتوا، كيف ما بِرِمْتوا، عَنجَدّ فيا إشيا كْتير حِلْوة. |
| 15 | The colors, life by the water, the people are all lovely. | الألْوان هيْك، كِلّ حَياة حَدّ المايْ، النّاس كِلّا بْتِنْحَبّ. |

| | | |
|---|---|---|
| 16 | The food is delicious. | الأكِل كْتير طيِّب. |
| 17 | And as we walk... I mean, when one walks down the street, the smell of food and spices is wonderful. | نِحْنا وماشْيين... يَعْني وَقِت الواحد ماشي هيْك عَ الشّارِع ريحِة الأكِل كْتير حِلْوة، ريحِة البْهارات كْتير حِلْوة. |
| 18 | I really enjoyed this trip and remember something that happened to me there. | عنْجدّ كْتير نْبسطِت بهَيْدي الرِّحْلِة وبْتذكّر شي صار معي أنا وهوْنيك. |
| 19 | I was at the big bazaar in Turkey—I think they call it the Grand Bazaar. | كِنِت بالْبازار الكِْبير يَلّي بِتِرْكيا، بِفْتِكِر بيسمّو the Grand Bazaar. |
| 20 | I wanted to buy a ring, and I went to buy this silver ring, which I still have and love very much. | وكِنِت بدّي إشْتري خاتِم ورِحِت تإشْتري الخاتِم وكان خاتِم فُضَّ، بعْدو عِنْدي بْحِبّو كْتير هَيْدا الخاتِم. |
| 21 | I wanted to buy it, and they gave me a price which was expensive. | وبدّي إشْتريه وعطْيوني سِعْر كان غالي. |
| 22 | Well, not too expensive, but I knew in such bazaars you haggle a bit, | هلَّأ ما كان هُوِّ كْتير غالي بسّ أنا بعْرِف إنّو بهيْك بازارات بيشارِع الواحد شْوَيّ عَ السِّعِر، |
| 23 | so I told them I couldn't pay that much and wanted to pay less. | بقى قِلِّتِلُّن ما فيِّ إدْفع هالْقدّ، بدّي إدْفع أقلّ. |
| 24 | The owner was an older man, and his son also worked in the shop. | كان هُوِّ زلمي كْبير بالْعُمْر وفي إبْنو كمان بْيِشْتِغِل بالْمحل. |
| 25 | His son came up to me and said, "Let's play a game, and if you win, I'll give you the ring for a lower price." | بيقوم بْيِجي إبْنو بيقِلّي: "بدّي إلْعب أنا ويّاكي لِعْبة، وإذا بْترْبحي إنْتي اللِّعْبة بعْطيكي الخاتِم بِسِعْر أقلّ". |
| 26 | I told him 'okay;' we agreed. And we played the game, and I won. | قِلْتِلّو أوْكيْ قْبِلْنا بقى لعِبْت اللِّعْبة معو ورْبِحِت أنا، |
| 27 | And they gave me the ring for a very good price, which made me very happy. | وعطْيوني الخاتِم بِسِعْر كْتير قليل وكْتير نْبسطِت. |
| 28 | And as I mentioned, I still have the ring. | وبعْدو الخاتِم مِتِل ما ذكرِت معي لهلَّأ. |
| 29 | And it reminds me of that beautiful trip. | هيْك بيذكِّرْني بهَيْدي الرِّحْلة والسَّفْرة الحِلْوة. |
| 30 | And also, it happened that, when I was there, some of my friends were also in Turkey, so I had dinner with them, and it was nice. | وكمان ساقبِت إنّو أنا وهوْنيك كان في حدا مِن أصْحابي كمان بِترْكيا، بقى تْعشّيْت عشا أنا ويّاهُن كمان كان حِلو. |
| 31 | Altogether, the whole experience was just amazing. | وهيْك كِلّا الفُرْصة عَ بعْضا عنْجدّ كانت بِتْجنِّن. |
| 32 | There was also another incident when I was there. | في كمان صار معي شغْلِة أنا وهوْنيك. |

| | | |
|---|---|---|
| 33 | I wanted to go to another area, a bit far from Istanbul. | كِنِت بَدّي روح عَ مَنْطِقة تانْيِة بْعيدِة شْوَيّ عَن إسْطنْبول. |
| 34 | I got on a bus and was lost. I didn't know where I was going or coming from or what I needed to do. | وطْلِعِت بِالْباص وضِعِت، ما أَعْرِف لا وين رايْحة، لا وين جايِة، لا شو لازِم أَعْمَل. |
| 35 | And I don't speak Turkish. | وما بِحْكي اللُّغة التَّرْكية. |
| 36 | Even though there are people who speak English there, not many people speak English; that is, it's not the majority who speak English. | مع إنّو في ناس تِحْكي إنْكْليزي هوْنيك، مِش كْتير في ناس تِحْكي إنْكْليزي، يَعْني مِش الأغْلبية ما بْيِحْكوا إنْكْليزي. |
| 37 | So, I couldn't communicate with anyone to ask. | بَقى ما كِنِت عَم أَعْرِف إتْفاهم مع حدا تَسْأَلُن. |
| 38 | Fortunately, there was an older woman and her daughter on the bus who, from what I understood, realized I was lost and helped me get back to Istanbul with gestures, | حرام في مرا كْبيرة بِالعُمُر وبِنْتا مِن اللي فْهِمْتو يَعْني كانوا عَلى الباص وعِرْفوا إنّو ضايْعة وساعدوني إرْجَع عَ إسْطنْبول هيْك بِالحركات وبِالتَّشْبير، |
| 39 | and wrote a note in Turkish saying I was lost and needed help getting back to Istanbul. | وعَطيوني وَرَقة كَتبوا عْلَيا بِالتّرْكي إنّو ضايْعة بْليز ساعْدوني إرْجَع عَ إسْطنْبول. |
| 40 | I don't remember the words exactly, | ما بِتْذكّر الكَلِمات عَ المَظْبوط، |
| 41 | But this situation was really like that, I mean, a situation I found myself in, | بَسّ هَيْدي الشّغْلة هيْك كانِت عِنْجدّ يَعْني وَضِع نْحطّيْت فيه، |
| 42 | and it showed me truly how kind and helpful the Turkish people are. | وفرْجاني إنّو عِنْجدّ كيف الشّعْب التّرْكي قَدّيش ناس طَيْبين وبيحِبّوا يْساعدوا، |
| 43 | And, of course, this doesn't mean one can generalize in this way. | وأكيد هَيْدي يَعْني ما في الواحد يِجْمُل بِهالطّريقة. |
| 44 | These were just two individuals that I happened to meet in this story and really liked a lot, | هَوْدي كانوا شَخْصيْن يِمْكِن بِهَيْدي القُصّة تْعرّفْت عْليْن وحبّيتُن كْتير، |
| 45 | but really, several things like this happened in Turkey that showed me how loving and helpful the people there are. | بَسّ عِنْجدّ صار كذا شَغْلة هيْك بْتِرْكيا بِتْفَرْجيني قَدّيش ناس هوْنيك مْحِبّين وبيحِبّوا يْساعْدوا. |
| 46 | I will never forget this trip. | ما رح إنْساها هَيْدي السَّفْرة أبداً. |

## Vocabulary

1. to travel[1] _____
2. traveling[2] _____
3. world[3] _____
4. trip[7] _____
5. man[24] _____
6. old[24] _____
7. to happen that...[30] _____
8. woman[38] _____
9. lost[39] _____
10. to show[45] _____

## Answers

**Main Idea:** b **True or False:** 1. F[3] 2. F[7] 3. T[10] 4. T[20-21] 5. F[33-34] **Multiple Choice:** 1. a[7-8] 2. d[19-28] 3. c[38-39] **Matching:** هالْقدّ / I can / فِيّي / still / بعْدو / there / هوْنيك / as / كَـ / so that, in order to / تَـ / truly, really / عنْجدّ / exactly / يَعْني / عَ المظْبوط / even though / مع إنّو / not / مِش / so / بقى / what / شو / with him/it / ويّاه / that much / كْبير **Vocabulary:** 1. سافر / 2. سفر / 3. دِني / 4. سفْرة / 5. زلمي / 6. I mean; that is / قدّيْش / how / ما رح / I will / 7. بالْعُمُر / إنّو ساقب / 8. مرا / 9. ضايع / 10. فرْجى

# Hobbies

## 16 Waleed's Hobbies

### Keywords

هواية hobby     كبر to grow up

### Main Idea

a. Waleed tells us about his lifelong dedication to reading and literature, overshadowing his other interests.
b. Waleed explains how his single hobby of soccer led him to a successful career in sports journalism.
c. Waleed tells us how he first fell in love with soccer as a hobby.
d. Waleed recounts his struggle to balance his passion for soccer with his academic pursuits in chemistry.

### True or False

1. Waleed's interest in reading began only in adulthood.
2. Waleed explains that his passion for soccer changed as he grew older, and he developed new hobbies.
3. Waleed's passion for soccer waned as he grew older, leading to an interest in reading mysteries and literature.
4. Waleed only developed an interest in technology after 2010.
5. Waleed indicates that he has remained indifferent to technological advancements and the internet.

### Multiple Choice

1. What initiated Waleed's interest in reading?

    a. A teacher who encouraged her students to read for pleasure

    b. Following sports magazines related to soccer

    c. A box of books he found at his aunt's house

    d. None of the above

2. Which of the following hobbies did Waleed pursue as he grew up?

    a. Reading various genres of literature    c. Delving into educational technology

    b. Developing an interest in documentaries    d. *All of the above*

3. Waleed's advice about hobbies suggests that:

   a. One should focus on hobbies related to one's academic background

   b. Hobbies are irrelevant in professional life

   c. People should explore a wide variety of hobbies

   d. *None of the above*

## Matching

|  |  |
|---|---|
| أنا وصْفير | and then |
| بسّ | but |
| ما بِالضّرورة | from a young age |
| مِش | not |
| مِن أنا وصفْير | not necessarily |
| وبعْديْن | related to |
| إلو علاقة بِـ | that I… |
| صار | this |
| إنّي | to become, start to |
| هَيْدي | when I was young |

## Text

1. مرْحبا أصْدِقائي، معْكُن وَليد عن جْديد. كيفْكُن اليوْم؟ انْشاالله تْكُونوا مبْسوطين وعم بْتِقضوا وَقِت حِلو بِمْمارسِةْ هِواياتْكُن وأنْشِطة مُفيدة.

   Hello, my friends! It's Waleed here again. How are you all today? Hopefully, you are happy and spending a nice time practicing your hobbies and engaging in beneficial activities.

2. بِالْحديث عن هِواياتْكُن، أنا وصْغير لمّا كان حدا بِيسْألْني عن هِواياتي، كِنِت قِلّو هِوايِة واحْدِة وهِيّ الفوتْبوْل.

   Speaking of your hobbies, when I was young and someone asked me about my hobbies, I would tell them I have only one hobby, which is soccer.

3. كِنِت فكِّر أنا وصْغير إنّو الشّخِص لازِم يْكون عِندو مِتِل وَلاء لهِوايِة واحْدِة، وممْنوع إنّو يْقول أكْتر مِن هِوايِة واحْدِة.

   I used to think when I was young that a person must be loyal to only one hobby, and you mustn't say more than one hobby.

| | | |
|---|---|---|
| بسّ أنا وعم بِكبَر، كْتشِفِت إنّو هَيْدا الشّي مِش صحيح. | 5 | But as I grew up, I discovered this wasn't true. |
| وكْتشِفِت إنّو نِحْنا وعم نِكبَر، مْنِكْتِسِب مهارات ومْنِكْتِسِب حُبّ لهوايات مُخْتِلفة. | 6 | I learned that as we grow, we acquire skills and develop a love for different hobbies. |
| وما بِالضّرورة إنّ تْكون هَيْدي الهواية... أوْ هَيْدي الهوايات في رابِط بَيْناتُن. | 7 | And it's not necessarily that this hobby... or these hobbies have a connection between them. |
| مُمْكِن إنّ تْكون هوايات ما بْتِشْبَهْ بَعْضا وما غير مُرْتِبطة بِبَعْضا. | 8 | They can be completely different hobbies, unrelated to each other. |
| مثلاً أنا. أنا وصْغير كان عِنْدي عِشق للْفوتْبوْل، على كبر هَيْدي الهواية تْغيّرت. | 9 | Me, for example. When I was younger, I had a love for soccer, but as I grew older, this hobby changed. |
| يَعْني العِشق نحْو الفوتْبوْل، لِعْب الفوتْبوْل، مُشاهدِة برامِج الفوتْبوْل، مُشاهدِة مُباريات والبرامِج اللي بْتِحْكي عن النّتايج وعن الرِّياضِيّين. | 10 | I mean the love for soccer, playing soccer, watching soccer programs, watching matches, and programs that talk about results and athletes. |
| وحتّى الجْرايِد اللي كان نِشتْريا اللي بْتِحْكي عن الدّوْر المحلّي بِلِبْنان ساعدِتْني إنّي إكتِسِب أوْ إتْعرّف على مهارات جْديدة. | 11 | Even the magazines that we used to buy, which talked about the local league in Lebanon, helped me to acquire or get to know new skills. |
| مِش جْديدة، مهارات تانْية وحبًّا، مِتِل الإطّلاع على هَيْدي الجْرايِد مثلاً، نمّى عِنْدي هوايةْ القراءة من أنا وصْغير. | 12 | Not new ones but different ones that I came to love, like keeping up with these magazines, for example, nurtured my hobby of reading from a young age. |
| وهَيْدي الهواية ما حصرْتا بسّ بِالمجلات الرِّياضية. | 13 | And this hobby wasn't limited to just sports magazines. |
| لأ، صِرْت تْوسّعِت ونْضاف إلى المجلات المْخصّصة للأطفال مِتِل كِنِت جيب كِلّ إسْبوع أكتر مِن مجلّة واحِدة. | 14 | No, it expanded, and I added to it children's magazines, like I used to get every week more than one magazine. |
| مثلاً نْهار الأرْبْعا كِنِت جيب ماجِد، نْهار الخميس كِنِت جيب سامِر. | 15 | For instance, I would get 'Majid' on Wednesdays and 'Samer' on Thursdays. |
| وبعْدين أنا وعم بِكْبر صِرْت إقْرا الألْغاز، المُغامرون الخمْسة، الشّياطين التْلاطعْش، المُغامِرون التّلاتة. | 16 | And then, as I grew older, I started reading mysteries, 'The Famous Five,' 'The Thirteen Devils,' 'The Three Investigators.' |
| كْبِرْنا شْويّ صِرْنا بِالْمدْرسِة، نِتْعرّف على الأدب والشِّعِر العربي. | 17 | As we grew a bit older and were in school, we started to learn about Arabic literature and poetry. |

| | | |
|---|:---:|---|
| صِرْت حِبّ إِقْرا لـ... شِعِر لِلْمُتَنَبّي، صِرْت حِبّ إِقْرا رْوايات كَمان مِتِل رْوايات لأَمين مَعْلوف، لـ... لِمَحْمود دَرْويش، لـ... كْتير مِن الشُّعَرا والأُدَبا. | 18 | I started enjoying poetry by Al-Mutanabbi and reading novels by authors like Amin Maalouf and Mahmoud Darwish... by a wide range of poets and writers. |
| كَمان القِراءة وَسّعِتْلي أَفاق الهْوايات. | 19 | Also, reading expanded the horizons of hobbies for me. |
| فا رِحِت صِرْت أَكْتَر روح لَكَمان لِلْبَرامِج الوَثائِقِية اللي إلا عَلاقة مَثَلاً بِالتَّحْقيقات، إلا عَلاقة مَثَلاً بِالحَرْب العالَمية، البَرامِج التّاريخية، الوَثائِقِيّات العِلْمية. | 20 | So, I became more inclined towards documentaries, for example, about investigations, or related to World War [II], historical documentaries, scientific documentaries... |
| يَعْني شوف كيف هْواية عَم تِفْتَحْلَك الأُفُق لِهْواية تانْية بِتْناسِب عُمْرَك وبِتْناسِب يِمْكِن الفَتْرة الزَّمْنية اللي نِحْنا عايْشين فيا. | 21 | So, I saw how a hobby can open up horizons to another hobby that suits your age and maybe the era we are living in. |
| هَيْدا الحُبّ لِلْمَعْرِفة تْحَوَّل مَثَلاً لـ... بِعَصْر التِّكْنولوجْيا، | 22 | This love for knowledge, for example, transitioned to the era of technology, |
| لَمّا صار في عِنّا ظُهور الإِنْتِرْنِت بْفَتْرة... بين الأَلْفين والأَلْفين وعَشْرة كان هَيْدي الفَتْرة هِيّ فَتْرِة ظُهور الإِنْتِرْنِت. | 23 | when the internet emerged in... between 2000 and 2010 was the period of the internet's emergence. |
| عَزَّزْتا مَثَلاً يَعْني بْحُبّ القِراءة صِرْت دافعْني إِنّي إبْحَث عَن الكُتُب على الإِنْتِرْنِت. | 24 | I reinforced it, for example, with my love for reading, and it drove me to search for books on the internet. |
| فا صار عِنْدي هَوْن هْواية جْديدة إِنّي إتْعَرَّف مَثَلاً على التِّكْنولوجْيا، | 25 | So, then I had a new hobby, which was to learn about the world of technology. |
| ومِن عالَم التِّكْنولوجْيا رِحِت تْعَرَّفِت على التِّكْنولوجْيا التَّعْليم اللي حَبّيت إِنّي غوص فيها أَكْتَر وتْحَوَّل هَيْدا الشَّغَف لِمِهْنة. | 26 | And from the world of technology, I went on to learn about educational technology, which I loved and wanted to delve into more, and this passion turned into a profession. |
| شوفوا كيف عَم تِتْحَوَّل مِن هْواية لِهْواية أَكْبَر لِهْواية أَكْبَر لِمَعْرِفة لِشَغَف لِمِهْنة. | 27 | See how it transforms from one hobby to another, to a bigger hobby, to knowledge, to passion, to a profession. |
| حِلْوة الهْوايات. فا نَصيحْتي لأَلْكُن إِنْتو وعَم تِكْبَروا، جَمّعوا أَكْبَر عَدَد مِن الهْوايات وتْعَرَّفوا على كِلّ هْواية وغوصوا فيها. | 28 | Hobbies are wonderful. So my advice to you as you grow up is to gather as many hobbies as possible, get to know each one, and dive into it. |
| مُمْكِن تِتْحَوَّل هَيْدي الهْواية لِشَغَف ومُمْكِن لِمِهْنِة المُسْتَقْبَل. | 29 | This hobby could turn into a passion and possibly a future profession. |

## Vocabulary

1. activities[2] _____
2. loyalty[4] _____
3. magazine[14] _____
4. league[11] _____
5. skill[11] _____
6. mysteries[16] _____
7. writers[18] _____
8. horizon(s)[19, 21] _____
9. to turn into[26] _____
10. passion[26] _____

_____

## Answers

**Main Idea: a True or False:** 1. F[12] 2. T[9] 3. T[9-10, 16-18] 4. F[23-24] 5. F[25-26] **Multiple Choice:** 1. b[11] 2. d[16-18, 20-21, 25-26] 3. c[28] **Matching:** مِن أنا / not / مِش / not necessarily / ما بِالضّرورة / but / بسّ / when I was young / أنا وصْفير / that I / إنّي / to become, start to / صار / related to / إلو علاقة بـ / and then / وبعْديْن / from a young age / وصْفير / this / هَيْدي **Vocabulary:** 1. أنْشِطة 2. وَلاء 3. مجلّة 4. دوْر 5. مهارة 6. ألْغاز 7. أدبا 8. أفاق (أُفُق) / 9. تْحوّل لـ 10. شغف

# 17 Mohammad's Hobbies

## Keywords

| إِشْيا things | بْسيط simple | أَشْعار poetry, poems |

## Main Idea

a. Mohammad enjoys writing science fiction and reading technical manuals, often spending his afternoons in libraries studying complex theories.
b. Mohammad is passionate about writing travel blogs and reading adventure novels, often drawing inspiration from his travels abroad.
c. Mohammad's hobbies are centered around writing poetry in classical Arabic and reading ancient historical texts, reflecting his deep interest in Lebanon's history.
d. Mohammad's hobbies include writing about his personal feelings and thoughts, primarily in English, and gradually exploring Arabic writing.

## True or False

1. Mohammad started writing in Arabic before English.
2. Mohammad typically starts his writing process by jotting down bullet points on his phone.
3. Mohammad has self-pubished a children's book.
4. Mohammad regularly buys and reads books randomly, not necessarily based on a specific genre or extensive research.
5. Mohammad likes to share some of his writings on social media.

## Multiple Choice

1. What is one of Mohammad's future goals related to his hobby?
   a. To become a journalist
   b. To open a bookstore
   c. To teach writing classes
   d. To write and publish several books

2. What sparked Mohammad's interest in improving his Arabic writing?
   a. A university course
   b. His realization of a weakness in Arabic
   c. A competition in Arabic poetry
   d. *None of the above*

3. Where does Mohammad enjoy reading books the most?
   a. In libraries   b. At home   c. In nature   d. In coffee shops

## Matching

| | |
|---|---|
| كطَريقة لَـ | as a way to |
| شْوَيّ شْوَيّ | everything |
| بَعْد | for myself |
| بدّي | gradually |
| كذا | I want |
| ما ضروري إنّو | immediately |
| دِغْري | not necessary that |
| طَبْعاً | of course |
| بِدون | several |
| شو | still |
| كِلّ شي | what |
| لإلي | why |
| ليْه | without |

## Text

| | |
|---|---|
| هِواياتي هِنّي الكِتابِة والقِراءة. | 1. My hobbies are writing and reading. |
| الكِتابِة بلّشِت فيا كطَريقة لـ... يَعْني ركِّلِج مشاعْري وأحاسيسي، بطَريقة إنّو فِشّ خِلْقي فيا لحالي. | 2. I started writing as a way to... I mean, to channel my feelings and emotions in a way that lets me express them by myself. |
| بلّشِت إكْتُب إشْيا بسيطة، أوّل شي بلّشِت بالإنْكْليش طَبْعاً. | 3. I began writing simple things, starting with English, of course. |
| إكْتُب إشْيا بسيطة توَصِّل شُعوري لحالي، يَعْني أنا... أنا بِكْتُب لحالي. | 4. I'd write simple things to express my feelings to myself; that is, I wrote for myself. |
| كِنِت... فا بلّشِت تِسْحب مِن شغْلة لشغْلة ومِش إنّو أشْعار يَعْني وهيْك، بسّ إشْيا خَواطِر بِتْكون عشْوائية. | 5. I was... So, it started evolving from one thing to another, not exactly poetry, but rather random inner thoughts. |
| يَعْني هيْك فجْأة بْكون قاعِد... صافِن بْشي منْظر حِلو، قاعِد مع رِفْقاتي، قاعِد بِمطْعم بِالجامْعة ويْن مكان، | 6. Like, suddenly, while sitting... admiring a beautiful view, sitting with friends, or at a restaurant at the university, wherever, |

| | |
|---|---|
| 7 | فجْأة بْيطْلع بْراسي شي، بْطلّع تِليفوْني وبلّش بِكْتُب، |
| 8 | لوْ بْحُطّ رُؤوس أقْلام يَعْني بسّ بلّش فيا بِرْجع بْكمّلا بعْدين. |
| 9 | وعن جْديد لاحظِت ضُعْفي باللُّغة العربية، فا صِرِت حِبّ كْتير العربي، بسّ ما إقْدر إكْتُب فيه ولا عِنْدي هالـ.. مُعْجم الكِلْمات الكِبير يَعْني. |
| 10 | فا صِرِت إتْعلّم شْوَيّ شْوَيّ، مِن خِلال الكِتابة، |
| 11 | يَعْني إكْتُب إشْيا بسيطة، إتْعلّم مِن وَراهُن كلِمات وقْواعِد جْديدة ناسيا. |
| 12 | بعْدْني ما وْصِلِت لمرحلِة الشّاعِر يَعْني الحمْدُلله بسّ إنّو على قدّي وشْوَيّ شْوَيّ، إنْشاالله بوصل. |
| 13 | بعْد بدّي إتْعلّم بْحور، وبدّي إتْعلّم كِلْمات أكْتر وبدّي شْوَيّ شْوَيّ إشْتغِل عَ حالي لحتّى أوْصل لهدفي. |
| 14 | يَعْني أنا هدفي إنّي إكْتُب كذا كْتاب، مِش بسّ كْتاب واحد، |
| 15 | كْتاب بالإنْكْليش، كْتاب بالْعربي، كْتاب للأطْفال، كذا شي يَعْني حابِب أعْملو أنا. |
| 16 | طبْعاً كِلّ النّاس اللي بِتكْتُب، كمان نفْس الوَقِت بِتْحِبّ القِراءة. |
| 17 | يَعْني أنا الكُتُب بعْشقا، بعْشق ريحِتا، بعْشق إشْتريْن، بعْشق حُطّن عِنْدي وأعْمل كولّكْشن. |
| 18 | بْحِبّ كْتير إشْتريْن وإقْرأن وبِطريقة رانْدُم يَعْني، وكمان ما ضروري إنّو بِقْرأ بسّ جانِر مْحدّد أوْ شي. |
| 19 | خلص، هَيْدا الكِتاب عجبْني، بسّ إقْرأ شْوَيّ عنّو دِغْري بِشْتريه وبلّش بِقْرأ فيه. |
| 20 | طبْعاً هيْدوْل الهِوايْتيْن اللي قِلْتُن قبِل، ما بِيْكْملوا بْدون ضهْرا كِلّ يوْم على محلّ نائي. |

| | |
|---|---|
| 7 | and suddenly, an idea comes to my mind, I take out my phone and start writing, |
| 8 | even if it's just jotting down bullet points, I start and then complete it later. |
| 9 | Recently, I realized my weakness in Arabic, so I started liking it a lot, but I can't write in it, nor do I have a large vocabulary. |
| 10 | So, I began learning gradually, through writing, |
| 11 | I mean, I write simple things and then learn new words and grammar that I had forgotten. |
| 12 | I haven't reached the level of a poet, praise God, but at my own pace, slowly but surely, hopefully, I'll get there. |
| 13 | I still want to learn about poetic meters, learn more words, and gradually work on myself to achieve my goal. |
| 14 | I mean, my goal is to write several books, not just one, |
| 15 | a book in English, a book in Arabic, a book for children, several things, you know, I'd like to do. |
| 16 | Of course, everyone who writes also loves to read. |
| 17 | I mean, I adore books; I love their smell; I love buying them; I love placing them in my home and creating a collection. |
| 18 | I really love to buy and read books in a random way, I mean, and it's also not necessary that I only read a specific genre or something. |
| 19 | Okay, this book has appealed to me, but just by reading a little bit about it, I'll immediately buy it and start reading it. |
| 20 | Of course, these two hobbies that I mentioned earlier aren't complete without going to a secluded place every day. |

|  |  |  |
|---|---|---|
| 21 | هيْك يكون في المنْظر رَواق عَ شي جبل، كاشِف الدِّني كِلّا. | Like, there's a calming view over some mountain, revealing the whole world. |
| 22 | ما بْتِكْمل بِدون قعْدِة هيْك. | It's not complete without sitting like this. |
| 23 | الواحد يقْعُد بَيْنو بيْن حالو بْعيد عن العالم، بْعيد عن القرف كِلّو، يقْعد يفكِّر بَيْنو بيْن حالو، يتْرْجِم أفْكارو، شو عم بيفكِّر، شو عم بيدور بِعقْلو. | One sits alone, away from the world, away from all the annoyances, sitting and thinking to oneself, interpreting one's thoughts, what they are thinking about, and what is going on in one's mind. |
| 24 | يتْرْجمُن ويِكْتِبُن، يْحُطُّن على... على وَرْقة وقلم يَعْني. | Interpreting them and writing them down, putting them on paper with a pen. |
| 25 | بعْد هالْمعْمعة كِلّا باخُد كِلّ شي كتبْتو... تقْريباً كِلّ شي، | After all this chaos, I take everything I wrote... nearly everything. |
| 26 | طبْعاً مِش كلّ شي بيْنكتب لازِم يتْفرْجا للعالم، | —Of course, not everything written should be shown to the world— |
| 27 | إنّو الأكْترية بْيتّاخدوا وبْحُطُّن على سوْشِل ميدْيا عِنْدي لإلي لغَيْري. | most of it is taken and put on my social media for myself, for others. |
| 28 | المُهِمّ، أنا عم حُطّن عِنْدي، يَعْني أنا مبْسوط فيْن مِش عارِف ليْه، الحمْدُلله. | The important thing is that I'm putting them on my page. I don't know why, but I am happy with them, thank God. |

## Vocabulary

1. to adjust[2] _____
2. to vent one's mood[2] _____
3. to begin[3] _____
4. feelings[4] _____
5. friends[6] _____

6. weakness[9] _____
7. vocabulary[9] _____
8. to adore[17] _____
9. world[21] _____
10. chaos[25] _____

---

## Answers

**Main Idea:** d **True or False:** 1. F[3] 2. T[7-8] 3. F[14-15] 4. T[18-19] 5. T[27-28] **Multiple Choice:** 1. d[14-15] 2. b[9] 3. c[20-21] **Matching:** لَـ كطريقة / as a way to / شْوَيّ شْوَيّ gradually / بعْد still / بدّي I want / كذا several / إنّو ما ضروري / not necessary that / دغْري immediately / طبْعاً of course / بِدون without / شو what / كِلّ شي everything / ليْه why **Vocabulary:** 1. ركْلج 2. فشّ خِلْقو 3. بلّش 4. شُعور 5. رِفْقاة 6. ضُعِف 7. مُعْجم كلِمات 8. عِشِق 9. دِني 10. معْمعة / لإلي for myself

# 18 Sandy's Hobbies

## Keywords

هواية hobby    موسيقى music    أحْلى better; sweeter

## Main Idea

a. Sandy is passionate about music because it offers her a career opportunity and financial stability.
b. For Sandy, music serves as an emotional outlet, a source of joy, and a way to express and heal herself.
c. Sandy views music primarily as a social activity to connect with friends.
d. Sandy is passionate about music due to its technical aspects and the challenge it presents.

## True or False

1. Sandy regularly schedules time at the recording studio to work on her music.
2. Sandy believes that music has the power to change moods and heal emotions.
3. Sandy only engages in music-related activities when she is at the recording studio.
4. Sandy describes music as a universal language, implying its importance beyond professional boundaries.
5. Sandy feels that there are other hobbies more enriching to the soul than music.

## Multiple Choice

1. Which of the following does Sandy include as part of her music-related activities?

    a. Writing lyrics    b. Composing melodies    c. Arranging music    d. *All of the above*

2. What is true of Sandy when she listens back to music that she has created herself?

    a. She usually feels it's never good enough the first time.

    b. She feels pride and joy.

    c. She always takes notes so she can improve it.

    d. She is eager to have her friends and family listen to it and give feedback.

3. According to Sandy, what role does music play in her life?

    a. A professional career only    c. A way to connect with others

    b. A source of entertainment    d. *None of the above*

## Matching

| | |
|---|---|
| دايْماً | always |
| بِالنِّسْبِةِ لإلي | even if |
| فينا | for me |
| حتّى إذا | I can |
| عنْجدّ | really, truly |
| أيْه | so much; to this extent |
| هَيْدي | that |
| يَلّي | that, which, who |
| فِيّي | these |
| كذا | various |
| إن كان... إن كان | we can |
| هوْلي | whether... or |
| هالْقدّ | yes |

## Text

| | |
|---|---|
| مرْحبا، اليوْم بدّي إحْكي عن هِوايةٍ مِن هِواياتي. | 1 Hello, today I want to talk about one of my hobbies. |
| رح إحْكي عن حُبّي وهِوايْتي وشغفي للموسيقى وكِلّ شي خصّو بِالموسيقى بعِمْلو بِحَياتي اليَوْمية. | 2 I'll talk about my love, hobby, and passion for music and everything I do related to music in my daily life. |
| كوْني أنا بغنّي، بِكْتُب، وبْلحّن، دايْماً عِنْدي قُصص أعْمِلا خصّا بِالموسيقى. | 3 Being someone who sings, writes, and composes, I always have stories, especially about music. |
| وأكيد كِلّ جُمْعة عِنْدي نْهار أوْ نْهاريْن مَوْعد بِسْتوديو التّسْجيل، بْروح وبْسجِّل فيه. | 4 And, of course, every Friday, I have a day or two scheduled at the recording studio where I go and record. |
| بِالنِّسْبة لإلي هَيْدا شِغِل، هِوايِة، شغف، كِلُّن مع بعْضُن. | 5 For me, this is a job, a hobby, and a passion all rolled into one. |
| لَيلّي بيغنّي رح يِفْهم شو عم جرِّب قول: هِيّي فشّةِ خِلِق شغف، هِيّي حُبّ للحَياةْ، هِيّي محلّ بِقْدر فضّي السْتريْس فيه. | 6 Anyone who sings will understand what I am trying to express: it's a release of emotions, a love for life, a place where I can let go of stress. |

| | |
|---|---|
| 7 | It's where I release my anger, unwind from my day, especially if it was a bad one, and let go of the negative energy I'm feeling. | فضّي غضبي، فضّي نْهاري، إذا كان بْشِع، فضّي الإنِرْجي البِشْعة يَلّي عم حِسّ فيا. |
| 8 | With music, everything gets better; everything falls into place. | بِالْموسيقى كِلّ شي بْيِتْحسّن، بِالْموسيقى كِلّ شي بْيِظْبط. |
| 9 | We can heal anything with music, not just when we're sitting at home doing nothing; we put on music and enjoy ourselves, and it changes the mood. | فينا نْداوي أيّ شي بِالْموسيقى، مِش حتّى إذا قاعْدين ما عم نعْمِل شي بِالْبيت، حطّيْنا موسيقى ونْبسطْنا فيا بْيِتْغيرّ الموْد. |
| 10 | If we're in the car on a long drive, we need to listen to music; it changes the entire mood. | إذا كِنّا بِالسّيّارة، عِنّا مِشْوار طَويل، بِدْنا نِسْمع موسيقى، كِلّ الموْد بْيِتْغيرّ. |
| 11 | Music is something great, truly a universal language that allows all people to communicate with each other. | الْموسيقى هِيِّ شي عظيم، عنْجدّ هيِّ لُغة عالمية لكِلّ النّاس تِقْدر تْتْواصل مع بعْضا. |
| 12 | So yes, it's an identity, but it's also a hobby when I have the inspiration to write. | فا أيْه، هيِّ هَوِية، وهِواية بسّ يْكون عِنْدي إلْهام إنّي إكْتُب. |
| 13 | It's a hobby when I write songs, compose music, arrange melodies, record, produce music with the producer who's helping me. | هَيْدي هِواية بسّ إكْتُب أغاني، بسّ إكْتُب موسيقى، بسّ لحّن، بسّ سجّل، بسّ أنْتِج هالْموسيقى مع المنْتج يَلّي عم بيْساعِدْني. |
| 14 | It's really wonderful. There's nothing better than this. | شي كْتير حِلو، ما في أحْلى مِن هيْك. |
| 15 | Whenever there's a sound that we feel like capturing, we record it, create something out of it, and make that song or music. | بسّ يْكون في أيّ صوْت ع بالْنا نْطلْعو، نْسجّلو، نْطلّع مِنّو شي وتِخْلق هَيْدي الغِنية أوْ هَيْدي الموسيقى. |
| 16 | Then you listen to it loudly and say, 'Can you believe I created this?' and feel proud of it. | وتِسْمعْوا ع صوْت عالي وتْقولوا: معْقول؟ أنا طْلع مِنّي هَيْدا الشّي وتِفْتخْروا فيا. |
| 17 | There's nothing sweeter than this feeling, truly. | ما في أحْلى مِن هَيْدا الشّعور، عنْجدّ. |
| 18 | For those who work with music, I don't think there's any hobby more important or beautiful or that brings more happiness than this. | الْموسيقى ويَلّي بْيِشْتِغِل بِالْموسيقى ما بِعْتِقد يْكون عِنْدو هِواية أهمّ وأحْلى وبِتْجِبْلو السّعادة أكْتر مِنّا. |
| 19 | I could talk about various other hobbies, whether it's the type of sports I do or nature and the outings I take in nature. | فيّي إحْكي عن كذا هِواية غيْر إن كان الرّياضة، نوْع الرّياضة يَلّي بعْملو، إن كان الطّبيعة والضّهْرات يَلّي بعْمِلا بِالطّبيعة. |

| | |
|---|---|
| All these are hobbies, but nothing enriches the soul quite like music does. | 20 هوْلي كِلُّن هِوايات، بسّ مِتِل الموسيقى ما في شي بْيِغْني الرّوح هالْقدّ. |

## Vocabulary

1. passion² _____
2. appointment⁴ _____
3. to empty, discharge⁷ _____
4. mood⁹ _____
5. great¹¹ _____

6. identity¹² _____
7. inspiration¹² _____
8. to record¹³ _____
9. loudly¹⁶ _____
10. to enrich²⁰ _____

---

## Answers

**Main Idea:** b **True or False:** 1. T⁴ 2. T⁸⁻¹⁰ 3. F¹²⁻¹³ 4. T¹¹ 5. F²⁰ **Multiple Choice:** 1. d³, ¹³ 2. b¹⁶ 3. d⁵⁻⁶, ¹¹ **Matching:** أيْه yes / really, truly عنْجدّ / even if حتّى إذا / we can فينا / for me بالنِّسْبِة لإلي / always دايْماً / these هوْلي / whether... or إن كان... إن كان / various كذا / I can فيّي / that, which, who يَلّي / that هَيْدي / so much; to this extent هالْقدّ **Vocabulary:** 1. شغف 2. مَوْعد 3. فضّى 4. مود 5. عظيم 6. هَوية 7. إلْهام 8. سجّل 9. عَ صوْت عالي 10. غنى

# Culture

## 19 Charbel: Dabke

### Keywords
رقْصة dance    جيل generation

### Main Idea
a. Dabke is a modern dance form that has recently become popular in Lebanon.
b. Dabke is a traditional Lebanese dance that is still enjoyed by many.
c. Dabke has evolved and become internationally famous.
d. Dabke is a dance known only in Lebanon and is losing its popularity among the younger generation.

### True or False
1. The dabke dance involves complex footwork and is usually performed in groups.
2. Dabke is typically performed to any kind of music and doesn't require specific tunes.
3. Dabke is still a popular dance at weddings and other celebrations in Lebanon.
4. Even the younger generation in Lebanon is widely familiar with and regularly performs the dabke.
5. According to Charbel, the specific steps and movements of dabke are the same in every country where it is performed.

### Multiple Choice

1. Where is dabke commonly performed in Lebanon according to Charbel?
   a. In schools and educational events
   b. In nightclubs and modern dance venues
   c. At weddings and village gatherings
   d. Exclusively in dance academies

2. How does Charbel describe the experience of people when they hear dabke music?
   a. They start to clap and ululate.
   b. They immediately start linking hands and dancing.
   c. They sing along to the music.
   d. *All of the above*

3. According to Charbel, who holds a strong attachment to dabke and traditional music?
   a. Expatriates and older generations
   b. The youth in Lebanon
   c. Tourists visiting Lebanon
   d. Modern Lebanese musicians

## Matching

| | |
|---|---|
| شْوَيّ | a little bit |
| مَثَلاً | also |
| كَذا | and then |
| إلا | because |
| دِغْري | especially |
| وبَعْدَيْن | even now |
| يِمْكِن | for example |
| حَتّى هَلَّأ | he wants |
| هَلَّأ | immediately, directly |
| كَمان | it/she has |
| لِأَنّو | long ago |
| مِن زَمان | may, might |
| بِدّو | now |
| أَكيد | of course, certainly |
| خاصةً | several |

## Text

1. وَقِت نِحْكي culture بِلِبْنان في كْتير قُصَص هيْك بْيِتْميَّز فيا، بَسّ أنا حبّيت إحْكي شْوَيّ عَلى الدَّبْكِة.

   When we talk about culture in Lebanon, there are many unique issues, but I want to talk a bit about the dabke.

2. الدَّبْكِة هِيِّ... يَعْني هِيِّ رقْصة كِلّنا مْنوعى عْلَيا نِحْنا وصْغار، لِأَنّو هِيِّ تُراث قديم.

   The dabke is... a dance that we're all aware of from a young age, as it's an ancient heritage.

3. وأنا خِلْقان بالضَّيْعة واللي بيقولوه إبن ضَيْعة، يَعْني لازِم يْكون يَعْرِف الدَّبْكِة.

   I was born in a village—what they call 'son of a village,' meaning you must know the dabke.

4. الدَّبْكِة هِيِّ رقْصة، هيْك يَعْني بْتِتِّكِل على الإجْران، هِيِّ سْتابْس للإجْران.

   The dabke is a dance, so, you know, it relies on footwork; it's steps for the feet.

5. مَثَلاً في عِنْدك كَذا دَبْكة بْيِنْلقطوا... مْنِشْبُك إدّيْن بَعْض كِلّنا ومْنِصير نِمْشي على اللَّحِن الدَّبْكِة.

   For example, there are several dabke dances where we join... we link hands together and start walking to the rhythm of the dabke.

6. مَثَلاً نْحُطّ إجْرا لقِدّام يَمين، إجِر لَوَرا.

   For instance, you put the right foot forward, the foot back.

|  |  |  |
|---|---|---|
| 7 | There are several movements, several steps for the dabke. | في كَذا موفْمِنْت، كَذا حَركِة بْتِنْعِمل للدَّبْكِة. |
| 8 | And it also has its own special music. | وكَمان إلا موسيقتا الخاصّة. |
| 9 | In every village, particularly if you see them at weddings, the most significant thing, as soon as they put on dabke music, everyone gets up and dances dabke. | وكِلّ... كِلّ ضَيْعة هُوِّ بِالأحْرى، يَعْني إذا بِتْشوفُن بِالأعْراس، أكْتَر شي دِغْري، بَسّ يْحُطّوا موسيقِةْ الدَّبْكِة، العالم كِلّا بِتْقوم بْتِرْقُص دَبْكِة. |
| 10 | And then I discovered that there are dabke dances in several countries, not just in Lebanon, | وبِعْدَيْن كْتِشفِت إنّو في دَبْكِة بِكَذا بَلد، مِش بَسّ لِبْنان، |
| 11 | but each country might have its own specific way of doing dabke. | بَسّ كِلّ بَلد يِمْكِن عِنْدو طَريقِة دَبْكِة مْعَيَّنة. |
| 12 | Even now, as I get older, no matter how much you age, as soon as you put on that specific music to which one dances the dabke, people immediately start linking hands and dancing dabke. | يَعْني حتّى هلّأ على كِبَر قَدّ ما... قَدّ ما بْتِكْبَر قَدّ ما بِتْضَلّا، مَثَلًا بَسّ نْحُطّ هَيْدي الموسيقى المْعَيَّنة يَلّي في الواحد يِرْقُص عْلَيا دَبْكة دِغْري بِتْصير العالم تْقوم تِشْبُك إيدَيا بِبَعض وتِدْبُك. |
| 13 | I'm talking about my generation, the 90s generation. | عَم بِحْكي أنا جيلي، جيل التِّسْعينات. |
| 14 | Now, I don't know if the 2000s generation and the current one know how to do the dabke, | هلّأ ما بَعْرِف إذا جيل الألْفيان وهلّأ لا يَلّي بْيِعْرْفوا... بْيِعْرْفوا يِدَبْكوا، |
| 15 | but I feel that, yes, this heritage of dabke is still with us. | بَسّ بْحِسّ إنّو أيْه كِلّ ما بَعْدا هَيْدي التُّراث الدَّبْكِة باقي مَعْنا. |
| 16 | And I also wanted to talk a bit about Mawawil and Ataba. | وكَمان بَدّي كِنِت إحْكي شْوَيّ كَمان عَ الـ... عَ المَواويل العَتابا. |
| 17 | Nowadays, it's rare because the music style in Lebanon has changed a bit. | هلّأ قَليل صارِت كَمان لأنّو تْغَيّرِت شْوَيّ السْتايْل الأغاني بِلِبْنان. |
| 18 | Ataba, back in the day, was when someone would sing a Mawwal, like expressing a grievance... | العَتابا مِن زَمان كَمان كان إنّو واحد يِطْلَع يْقول المَوّال، مِتِل بِيْعاتِب إنّو شو... |
| 19 | I mean, for example, wanting to sing, to express something through song, they would sing Ataba. | يَعْني مَثَلًا بَدّو يِحْكي، بَدّو يْغَنّي، بَدّو يْقول مَوّال، بِيْقول عَتابا. |
| 20 | And this was very popular a long time ago with the older generation, who have now, may God rest their souls, passed away. | وهَيْدي كانِت مَشْهورة كْتير مِن زَمان بالعالم القَديمة يَلّي هلّأ كَمان الله يِرْحمُن تْوَفّوا. |
| 21 | They used to sing Ataba, and it wasn't very popular because, of course, there was no social media. | وكانوا يْغَنّوا عَتابا وما كانِت مَشْهورة كْتير، لأنّو أكيد ما كان في هالسّوشيْل ميدْيا. |

| | |
|---|---|
| لِأنّو الواحد يْنزِّل شي دِغْري على الإنْسْتغْرام أوْ على فايْسْبوك أوْ على تيكْتوك دِغْري بْتِنْشر. | 22 Because now, anyone can post something quickly on Instagram, Facebook, or TikTok, and it spreads rapidly. |
| كان... كان قليل هَيْدا هَيْدي السّوْشيْل ميدْيا مِن قبِل. | 23 Social media like this didn't exist back then. |
| فا الدّبْكِة والعتابا وكِلّ هالقُصص الموسيقية بيذكّرونا بِلِبْنان، | 24 So, dabke, Ataba, and all these musical stories remind us of Lebanon, |
| وخاصةً مين بْيِتْذكّر هوْل القْصص، بْيِتْذكّر المِغْتربْين يَلّي فلّو مِن لِبْنان اللي سافروا على أُسْتراليا، على فِنِزْويْلا وهِنّي كانوا مِن جيل الحرِب وما قبِل الحرِب. | 25 especially those who remember these things, they remind the expatriates who left Lebanon for Australia, Venezuela, and they were from the generation of the war and before the war. |
| كْتير مِتْعلّقين بالدّبْكِة وبِهالْموسيقى التّراثية المِتْعلّقة بِلِبْنان. | 26 They are very attached to the dabke and to this traditional music associated with Lebanon. |

---

**Answers**
**Main Idea:** b **True or False:** 1. T[4-7] 2. F[8] 3. T[9] 4. F[14] 5. F[11] **Multiple Choice:** 1. c[9] 2. b[12] 3. a[25-26]
**Matching:** شْوَيّ a little bit / مثلاً for example / كذا several / إلا it/she has / دِغْري immediately, directly / مِن زمان long ago / بدّو he wants / أكيد of course, certainly / خاصةً especially / لِأنّو because / كمان also / هلّأ now / حتّى هلّأ even now / يِمْكن may, might / وبعْدين and then /

86 | Lebanese Arabic Voices

# 20 Nisrine: Festivals

## Keywords

مِهْرجان festival     خَفْلة (خفلات) concert

## Main Idea

a. Nisrine highlights the Lebanese people's love for simplicity, joy, and optimism.
b. Nisrine offers a detailed guide to the Baalbek festivals.
c. Nisrine focuses on the culinary aspects of Lebanese festivals.
d. Nisrine tells us about the historical significance of Lebanese festivals.

## True or False

1. Nisrine describes the Lebanese people as generally optimistic, trying to make themselves happy even in difficult times.
2. According to Nisrine, summer is the season when festivals and parties are most prevalent in Lebanon.
3. Concerts and festivals in Lebanon are limited to major cities with large populations.
4. Nisrine has never personally attended any concerts or festivals in her local area.
5. The Lebanese revolution was characterized by violence and unrest.

## Multiple Choice

1. Which artist does Nisrine recall seeing at a concert in Beit Mellat?
   a. Elissa   b. Fairuz   c. Joseph Attieh   d. *None of the above*

2. Which of the following is true about the Baalbek festivals according to Nisrine?
   a. They are small, local events.
   b. They provide a sophisticated and fine portrayal of Lebanese art to the world.
   c. They are exclusively for Lebanese citizens.
   d. *None of the above*

3. How does Nisrine describe the Lebanese people's response to challenges such as the revolution?

   a. By maintaining a spirit of joy and optimism

   b. By voicing despair and anger

   c. By distracting themselves with festivals and other social events

   d. By using festivals as a way to protest government policies

## Matching

| | |
|---|---|
| قدّيْش | a couple of years ago |
| حتّى لَوْ | always |
| عَ طول | among others |
| لِأنّو | because |
| كِلّ العالم | even during |
| بسّ كِرْمال | even when |
| بكِلّ العالم | everyone |
| وبَيْنو | how much |
| مِن شي سْنين | in the whole world |
| حتّى وَقِت | just to |
| مع هيْك | nevertheless |

## Text

| | | |
|---|---|---|
| أكتر شي بْحِبّو بِلِبْنان، بالشّعْب اللّبْناني، قدّيْش نِحْنا شعِب بيحِبّ البْسِط، بيحِبّ الفرح، وعِنّا أمل كْتير كبير. | 1 | What I love most about Lebanon and the Lebanese people is how much we love simplicity and joy, and we have great hope. |
| قدّيْش نِحْنا شعِب كْتير مِتْفائل، دايماً نِحْنا مِنْحِبّ نِبْسُط حالْنا بِحالْنا، وحتّى لَوْ كِنّا زِعْلانين ومِتْدايْقين. | 2 | We are a very optimistic people, always trying to make ourselves happy even when we're upset or bothered. |
| بِتْلاقي الشّعْب اللّبْناني عَ طول بيروح على البْسِط، على السّهر، على الحفلات، على الأجْواء الحِلْوة. | 3 | You'll always find the Lebanese people heading to enjoy themselves, to stay out late, to parties, and to enjoy beautiful atmospheres. |

| | |
|---|---|
| 4 | My favorite season in Lebanon is summer because that's when festivals and parties start. | وأكْتَر مَوْسَم بْحِبّو بِلِبْنان هُوّ مَوْسَم الصَّيْف، لأنّو بْوَقْتا بِتْبلِّش المهْرَجانات والحفلات. |
| 5 | You'll find all of Lebanon, from north to south, staying out late. | مِنْلاقي لِبْنان كِلّياتو، مِن شْمالو لجْنوبو سهْران. |
| 6 | Everyone is happy, everyone is dancing, everyone is singing. | كِلّ العالم سِهْرانة، كِلّ العالم مبْسوطة، كِلّ العالم، عم تِرْقُص. |
| 7 | You'll see Lebanon all lit up, radiant, with the best atmosphere, the atmosphere of staying out late, of parties. | كِلّ العالم عم بِتْغنّي وبِتْلاقوا لِبْنان مْضَوّى كِلّو، ومْشعْشِع وأحْلى أجْواء، أجْواء السَّهر، أجْواء الحفلات. |
| 8 | The very most important and famous thing in Lebanon is the Baalbek festivals, | وأهمّ أهمّ شي وأشْهر شي بِلِبْنان معْروفين بمِهْرَجانات بعلْبك، |
| 9 | the festivals that give a very beautiful image of Lebanon, | المِهْرَجانات اللي بتعْطي صورة كْتير حِلْوة عن لِبْنان، |
| 10 | which attract tourists from all over the world—from the West and Arabs—to Lebanon, just to attend the most beautiful, famous concerts that take place in Baalbek, | اللي بِتِسْتقْطب كِلّ السِّيّاح مِن كلّ أنْحاء العالم بْيجوا عالم وأجانِب وعرب عَ لِبْنان بسّ كِرْمال يحْضروا أجْمل الحفلات اللي بِتْصير ببعلْبك المشْهورة، |
| 11 | providing the best image of Lebanon, reflecting sophisticated art and the finest performances in the world, all happening at the Baalbek celebrations and festivals. | اللي بْتعْطي أحْلى صورة عن لِبْنان، اللي بِتعْكُس الفنّ الرّاقي وأحْلى فنّ بيصير بكلّ العالم، هنّي بإحْتفالات ومهْرَجانات ببعلْبك. |
| 12 | Here in Akkar, we have many concerts close to us, | ونِحْنا هوْن عِنّا بعكّار كْتير بِتْصير حفلات قريبة مِنّا، |
| 13 | in the villages... in the villages around us like Rahbe, and Beit Mellat, among others. | مِن الضِّيَع... في ضِيَع حدُّنا مِتِل رحْبة، مِتِل بيْت ملّات وبيْنو. |
| 14 | They organize many concerts and festivals in the summer. | كْتير بالصَّيْف بْيَعْملوا حفلات ومهْرَجانات. |
| 15 | These festivals also attract people from Beirut and Tripoli, who just come to attend the concerts. | هيْدول كمان المِهْرَجانات بْيجوا علْيَا عالم مِن بيْروت، عالم مِن طرابُلْس بْيجوا بسّ كِرْمال يحْضروا الحفلات. |
| 16 | Lebanese and foreign artists come here to perform in these villages. | بْيجوا فنّانين لِبْنانيّين وأجانِب بْيجوا لعنّا لهوْن على الضِّيَع. |
| 17 | I remember once, a couple of years ago, I went with my family and friends to a concert in Beit Mellat. | بِتْذكَّر مرّة، مِن شي سنتيْن رِحِت أنا وأهْلي ورفْقاتي حضرْنا... حْضِرْنا الحفْلِة اللي صارِت في بيْت ملّات. |

|  |  |  |
|---|---|---|
| 18 | إجا جوزيْف عطية، وَقْتا كْتير نْبسطْنا، | Joseph Attieh was performing [lit. came], |
| 19 | وكانِت الأجْواء كْتير كْتير حِلْوِة. | and we had a lot of fun; the atmosphere was very enjoyable. |
| 20 | هَيْدي... هَيْدي الإيّام كْتير بْحِبّا أنا، | I really love these days, |
| 21 | كْتير بْحِبّ وَقْت بيبلّش الصّيْف كرْمال تْبلّش الحفْالات، وتْبلّش المهْرجانات، | I love when summer starts because that's when the parties and festivals begin, |
| 22 | ونِنْبسِط ونْشوف العالم ونِفْرح بالعالم ونِفْرح بالأجْواء الحِلْوِة والرّقْص والغِني والسّهر. | and we have fun, see people, and enjoy the people and enjoy the wonderful atmosphere, and dancing, singing, and staying out late. |
| 23 | لِبْنان كْتير كْتير بيْعْطي صورة حِلْوة لكِلّ العالم قدّيْش نِحْنا شعْب منْحِبّ نِنْبسِط، منْحِبّ الفرح. | Lebanon gives a very beautiful image to the whole world of how much we, as a people, love to be happy and enjoy joy. |
| 24 | عَ طول مِتْفائلين، عَ طول مِنْطْلِع نِحْنا اللّبْنانية بأحْلى صورة قدّام كِلّ العالم، | We are always optimistic, always presenting the best image of Lebanese to the entire world. |
| 25 | حتّى وَقْت الثّوْرة ووَقْت أصْعب إيّام حَياتْنا، | Even during the revolution and the toughest days of our lives, |
| 26 | عْطيْنا صورة لكِلّ العالم إنّو نِحْنا اللّبْنانية عم نمرْق بأزْمِة، بـ... بإيّام صعْبِة كْتير، ومع هيْك نِحْنا عْمِلْنا الثّوْرة، عْمِلْناها سِلْمية. | we showed the world that we, the Lebanese, were going through a crisis, very difficult days, and yet, we conducted the revolution, we made it peaceful." |
| 27 | وعْمِلْناها ثَوْرِة رقْص وثَوْرِة فرح لنعْطي الأمل لكِلّ الشّعوب، | We made it a revolution of dance and joy to give hope to all people, |
| 28 | إنّو حتّى نِحْنا وعم نْثور نِحْنا بدّنا نْثور نِحْنا وفرْحانين بدّنا نْثور بطريقة كْتير سِلْمية. | showing that even in our uprising, we wanted to do so joyfully and in a very peaceful way. |
| 29 | وعبّرْنا عنّا بالرّقْص والغِني والفرح. | And we expressed ourselves through dancing, singing, and happiness. |

---

**Answers**
**Main Idea:** a **True or False:** 1. T[1-2] 2. T[4] 3. F[12-14] 4. F[17-19] 5. F[26-28] **Multiple Choice:** 1. c[18] 2. b[11] 3. a[25-29]
**Matching:** قدّيْش how much / حتّى لَوْ even when / عَ طول always / لأنّو because / كِلّ العالم everyone / بكِلّ العالم in the whole world / وبيْنو among others / مِن شي سْنين a couple of years ago / بسّ كِرْمال just to / مع هيْك nevertheless / حتّى وَقْت even during

**90 | Lebanese Arabic Voices**

# 21 Waleed: The Book Fair

## Keywords

معْرض بيْروت للكِتاب الدُّوَلي the Beirut International Book Fair
فعّالية = حدث = ظاهْرة = نشاط event
قِصّة story(book)   نقل to move   دوْر نشِر publisher

## Main Idea

a. Waleed presents a critique of the current state of the fair.
b. Waleed shares a nostalgic recollection of his childhood experiences at the fair.
c. Both a and b
d. Neither a nor b

## True or False

1. The Beirut International Book Fair is a relatively new event, starting in the 2000s.
2. Waleed felt amazed the first time he visited the book fair.
3. Waleed's first visit to the Beirut International Book Fair was with his family.
4. The location of the fair changed from to Biel, by the sea, to the Ministry of Tourism in Hamra.
5. The fair had booths by over 100 publishers from all over the world.

## Multiple Choice

1. What was the initial purpose of Waleed's school trip to the book fair?

    a. To explore the fair without any specific agenda

    b. To purchase and read a specific storybook for a test

    c. To meet famous authors

    d. *None of the above*

2. Which of these elements did Waleed mention as new additions to the Beirut International Book Fair?

    a. Video games   b. Food court   c. Games area   d. *All of the above*

3. What are Waleed's sentiments towards the changes at the Beirut International Book Fair?

    a. He is pleased with the diversification.   c. He is indifferent to the changes.

    b. He appreciates the modernization.   d. *None of the above*

## Matching

| | |
|---|---|
| مِتِل ما | according to |
| حسب ما | among |
| بِحْدود | around |
| تَـ | as |
| بِفتِرْتا | back then |
| فيني | I can |
| ضِمِن | in order to, so that |
| بعْدو | still |
| على | to |
| ليْش | why |

## Text

1. مرْحبا، كيفْنا؟ شْتقْتولي؟ معْكُن وَليد.
   Hello, how are you? Did you miss me? This is Waleed.

2. اليوْم كِنِت حابِب إحْكيكُن مِتِل ما بْتعِرْفوا، نِحْنا بِشهْر كانون الأوّل، وبِبيْروت كِلّ سِنة بِشهْر كانون الأوّل بيصير فيها نشاطي ثقافي كْبير.
   Today, I wanted to tell you, as you know, we are in the month of December, and in Beirut, every year in December, there is a significant cultural event.

3. وهُوّ معْرِض بيْروت للْكِتاب الدُوَلي. معْرض بيْروت كان واحد مِن أهمّ المعارِض اللي إلا علاقة بالْكِتاب العربي بالْوَطن العربي.
   It's the Beirut International Book Fair. The Beirut fair has been one of the most important fairs related to Arabic books in the Arab world.

4. ويمْكِن فينا نْقول إنّو هُوّ مِن أقدم المعارِض اللي بِتْصير بالْوَطن العربي، واللي إلا علاقة بِعالم الكُتُب.
   It's probably one of the oldest fairs in the Arab world that deals with the world of books.

5. أنا زْيارْتي الأولى لمعْرض الكِتاب العربي كانِت بِتسْعينِيّات القرْن الماضي.
   My first visit to the Arab Book Fair was in the nineties of the last century.

6. ويَعْني تقْريباً حسب ما بِتْذكّر، كِنِت بِصفّ التّالِت مُتَوَسِّط، اللي هُوّ حاليّاً بيقولوا عنّو الصّف التّامِن.
   If I remember correctly, I was in the third intermediate grade, which is now called the eighth grade.

7. وكان هَيْدا الشّي بِحْدود السِّنة التْنيْن وتِسْعين.
   It was around 1992.

8. بِهيْدي السِّنة، المدْرسة قرّرِت إنّو تاخِدْنا... تاخُد التّلاميذ على بِزْيارة لمعْرض الكِتاب العربي.
   That year, our school decided to take us... take the students, on a visit to the Arab Book Fair.

| | | |
|---|---|---|
| 9 | At that time, they asked us to buy a storybook. | وطلبوا مِنّا وَقْتا إنّو نِشْتري قُصّة. |
| 10 | This story was required for us to read, and then we would take a kind of test about it, about the subject to make sure we had actually read it. | هَيْدي القُصّة كان في مطْلوب مِنّا إنّو نِقْراها ونِرْجع نعْمِل مِتِل إخْتِبار حَوْلا، حَوْلَ المَوْضوع تَيِتْأكّدوا إنّو نحْنا قْريناها. |
| 11 | Back then, the fair was held at the Ministry of Tourism, in the Hamra area, the hall... in a large hall. | كان بِفتْرِتا أُقيم المَعْرض بِوزارةِ السِّياحة، بِمنْطِقةِ الحمْرا القاعة... في قاعة كْبيرة. |
| 12 | It was called the Glass Hall. | كان إسْما القاعة الزُّجاجية. |
| 13 | When we arrived, I was amazed by this world. | نْزِلْنا بُهِرْت أنا بهَيْدا العالم. |
| 14 | I mean, I can say that this might have been my first journey not with my family or parents, but with the school, with my classmates. | يَعْني فيني قول إنّو هَيْدي يِمكِن كانت أوّل مِشْوار لإلي مِش مع عايْلْتي مِش مع أهْلي، ضِمْن المدْرسة، مع رِفْقاتي بالْمدْرسِة بالصّف. |
| 15 | I was amazed by this world, entering a large place. | بُهِرْت بهَيْدا العالم، بْتْفوت عَ مكان كْبير. |
| 16 | As a boy of 12 or 13 years old, I was seeing books, covers, and authors' names. | وَلد عُمْرو طْنعْش تْلِطعْش سِنِة، عم بيشوف كُتُب وغِلافات وأسْماء كُتّاب. |
| 17 | Names of novels by Mikhail Naimy, 'Birds of September,' Amin Maalouf, Gibran Khalil Gibran. | أسْماء روايات مْخائيل نْعَيْمة، طْيور أيْلول، أمين معْلوف، جُبْران خليل جُبْران. |
| 18 | Books in English, Arabic, books in all languages. | كُتُب بالْإنْكْليزي، كُتُب بالْعربي، كُتُب بِكِلّ اللُّغات. |
| 19 | It was a significant cultural and literary event in Lebanon. | كانت ظاهْرة فنّية أوْ حدث أدبي ثقافي كْتير كْبير بِلِبْنان. |
| 20 | This event is still held annually in Lebanon, but the location has changed, where... | وبعْدو هَيْدا النّشاط يُقام سنَويّاً بِلِبْنان، ولكِن تْغيَّر المكان اللّي صار... |
| 21 | The fair moved to a new location by the sea, on the Beirut waterfront, at a place called Biel. | يِتِمّ تنْظيم في هَيْدا المَعْرض صار نقل على منْطِقة تانْية على البحْر، على واجْهةْ بيْروت البحْرية، على مكان إسْمو بْيال. |
| 22 | This new venue was enormous and right by the sea in Beirut. | هَيْدا المكان كْتير كْبير ومُقابِل بحِر بيْروت. |
| 23 | Publishers started coming from Lebanon, Algeria, Cairo, the Gulf, universities, European publishers, and from America. | صار يِجي علَيْه دوْر نشْر مِن لِبْنان، الجزائِر، مِن القاهِرة، مِن الخليج، جامعات، دوْر نشْر أوروبّية، ومِن أميرْكا. |
| 24 | There were over 150 to 250 publishing houses every year. | صار في كْتير يَعْني فوْق المِيّة وخمْسين ميتيْن وخمْسين دار نشْر كِلّ سِنِة. |

|  |  |  |
|---|---|---|
| 25 | ولكِن لِلأسَف، صِرْنا نِشْهد بهَيْدا المَعْرض وُجود دوْر نشِر يَعْني أوْ وُجود مُؤسّسات ما إلا علاقة بالكِتاب بإصدار الكُتُب أوْ بنشر الكُتُب. | Unfortunately, we've started to see at this fair the presence of publishers or institutions that have nothing to do with books or book publishing. |
| 26 | صِرْنا نْشوف يَعْني مكان لِلألْعاب، مكان بقلْب المَعْرض coin لِلأكِل ولألْعاب الفيديو غايمْز لـ... يَعْني شغْلات. | We've started to see places for games, a food court in the heart of the fair, and video games, among other things. |
| 27 | بِتْطلّع فيا يَعْني أنا هلّأ مثلاً إذا بْتِتْذكّروا كِنت عم قول إنّو أنا بشْتِغل بمدْرسة. | It seems to me, for example, if you remember, I was saying that I work at a school. |
| 28 | فا كِنّا كمان نْنظّم رحْلات ثقافية لهالتّلاميذ نزّلْن على المَعْرض، فا الوْلاد ما يِشْتروا كُتُب ما يِشْتروا روايات | So we also organized cultural trips for these students to the fair, but the kids wouldn't buy books or novels. |
| 29 | يْروحوا على هَيْدي... التّجمُّعات ويشْتروا أشْيا يَعْني لا علاقة إلا بالكُتُب. | Instead, they would go to these gatherings and buy things that had nothing to do with books. |
| 30 | لِلأسف لمّا كِبِر المَعْرض تأمّلْنا إنّو يْصير في إلو قيمة أكْبر بعالم الكُتُب وبعالم الثّقافة ولكِن لِلأسف فقد هَيْدي القيمة. | Sadly, as the fair grew, we hoped it would gain more significance in the world of books and culture, but unfortunately, it lost its value. |
| 31 | هوْن السُّؤال ليْش صار هيْك؟ | The question is, why did this happen? |
| 32 | يَعْني ليْش ما ضلّ المَعْرض عم بيحافِظ على سمِعْتو التّرْويجية للثّقافة وللكُتُب؟ | Why didn't the fair maintain its reputation for promoting culture and books? |
| 33 | سُؤال لازم مِن المُنظّمين يوقفوا عِنْدو ويْحاوْلوا يْلاقولوا إجابة، ويْحاوْلوا يسْعوا لإرْجاع الصِّفة الثّقافية لهالـ... الفعّالية السّنَوية اللي كانِت مْهِمّة. | It's a question for the organizers to consider and find answers to, to restore the cultural significance of this... annual event that had been so important. |
| 34 | ولِلأسف وْصِلْت أنا لَوَقِت مِن أكْتر مِن خمْس سْنين، سِتّة سْنين، ما عِدِت نْزِلِت على المَعْرض، لأنّي بعْرِف إنّو حشوف شغْلات تْضايقْني. | Unfortunately, for more than five or six years, I haven't gone to the fair because I know I'll see things that upset me. |
| 35 | وإنْتو شو رأيْكُن بهَيْدا المَوْضوع؟ | What do you all think about this issue? |

---

**Answers**

**Main Idea:** c **True or False:** 1. F[5] 2. T[13, 15] 3. F[14] 4. F[21] 5. T[23-24] **Multiple Choice:** 1. b[9-10] 2. d[25-26] 3. d[30, 34]

**Matching:** مِتِل ما / as حسب ما / according to بحْدود / around تَـ / in order to, so that بفترْتا / back then / ليْش why / على to / بعْدو still / ضمِن among / فيني I can

# 22  Rita: Lebanese Food

## Keywords

مَطْبَخ cuisine    طَعْمة flavor

## Main Idea

a. Rita discusses the international appeal and variety of Lebanese cuisine and her personal favorites.
b. Rita describes the evolution of Lebanese cuisine over centuries and its influence on other culinary traditions.
c. Rita focuses on the decline of traditional Lebanese dishes in favor of modern cuisine.
d. Rita talks about her personal journey in learning to cook various Lebanese dishes.

## True or False

1. Rita expresses a strong preference for Lebanese food despite traveling and experiencing other cuisines.
2. Rita's American friends are generally unfamiliar with Lebanese cuisine.
3. Rita mentions that Lebanese cuisine offers limited options for vegetarians.
4. In recent years, the variety of food options in Lebanon has increased, including cuisines like sushi and Mexican.
5. Rita argues that the flavors in Lebanese food are familiar and loved, not strange or entirely new.

## Multiple Choice

1. Which of the following is **not** mentioned by Rita as a favorite Lebanese dish?

   a. Hummus   b. Mujaddara   c. Kibbeh   d. Tabbouleh

2. What aspect of Lebanese cuisine does Rita highlight as particularly appealing?

   a. Its complex cooking methods    c. The focus on seafood dishes
   b. The use of exotic ingredients    d. Its visual appeal and delicious flavors

3. How has the dining culture in Lebanon changed according to Rita?

   a. It has shifted to fast food.
   b. People now consider a wider variety of cuisines.
   c. Lebanese food is no longer popular.
   d. Traditional Lebanese dining has completely disappeared.

## Matching

|  |  |
|---|---|
| بِنَظَري | a few |
| قدّ ما | at least |
| بِيَوْم مِن الإيّام | even |
| حتّى | in my opinion |
| عَ قليلة | no matter, how much ever |
| كم | one day, someday |
| شو | so (much) |
| هالْقدّ | somewhere |
| ما رح | that's why |
| مِن هيْك | we have |
| عنّا | what |
| كلّ ما | whenever |
| شي مطْرح | will |
| رح | will not |

## Text

|  |  |  |
|---|---|---|
| 1 | المَطْبخ اللّبْناني بِنَظَري مِن أطْيَب المَطابخ بِالْعالم. | Lebanese cuisine, in my opinion, is one of the most delicious cuisines in the world. |
| 2 | قدّ ما بِرمِت وسافرِت وشِفِت ودِقِت وأكلِت ما بِفْتِكِر بِيَوْم مِن الإيّام رح إزْهق مِن الأكِل اللّبْناني. | No matter how much I travel, see, taste, and eat, I don't think I'll ever get tired of Lebanese food. |
| 3 | حتّى أصْحابي. بسّ كِنِت عايْشِة بِالإمارات، كان في ناس مِن حْوال العالم، | Even my friends. When I was living in the UAE with people from all around the world, |
| 4 | وهلّأ بِأميرْكا، حتّى أصْحابي الأميرْكان، أوْ حتّى أصْحاب مِن غيْر محلّات، | and now in America, even my American friends, or friends from other places, |
| 5 | دايماً بسّ كون شي مطْرح وإذْكُر الأكِل اللّبْناني أوْ شي أكْلِة لِبْنانية، | always wherever I am and mention Lebanese food or some Lebanese dish, |
| 6 | عَ القليلِة بيكون في كم شخِص عارْفين عن شو عم بِحْكي. | at least a few people know what I'm talking about. |

| | | |
|---|---|---|
| 7 | Lebanese cuisine has truly made a name for itself internationally, with really delicious food. | المَطْبَخ اللِّبْناني عنْجدّ مِتِل عِمِل لحالو إسِم عالميّاً، أكِل كْتير طيِّب. |
| 8 | But I also think another reason why it's so famous and so many people love it | بسّ بفْتِكِر كمان سبب تاني مِن الأسْباب، إنّو نْشهر هالقدّ وهالقدّ في ناس بْيحِبّوه، |
| 9 | is that its flavors are very familiar; our spices are familiar. | هوّ إنّو طعْماتو كْتير مألوفة، بْهاراتْنا مألوفة. |
| 10 | The sourness, garlic, oil—these are flavors people love and recognize. | الحامُض، التّوم، الزَّيْت، هوْدي كِلّا طعْمات النّاس بتْحِبّا وبْتعْرفا. |
| 11 | It's not like if someone tries Lebanese food for the first time, they won't know. | ومِش إنّو مثلاً إذا حدا عم بيدوق الأكِل اللِّبْناني لأوّل مرّة، ما رح يَعْرِف. |
| 12 | I mean, they won't find it strange or taste something they've never experienced before. | يَعْني... ما رح يْحِسّوا غريب، أوْ شي مِش دايِق مِنّو قبل. |
| 13 | The flavors are familiar and loved. | يَعْني طعْمة مألوفة وطعْمة بْنْحِبّ. |
| 14 | That's probably why it's so famous and internationally recognized. | ومِن هيْك يِمْكِن مشْهور هالقدّ عالميّاً. |
| 15 | But I also think it's because Lebanese cuisine offers a lot of options for people who, for example, might not eat meat. | بسّ كمان بفْتِكِر إنّو لأنّ المَطْبَخ اللِّبْناني عنْدو كْتير مجال لحتّى النّاس يلّي مثلاً ما بْياكْلوا يِمْكِن لحْمة. |
| 16 | We have hummus, baba ghanoush, tabbouleh, fattoush. | في عنّا الحمُّص، البابا غنّوج، التّبّولي، الفتّوش. |
| 17 | There are many famous dishes in Lebanon. | في عنّا كْتير أكْلات كْتير مشْهورة بِلِبْنان. |
| 18 | I feel that many people who don't eat meat, for instance, love Lebanese food because we have these options to choose from. | بْحِسّ كْتير ناس اللي ما بْياكْلوا لحْمة مثلاً بيحِبّوا إنّو ياكْلوا أكِل اللِّبْناني، لأنّو في عنّا هالخَيارات يْنقّوا مِنّا. |
| 19 | From among the tastiest Lebanese dishes, I personally really love kibbeh. | مِن أطْيَب الأكْلات اللِّبْنانية، أنا شخْصيّاً بْحِبّ كْتير الكبّة. |
| 20 | Kibbeh in a tray or fried kibbeh. | الكبّة بالصّايْنية، أوْ كِبّة مِقْلية. |
| 21 | I also love mujaddara, if someone wants, for example, a homemade dish. | بْحِبّ كْتير المِجدّرة إذا حدا عبالو مثلاً هيْك طبْخِة بيْت. |
| 22 | I love tabbouleh, and I love grills, especially chicken taouk or kofta. | بْحِبّ التّبّولي، بْحِبّ المشاوي خْصوصية الطّاووق، أوْ الكفْتة. |
| 23 | But I want to go back to kibbeh because this is something that sometimes makes my American friends laugh. | بسّ بدّي إرْجع عَ الكبّة، لأنّو هيْدا شي إيّام بيضحِّك أصْحابي الأميرْكان. |

|  |  |  |
|---|---|---|
| 24 | بيحِسّوا إنّو الكِبّة هيِّ مِتل كأنّو حدا عم ياكُل معْكاروني بخِبز، لأنّو هيِّ الكِبّة عِبارة عن لحْمة محْشية لحْمة. | They feel like kibbeh is like eating pasta with bread because it is basically meat stuffed with meat. |
| 25 | وأنا هَيْدا أطْيَب شي عِنْدي، | And for me, this is the tastiest thing. |
| 26 | بقى عنْجدّ كْتير كْتير كْتير بْحِبّ الأكِل اللِّبْناني. | So, I really, really love Lebanese food. |
| 27 | وشي كمان هيْك شْوَيّ بيحِسّوه مُلْفِت للنّظر. | And it's also visually appealing. |
| 28 | إنّو هوْن بلِبْنان مثلاً، مِش هلاّ وإنّو هلاّ بآخِر سِنْتيْن يمْكِن تْغيّرِت شْوَيّ الأوْضاع. | Here in Lebanon, for example, not now but maybe in the last couple of years, things might have changed a bit. |
| 29 | بسّ قبِل هيْك كلِّ ما حدا مثلاً بدّو يِضْهر ياكُل شي مطرح يْروح يِتْغدّى ويتْعشّى بمطْعم ما كان بِنْسأل سُؤال شو بدّكُن تاكْلوا. | But before that, whenever someone wanted to go out to eat somewhere, to have lunch or dinner at a restaurant, they weren't asked what you would like to eat. |
| 30 | لإنّو دايماً الجَواب كان أكِل اللِّبْناني. | Because the answer was always Lebanese food. |
| 31 | يَعْني غيْر مثلاً بغيْر محلاّت بالْعالم، بسّ حدا يْكون رايِح ياكُل دايماً بِنْسأل إنّو شو عَ بالكُن أيّ مطْبخ، | Unlike in other places in the world, where you're always asked what kind of food you want to eat, |
| 32 | هوْن بلِبْنان، يمْكِن قدّ ما الشّعْب اللِّبْناني فخور بأكْلو وقدّ ما ثقافةِ الأكِل قَويّة بلِبْنان وقدّ ما النّاس بيحِبّوا الأكِل اللِّبْناني ما بْيِزْهقوا مِنّو. | here in Lebanon, maybe because howmuchever the Lebanese people are proud of their food and the food culture is strong, people never get tired of it. |
| 33 | دايماً الجَواب كان إنّو... ما في سُؤال أصْلاً، يَعْني دايماً ضاهْرين تاكْلوا أكيد لِبْناني مِش سُؤال بْينْسأل. | The answer was always that... there wasn't actually a question, that is, whenever going out to eat, it's definitely Lebanese food; it's not a question that gets asked. |
| 34 | هلاّ شْوَيّ يمْكِن غيْر ثقافات أثّرِت شْوَيّ. | Now, maybe other cultures have influenced a bit. |
| 35 | يمْكِن الشّباب بلِبْنان والطّريقة اللي بْ... بْيِضْهروا فيا وبْيِسْهروا فيا... صار بِيْنْسأل شْوَيّ أكْتر إنّو: "عَ بالكُن سوشي؟ عَ بالكُن أكِل مكْسيكي أوْ صيني؟" | Maybe the youth in Lebanon and the way they go out and spend their evenings... it's asked a bit more now, like, "Do you feel like sushi? Do you feel like Mexican or Chinese?" |
| 36 | بسّ هَيْدا الشّي كْتير جْديد، يَعْني بكِلّ سْنيني اللي أنا كِنْتُن لِبْنانية، هَيْدا السُّؤال ما كان يَعْني بْينْطرح. | But this is very new; I mean, in all my years of being Lebanese, this question was never really asked. |
| 37 | بقى هَيْدا الشّي بِفْتِكِر مُلْفِت وعنْجدّ بيفرْجي قدّي الشّعْب اللِّبْناني بيحِبّ أكْلو. | So, I think this is striking and really shows how much the Lebanese people love their food. |

| | | |
|---|---|---|
| 38 | انشاالله يْكون هالْمعْلومات الصْغيرة اللي عطيتْكُن ياها هيْك تْحمِّسْكُن إنّو تْنبْشوا أكْتر على المطْبخ اللِّبْناني. | Hopefully, these little bits of information I've given you encourage you to explore Lebanese cuisine more. |
| 39 | وإذا مِش دايْقين الأكِل اللِّبْناني تْروحوا تْدوقوه لِأنّو عنْجدّ، مِن أطْيَب الأكْلات اللي رح تاكْلوه بِحَياتْكُن. | And if you haven't tried Lebanese food, you should go taste it because it's truly one of the best cuisines you'll ever experience in your life. |

---

### Answers

**Main Idea:** a **True or False:** 1. T[2] 2. F[4-6] 3. F[15-18] 4. T[34-36] 5. T[11-13] **Multiple Choice:** 1. c[19-22] 2. d[27] 3. b[34-36]
**Matching:** بِنظري / in my opinion / قدّ ما no matter, how much ever / بيوْم مِن الإيّام one day, someday / مِن هيْك that's why / رح ما will not / هالْقدّ so (much) / شو what / كم a few / عَ قليلة at least / حتّى even / رح will / شي مطْرح somewhere / كِلّ ما whenever / عنّا we have

# 23 Mohammad: The Arabic Language

## Keywords

ثَقافة culture    لَهْجة dialect    بُلْدان countries    تَأثير impact, effect

## Main Idea

a. Mohammad suggests that the Arabic language has limited impact on Lebanese culture and is declining in usage.
b. Mohammad argues that Modern Standard Arabic should replace the local dialect to promote pan-Arab unity.
c. Mohammad believes foreign Arab culture and language has negatively impacted Lebanese cuisine and traditions.
d. Mohammad highlights the Arabic language as a unifying cultural force in Lebanon despite the differences in dialects.

## True or False

1. Mohammad considers Lebanese an entirely separate language from Modern Standard Arabic.
2. Lebanese writers and poets have been influenced by Arabic writers and poets.
3. According to Mohammad, Arabic literature and poetry have played a significant role in shaping Lebanese literature.
4. Lebanese society is influenced by ancient Arab customs like hospitality and generosity.
5. Lebanese cuisine is completely independent of Arab influences.

## Multiple Choice

1. According to Mohammad, how is Arabic taught in Lebanese schools?

    a. As an optional language
    b. As a core subject throughout schooling
    c. Only in higher education
    d. *None of the above*

2. What role does the Arabic language play in Lebanese media and entertainment?

    a. It is used occasionally.
    b. Only foreign languages are used.
    c. Arabic is used less than French and English nowadays.
    d. Arabic is predominantly used.

3. How does Mohammad describe Lebanon's relationship with the Arab world?

   a. Integral, participating in regional affairs
   c. Based solely on trade

   b. Distant and unrelated
   d. *None of the above*

## Matching

| | |
|---|---|
| أكيد | after |
| حاليّاً | all |
| لحتّى | and others |
| وغَيْرو | but |
| كان إلُن | currently |
| بعْد ما | definitely |
| حدا | in order that, so that |
| هوْل | someone |
| كلّ | these |
| بسّ | they had |

## Text

1. اللُّغة العربية، متِل ما كلُّنا مْنعْرِف، تركِت بصْمة وكان إلا تأْثير كْتير كْبير على الثّقافة والتُّراث اللي كْتير مِن البُلْدان هوْن بالشّرْق الأوْسط،

The Arabic language, as we all know, has left a significant mark and had a great impact on the culture and heritage of many countries here in the Middle East.

2. واحد مِن هَيْدي البُلْدان هُوّ لبْنان أكيد.

One of these countries is definitely Lebanon.

3. أبْسط مِثال على تأْثير اللُّغة العربية هُوّ إنّي أنا حاليّاً عم بحْكيكِن باللّهْجة اللُّبْنانية.

A simple example of the influence of the Arabic language is that I am currently speaking to you in the Lebanese dialect.

4. هَيْدي اللّهْجة لوْ قدْ ما كانت مِخْتِلْفة عن اللّهْجة البُلْدان المُجاوْرة، متِل الأُرْدُن وفلسطين وسوريا والعراق مثلاً،

This dialect, no matter how different it is from the dialects of neighboring countries like Jordan, Palestine, Syria, and Iraq,

5. وقدْ ما كانت مِخْتِلْفة عن اللُّغة العربية الفُصْحة، بتْضلّ جُزْء مِنّو.

and as different as it is from Modern Standard Arabic (MSA), it remains a part of it.

|  |  |  |
|---|---|---|
| 6 | ومِنِتْعلّم هَيْدي اللُّغة نِحْنا بِالْمدارس مِن... يَعْني، أوّل شي مِن الكِنْدر جارْدِن لآخِر السِّنين الدِّراسي. | And we learn this language [MSA] in schools from kindergarten to the final years of study. |
| 7 | مِنْضلّنا عم نِدرُس عربي، يَعْني مادّة أساسية ولازِم تِنْجحا لحتّى تْكمِّل. | We continue to study Arabic; that is, it's a core subject, and we must pass it to proceed. |
| 8 | مِنْتعلّم فيا كِلّ شي: إعْراب، أفْعال، قْواعِد، بْحور، شِعِر. | We learn everything about it: syntax, verbs, grammar, poetic meters, poetry. |
| 9 | كمان حتّى مِنْتعلّم... يَعْني مِنْتعلّم إشْيا كْتير فيّا هَيْدي اللُّغة. | We even learn... well, we learn lots of things in this language. |
| 10 | حتّى وسائِل الإعْلام والتّرْفيّه كِلّا بْتِسْتعْمِل اللُّغة العربية، يَعْني النّشْرات الأخْبار، الصّحافة، المُسلْسلات، الأفْلام كِلّ شي بْيِسْتعْمِل اللُّغة العربية. | Even the media and entertainment industries use Arabic, like news bulletins, journalism, series, movies–everything uses Arabic. |
| 11 | حتّى هِيِّ اللُّغة الرّسْمية بْدوائِر الحُكومية وهِيِّ اللُّغة اللي بْيِنْكتبوا فيا الوثائِق الرّسْمية. | It's even the official language in government departments and the language in which official documents are written. |
| 12 | حتّى الأدبا والشّعرا اللُّبْنانية تْأثّروا كْتير بِالأدبا والشُّعرا العرب، مِتِل عنْطرة بِن شدّاد وغَيْرو. | Even Lebanese writers and poets were greatly influenced by Arabic writers and poets, like Antarah ibn Shaddad and others. |
| 13 | وكان إلُن تأْثير كْتير كْبير على يَعْني الشِّعِر العربي. | They had a significant impact on Arabic poetry. |
| 14 | يَعْني اللُّبْنانية بعْد ما تْعلّموا العربي وصاروا يِكْتْبوا بِالعربي، صار إلُن تأْثير كْتير كْبير عْليا، | That is, after the Lebanese learned Arabic and began writing in Arabic, they had a significant impact on it, |
| 15 | لأنُّن أبْدعوا بِهَيْدا المجال كمان. | because they excelled in this field as well. |
| 16 | وفي شغْلِة تْأثّر فيا المُجْتمع اللُّبْناني مِن اللُّغة هِيِّ عادات والتّقاليد العرب القُداما، يَعْني العرب القُداما هِنِّ أساس العربي وكانوا معْروفين بِحُسِن الضّيافة والكرم. | One aspect of the Lebanese society that was influenced by the language is the ancient Arab customs and traditions, like the ancient Arabs, who were the foundation of Arabic and known for their hospitality and generosity. |
| 17 | يَعْني كان لمّا أيّ حدا يِجي لعِنْدُن ويكون بدّو بسّ هيْك، يَعْني مارِق مرْقِة طريق، واجِب عْلَيُن إنّو يِسْتضيفوا تْلات إيام بْبَيْتُن، يْطعْموا، يْشرْبوا، ويْنيْموا عِنْدُن. | Meaning that whenever someone visited them, even just passing by, they were obliged to host them for three days in their home, providing food, drink, and accommodation. |

| | |
|---|---|
| 18 | Lebanese people are also influenced by this– thankfully most of them are like this–meaning you enter their home, and they are generous with you and offer you everything and don't accept you leaving, wanting you to stay with them, such beautiful things. |
| 19 | Even the food, if one notices, in all these neighboring countries, the dishes vary among each other, meaning they are mixed. |
| 20 | So, for example, there are dishes we eat in Lebanon that we consider Lebanese but are originally Arab, |
| 21 | like knafeh, which is originally Palestinian, |
| 22 | but since everyone is connected by the same language, they take and give from each other, even the dishes vary among each other. |
| 23 | Of course, we're not talking about all dishes, because Lebanon has a very rich history with many cultures, not just the Arab culture. |
| 24 | But I am talking about Arab dishes. |
| 25 | Currently, Lebanon has historical ties with the Arab world. |
| 26 | It is a part of the Arab world because it participates in regional affairs and in most of the events that happen in the region. |
| 27 | So now, Lebanon has an Arab identity. |

فا اللُّبْنانية كمان مِتْأَثّرين بِهَيْدا الشّي والحمْدُلله أكترِيِّتُن هيْك، يَعْني بِتْفوتي لعنْدُن، بيكونوا كُرما معك وبيضَيّفوك كِلّ شي وما بيِقْبلوا ما تْفِلّي بدِّك تضلِّك قاعْدة معُن، يَعْني هيْك إشْيا حِلْوة.

حتّى الأكل، إذا الواحد بيلاحِظ بِكِلّ هوْل البُلْدان القُراب مِن بعْض الأكْلات مِتْفاوْتة بيْن بعْضا، يَعْني ومِنْدمِجة.

يَعْني مثلاً في أكْلات مْناكُلا نِحْنا بِلُبْنان مِنْفكِّرا لُبْنانية هِيِّ بِتْكون أصْلا عربي،

يَعْني مِتِل فـ... الكْنافة مثلاً أصْلا فلسْطيني،

بسّ لأنّو كِلُّن مِتْرابْطين بِنفْس اللَّغة بيصيروا بْياخدوا ويْعْطوا مِن بعْض، يَعْني حتّى الأكْلات بْتِتفاوَت مع بعْضا.

طبْعاً مِش عم نِحْكي عن كِلّ الأكْلات، لأنّو لبْنان إلو تاريخ كْتير عريق مع كْتير مِن الثّقافات، مِش بسّ الثّقافة العربية.

بسّ أنا عم بِحْكي عن الأكْلات العربية.

لُبْنان حاليّاً بْترْبطو علاقات تاريخية مع الوَطن العربي،

هوِّ جِزْء مِن الوَطن العربي، لأنّو بيشارك بِالشُّؤون الإقْليمية وبيشارك بِالأكْترِيّة الإشْيا اللي بِتْصير بِالمنْطقة.

فا هلّأ صارِت لُبْنان هوِيْتو عربية.

---

### Answers

**Main Idea:** d **True or False:** 1. F[5] 2. T[12] 3. T[12-14] 4. T[16-18] 5. F[20-24] **Multiple Choice:** 1. b[6] 2. d[10] 3. a[26]
**Matching:** أكيد definitely / حاليّاً currently / لحتّى in order that, so that / وغَيْرو and others / إلُن كان they had / بعْد ما after / حدا someone / هوْل these / كِلّ all / بسّ but

# 24 Sandy: Lebanese Cinema

## Keywords

البان أرب Pan-Arabism    خصّ بالذّكر to mention specificaly

## Main Idea

a. Sandy talks exclusively about modern commercial films in Lebanese cinema.
b. Sandy focuses on the history and evolution of Lebanese cinema, highlighting key periods, films, and filmmakers.
c. Sandy gives us a detailed biography of the Rahbani brothers and their contributions to cinema.
d. Sandy discusses the technical aspects of filmmaking in Lebanon.

## True or False

1. Lebanese cinema started in the early 20th century with the opening of the first theater in Beirut.
2. Lebanese cinema declined after the Lebanese War, with few notable films.
3. Nadine Labaki's 'Capernaum' received global recognition, including a nomination at the Cannes Film Festival.
4. Sandy credits Egyptian cinema as having a significant influence on Lebanese cinema during its developmental stages.
5. Sandy believes that the early 2000s marked a decline in the quality of Lebanese cinema.

## Multiple Choice

1. Which period saw an influx of Egyptian filmmakers to Beirut?

    a. During the French Mandate
    b. After the Lebanese War
    c. After Gamal Abdel Nasser nationalized Egyptian cinema
    d. The early 2000s

2. Which of the following achievements is associated with Lebanese cinema?

    a. 'The Insult' by Ziad Doueiri nominated at the Academy Awards
    b. Maroun Baghdadi winning the Special Jury Prize at Cannes
    c. 'Capernaum' by Nadine Labaki nominated for the Palm d'Or
    d. *All of the above*

3. Sandy's personal inspiration to adore cinema came from which film?
   a. 'West Beirut' by Ziad Doueiri
   b. 'Caramel' by Nadine Labaki
   c. 'The Ring Seller' by the Rahbani brothers
   d. *None of the above*

## Matching

| | |
|---|---|
| فِعْلِيّاً | actually, in reality |
| مِن قِبِل | after ___ing |
| أَصْلاً | after |
| مِن بَعْد ما | by the way |
| مَع الوَقِت | in this way |
| تَبَع | indeed, really |
| بِطَبيعة الحال | of course |
| عَ فِكْرة | of, belonging to |
| بِهَيْدا الشَّكِل | on behalf of |
| عَنْجَدّ | originally |
| مِن بَعْد | over time |
| فِعْلاً | seriously, for real |

## Text

1. مَرْحبا، اليوْم بِدّنا نِحْكي عن السّينِما اللّبْنانية وهَيْدا المَوْضوع كْتير عزيز عَ قَلْبي.

   Hello, today we want to talk about Lebanese cinema, a topic very dear to my heart.

2. كَوْني أنا خِرّيجِةْ سينما وشَخِص بيتابِع وبيحِبّ السّينِما كْتير،

   Being a cinema graduate and someone who follows and loves cinema a lot,

3. لنْلَخِّص القِصّة، إذا بِدّنا نِحْكي كيف بلّشِت السّينِما اللّبْنانية.

   let's summarize the story of how Lebanese cinema started.

4. بلّشِت بالأْلْف وتِسِعْميّة وتِسْعة فِعْلِيّاً بِأوّل مسْرح فْتَح بِبيروت مِن قِبِل ناس كْتشفوا مدينِةْ بيروت.

   It actually began in 1909 with the opening of the first theater in Beirut by people who discovered the city of Beirut.

5. كانوا جايين مِن قِبِل Lumière brothers يَلّي هِنّي أصْلاً أنْتجوا أوّل فيلِم سينما بِالْعالم.

   They came on behalf of the Lumière brothers, who originally produced the first cinema film in the world.

|  |  |  |
|---|---|---|
| 6 | مِن بَعْد ما كْتشفوا مدينةْ بيْروت وفْتحوا هَيْدا المسْرح، مع الوَقِت، يَعْني عم نِحْكي ألْف وتِسْعميِّة وتِسْعة وطْلوع، بلّشِت فِكْرِة السّينما تِتْداوَل أكْتر وأكْتر وفِكْرِة المسارِح. | After they discovered the city of Beirut and opened this theater, over time, specifically from 1909 and onwards, the idea of cinema and theaters started to spread more and more. |
| 7 | لوْ وصِلْنا لفتْرِة الإنْتِداب الفرنْساوي، فتْرِة الإنْتِداب الفرنْساوي شهدِت على يَعْني تصاعُد كْتير كْبير بدوْر السّينما. | Moving on to the French Mandate period: The French Mandate witnessed a significant rise in cinema houses. |
| 8 | صار في كْتير مُخْرِجين، صارِت فِكْرِة السّينما والمسارِح موْجودِة كْتير. | There were many directors, and the concept of cinema and theaters became very prevalent. |
| 9 | إذا فينا نْخِصّ بِالذِّكِر، كْريسْتِل سينما بِبيْروت كانِت، تقْريباً مِن ألْف وتِسْعميِّة وخمْس وعِشْرين، | If we were to mention a specific example, there's the Cinema Cristal in Beirut, around since 1925, |
| 10 | المقَرّ الرّئيسي لكِلّ الإجْتِماعات اللي بدّا تْصير عِنْد الأحْزاب السّياسية، أوْ الشّخْصيات السّياسية مِتِل الحِزْب الشّيوعي كان يَعْمل كِلّ إجْتماعاتو تحْت. | the main venue for meetings held by political parties, or political figures like the Communist Party used to hold all their meetings there. |
| 11 | إذا بِدّنا نِحْكي شْوَيّ مِن بَعْد هَيْدي المرْحلة، مرْحلِةْ الإنْتِداب، فينا نِحْكي عن العصر الدّهبي actually أوْ Golden Age تبع السّينما بِلِبْنان. | If we want to talk a bit about the period after the Mandate era, we can discuss the golden age, or actually, the Golden Age of cinema in Lebanon. |
| 12 | هِيّ الفتْرة اللي جمال عبْد الناصر صار رئيس الجُمْهورية المِصْرية وقرّر إنّو يْخلّي السّينما تْكون تابْعة للدّوْلة. | It was the period when Gamal Abdel Nasser became the President of Egypt and decided to nationalize the cinema industry, making it state-controlled. |
| 13 | بْطبيعةْ الحال كِلّ المُخْرِجين وكِلّ المُنْتِجين يَلّي كانوا بْيِشْتِغْلوا على حْسابُن أوْ مِسْتقِلّين ضْطرّوا إنّو يْفِلّوا ويِنْزحوا عَ بيْروت. | Of course, all the directors and producers who were working independently or on their own account were forced to leave and migrate to Beirut. |
| 14 | ويوسِف شاهين كان واحد مِنُّن عَ فِكْرة. | Youssef Chahine was one of them, by the way. |
| 15 | وبِهَيْدا الشّكِل صارِت السّينما بَعْد تِكْبر أكْتر وأكْتر بما إنّو السّينما المِصْرية كانِت الرّائدة بِالْعالم العربي. | In this way, cinema continued to grow even more since Egyptian cinema was leading in the Arab world. |
| 16 | فا نُزوح هوْل الأشْخاص المِصْريّين خلّى السّينما بَعْد تْصير أهمّ وأقْوى ومُتداولِة أكْتر. | So, the migration of these Egyptian individuals made the cinema in Lebanon even more significant, stronger, and more widespread. |
| 17 | الأخويْن الرّحْباني يَلّي كمان بِهَيْديك الفترة نعْرفوا كْتير وأكيد فيْروز كانِت النّجْمة تبع هوْلي الفِلْومة. | The Rahbani brothers, who were also well-known during that period, and of course, Fairuz was the star of their movies. |

| | |
|---|---|
| 18 | فينا نْخِصّ بِالذِّكِر، بِيّاع الخَواتِم، سفر برْلِك. |
| 19 | طبْعاً الفِلْومِة تبع الرَّحْباني كانوا يَعْني بْيِحْكوا عن لِبْنان أكْتر أوْ جبل لِبْنان أكْتر. |
| 20 | بِحْكوا عن الضِّيَع، عن القُرى، عن جمال لبْنان. |
| 21 | ما كانوا أكيد يْخاطْبوا العرب ككلّ مِتِل الفِلْومِة اللي كانِت تُنْتج مِن المُنْتِجين المِصْريين ويَلّي مِن وَراهُن. |
| 22 | بلّشْنا نِسْمع شْوَيّ بِالبان أرب. البان أرب يَعْني بسّ يْكون الفيلم أوْ المْسلْسل أوْ أيّ عمل عم بيخاطب كذا مُشاهد عربي مِش بسّ مِن جِنْسية واحْدِة. |
| 23 | مِن بَعْد هَيْدي الفِتْرة، فينا نِحْكي شْوَيّ عن ما بَعْد الحرْب اللّبْنانية وأنا صراحة هَيْدي الفِتْرة بِالسّينما هِيِّ مِن الأجْمل بِالنِّسْبة لإلي. |
| 24 | فينا نْخِصّ بِالذِّكِر ويسْت بيْروت زياد دْوَيْري. ويسْت بيْروت كان فيلِم عنْجدّ أوّل فيلم لبْناني أنا حْضرْتو بحَياتي. |
| 25 | هوِّ يَلّي خلّاني حِبّ وإعْشق السّينما. فظيع هَيدا الفيلِم! |
| 26 | فينا نِحْكي عن جوْسْلين صعْب Once Upon a Time in Beirut، مارون بغْدادي عِمِل Hors La Vie، ربِح Special Jury Prize بْكان بِالألف وتِسعْميّة وواحْدة وتِسْعين. |
| 27 | كْتير فْلومِة غيْرا. حتّى بِالسّبْعة وتِسْعين يوسف شاهين كمان عِمِل فيلْم Destiny وتْصوّر بِبيْت الدّين كمان أخد جْوايِز. |
| 28 | مِن بَعْد هَيْدي الفِتْرة فينا نِحْكي عن الرّونيسانْس أوْ أوّل الألْفين بسّ بلّشوا الفْلومِة الشّوَيّ فينا نْقول تِجارية أكْتر إنّا تْطْلع. |
| 29 | فينا نِحْكي عن كراميْل لنَدين لبَكي فينا نِحْكي عن بوسْطة لفيليب عرقْتنْجي، مْنِحْكي شْوَيّ عن رْصاصة طايْشة. |

| | |
|---|---|
| 18 | We can specifically mention films like 'Bayya3 El Khawatem' (The Ring Seller) and 'Safar Barlik' (The Exile). |
| 19 | The Rahbani movies spoke more about Lebanon or the mountains of Lebanon. |
| 20 | They depicted the villages, the rural areas, and the beauty of Lebanon. |
| 21 | Certainly, they weren't addressing the entire Arab world like the movies produced by Egyptian producers and those after them. |
| 22 | We started to hear a bit about 'Pan-Arab.' Pan-Arab means when a film, series, or any work addresses various Arab audiences, not just from one nationality. |
| 23 | Talking about the period after the Lebanese War, personally, I find this era in cinema to be one of the most beautiful. |
| 24 | I can specifically mention Ziad Doueiri's 'West Beirut.' 'West Beirut' was actually the first Lebanese film I ever watched in my life. |
| 25 | It's what made me fall in love with and adore cinema. This film is incredible! |
| 26 | We can talk about Jocelyne Saab with 'Once Upon a Time in Beirut' and Maroun Baghdadi, who made 'Hors La Vie' and won the Special Jury Prize at Cannes in 1991. |
| 27 | There were many other films. Even in 1997, Youssef Chahine also made the film 'Destiny,' which was shot in Beit ed-Dine and won awards. |
| 28 | After this period, we can discuss the renaissance or the early 2000s, when more commercial films started to emerge. |
| 29 | We can talk about 'Caramel' by Nadine Labaki, 'Bosta' by Philippe Aractingi, and also mention 'Stray Bullet.' |

|  |  |  |
|---|---------|--------|
| 30 | We can discuss 'Where Do We Go Now?' also by Nadine Labaki and move on to 2018 with 'The Insult' by Ziad Doueiri, which was nominated for the Palm d'Or and for Best Foreign Language Film, sorry, at the Academy Awards. It was the first Lebanese film to reach such recognition at the Oscars. | مْنِحْكي عن هلّاً لَوَيْن لنادين لبكي وْصولاً للألْفيْن وتمْنْطعِش مع الفيلْم The Insult لِزياد دْويري يَلّي كمان تْرشّح للـ Palm d'Or وللـ Best Foreign Language Film سوْري بالـ Academy Awards. كان أوّل فيلْم لبْناني بْيوصل هالْقد للأُسْكارات. |
| 31 | We have the film 'Capernaum' by Nadine Labaki, which was also nominated for the Palm d'Or at the Cannes Film Festival in 2018. | عنّا فيلْم كْفرْنحوم لنادين لبكي يَلّي كمان بالألْفيْن وتمْنْطعِش تْرشّح للـ Palm d'Or بالـ Cannes Film Festival. |
| 32 | Indeed, Lebanese cinema has remarkably developed despite all the difficulties in Lebanon, reaching global recognition and continues to do so. | فِعْلاً السّينما اللّبْنانية مِنْشوف كيف عنْجدّ مع كلّ شي يِقْطع في لِبْنان تْطوّرِت وقِدرِت توصل وبعْدا عم توصل. |
| 33 | It is a field that we should all be proud of and always support. | هيْدا مجال لازِم كلّنا نْكون فخورين فيه ومِن شجّعو دايْماً. |

___

**Answers**

**Main Idea:** b **True or False:** 1. T[4] 2. F[23-27] 3. T[31] 4. T[15-16] 5. F[28] **Multiple Choice:** 1. c[12-16] 2. d[26, 30-31] 3. a[24] **Matching:** فِعْليّاً actually, in reality / مِن قبِل on behalf of / أصْلاً originally / مِن بعْد ما after / مع الوَقِت over time / تبع of, belonging to / بْطبيعة الحال of course / عَ فِكْرة by the way / بهيْدا الشّكِل in this way / فِعْلاً indeed, really / مِن بعْد after / عنْجدّ seriously, for real

# Social Issues

## 25 Charbel: The Beirut Explosion

## Keywords

إنْفِجار explosion     مَرْفَأ port

## Main Idea

a. Charbel explains how the Lebanese people held the government to account after the explosion.
b. Charbel shares his personal trauma of family members killed in the explosion.
c. Charbel relates his personal experiences of the events on the day of the explosion.
d. Charbel tells us his theories as to how and why the explosion happened.

## True or False

1. The loud noise Charbel and his father heard a loud noise but couldn't comprehend what had happened initially.
2. Charbel's first reaction was to turn on the TV and call to check on the safety of his family members.
3. The explosion happened in the early morning hours.
4. Charbel mentions that even now no one knows exactly what happened or the reason behind the explosion.
5. Charbel describes Beirut as being lively and bustling when he returned two days after the explosion.

## Multiple Choice

1. What was Charbel doing when he heard the loud noise?
   a. Driving in Dora
   b. Watching TV at home
   c. Fixing up his rented house in Bsalim
   d. Working at his office in downtown Beirut

2. How did Charbel describe the scenes on the road after the explosion?
   a. Like a warzone with dead bodies everywhere
   b. Quiet and deserted
   c. Unaffected and normal
   d. Full of shattered glass and chaos

3. What does Charbel express at the end?
   a. That no other country should ever have to endure such a tragedy
   b. Heartbreak over the tragic event and a wish for it not to be repeated
   c. Satisfaction with the government's response
   d. A desire for those responsible to be brought to justice

## Matching

|  |  |
|---|---|
| قبِل ما | a few |
| كم | and even now |
| وإذ | any |
| إذا | as much as |
| حيّلا | as soon as |
| ما... بعْد | before |
| شي | if |
| أوّل ما | never |
| لحدّيت | nobody |
| وَلا مرّة | not... yet |
| ما حدا | something |
| شو | up to, as far as |
| وبعْد لهلّأ | what |
| قدّ ما | when suddenly |

## Text

|  | |  |
|---|---|---|
| بِتْذكّر كِنِت قبِل ما إتْجوّز، بدّي ظبِّط البيْت اللي أخدْتو اللي سْتأجرْتو. | 1 | I remember before I got married, I needed to fix up the house I had taken, the one I rented. |
| سوْ كِنِت أنا وبيّي بِبْصاليم، عم نْظبِّط كم شغْلِة بِالبيْت، | 2 | So, my father and I were in Bsalim, fixing a few things in the house, |

| | | |
|---|---|---|
| 3 | and it was around six o'clock when we suddenly heard a very loud noise. | كانِت تِقْريباً شي ساعة سِتّة، وإذ مِنِسْمَع صوْت كْتير قَوي. |
| 4 | We were thinking that we couldn't comprehend what had happened. | مِنْفَكِّر ما مِنِسْتَوْعِب شو صار. |
| 5 | So we quickly turned on the TV, as we are used to... because if something happens in Lebanon, or any news, the news about it immediately comes on TV in the news [broadcast]. | سوْ مِنِرْكُض دِغْري على التِّيفي لأِنّو مِتعَوّدين... لأِنّو إذا صار شي بِلِبْنان، أوْ حيّلا شي نْيوز دِغْري على التّيفي بْيَعْطوا النْيوز تبعا عَ الأخْبار. |
| 6 | They hadn't put anything on yet, so we started calling around... I called my wife to make sure she was alright. | ما حَطّوا شي بَعْد كان، سوْ مِنْبَلِّش نْدَقْدِق لَـ... دَقّيت لمرْتي تأكّدِت إنّو هيِّ بْخيْر. |
| 7 | The situation was a bit tense. | كان... كان الوَضِع شْوَيّ tensed. |
| 8 | My mother called my father, and they thought there had been bombings. | إمّي عم بِتْدِقّ لبَيّي مْفَكْرين إنّو في قَصِف. |
| 9 | Everyone was thinking something. | كِلّ واحِد مْفَكِّر شي. |
| 10 | The sound and the idea of it, it was indescribable. | كان الصّوْت والفِكْرة، كان شي لا يوصف. |
| 11 | We got in the car and went down to Dora, where my parents live. | مِنْدَوِّر السِّيارة ومْنِنْزِل على الدّوْرة مَطْرح ما ساكْنين أهْلي. |
| 12 | We saw... we started to see the scenes on the road, the shattered glass. | مِنْشوف... مِنْبَلِّش نْشوف المناظِر على الطّريق، الإزاز المْكَسّر. |
| 13 | My parents' house is near a hospital. | نِحْنا بيْت أهْلي قاعْدين حدّ مِسْتَشْفى. |
| 14 | So, as soon as we arrived near my parents' house, we saw crowds gathered at the hospital, where there had never been blood on the ground before, a shocking scene. | سوْ أوّل ما وْصِلْنا لحدّيت بيْت أهْلي، مِنْشوف العالم المِتْجَمّعا بقَلْب هالمِسْتَشْفى يَلّي ولا مرّة صاير الدّم على الأرْض، مَشْهَد يَعْني shocking كان، وبَعْد مِش مِسْتَوعْبين شو صايِر. |
| 15 | What was this? Nobody knows what is going to happen. | شو يَعْني؟ ما حدا بْيَعْرِف شو في بَعْد. |
| 16 | I'm telling you this, and within ten minutes as we turned on the TV, we were confirming that all of us, those we know, that we are related to among our families, my wife, my wife's family, all our friends, that we were safe. | يَعْني عم بِحْكيك هوْلي وبِقَلْب العشر دْقايِق وإذ مِنْدَوِّر التّيفي، ومْنِتْأكّد إنّو نِحْنا كِلّنا واللّي مْنَعْرِفْن، اللي بْيِقْربونا بيْن أهْلي، بيْن مرْتي بيْن أهْلا لمرْتي، بيْن كِلّ أصْحابْنا إنّو كِلّنا we are safe. |
| 17 | But then the news started to come in about a big explosion at the port. | بَسّ بِتْبَلِّش النْيوز تِطْلَع إنّو إنْفِجار كْبير على المَرْفأ. |

|  |  |  |
|---|---|---|
| 18 | This explosion was the third largest in human history, with more than 250 fatalities, and it was around six o'clock. | هَيْدا الإنْفِجار هُوِّ مِن تِقْريباً تالِت أكْبر إنْفِجار صار بِتاريخ البشرية، راح فيا أكْتر مِن مِتيْن وخمْسين قتيل وكانِت السّاعة سِتّة. |
| 19 | And more than two to three thousand injured. | وأكتر مِن ألفيْن لتْلات آلاف جريح. |
| 20 | There were explosive materials at the port, a fire broke out, and then the port exploded. | كان في مَوادّ مُتفجِّرة بِالْمرْفأ، وصار في إشْتِعال ونْفجر البور. |
| 21 | And still now, no one knows exactly what happened or the reason behind it. | وبعْد لهلّأ ما حدا بْيَعرِف شو صار exactly وشو الفِكْرة. |
| 22 | But many people died and were lost in it. | بسّ في عالم تْوَفّت وراحِت فيا هيْك. |
| 23 | And the damage in Beirut was frightening, honestly. It was traumatic. | والأضْرار اللي صارت بْبيْروت بِبيخوّف كانِت صراحة، كانِت تْروما. |
| 24 | And when I went back two days later, it was like a ghost town. | وكان عِنْدي أنا شِغِل بعْد يوْميْن، نْزلِت لتحِت مِتِل مدينِة أشْباح. |
| 25 | The scene was heartbreaking and unforgettable; may it never be repeated, and God rest the souls of those who died. | المشْهد مُبْكي وتِنْذكر، ما تِنْعاد، والله يرْحم اللي ماتوا. |
| 26 | And this is Lebanon. Every so often, sad events happen. | وهيْدا لِبْنان، يَعْني كِلّ فترة بيصير في قُصص حزينة. |
| 27 | As beautiful as it is, at the same time, it has its bad memories. | قدّ ما هُوِّ حِلو وقدّ ما هُوِّ كمان بِذات الوَقِّت فيو bad memories. |

---

**Answers**

**Main Idea:** c **True or False:** 1. T³⁻⁴ 2. T⁶ 3. F¹⁸ 4. T²¹ 5. F²⁴ **Multiple Choice:** 1. c¹⁻² 2. d¹² 3. b²⁵⁻²⁷

**Matching:** ما... بعْد / not... yet / إذا if / وإذ when suddenly / كم a few / قبل ما before / حيّلا any / ما حدا nobody / شو what / وَلا مرّة never / لحدّيت up to, as far as / أوّل ما as soon as / شي something / قدّ ما as much as / وبعْد لهلّأ and even now

**112** | Lebanese Arabic Voices

# 26 Nisrine: The Economic Crisis

## Keywords

أَزْمِة إِقْتِصادية economic crisis    تْفاقَم to worsen    بَلَد country

## Main Idea

a. Nisrine highlights the successful recovery of Lebanon from the economic crisis through international aid.
b. Nisrine discusses the crisis's impact on Lebanon's education system.
c. Nisrine focuses on the economic crisis's impact on Lebanon's tourism industry.
d. Nisrine shares her personal experience as well as the broader societal impact of the economic crisis in Lebanon.

## True or False

1. Only the poor segments of Lebanese society were seriously affected by the economic crisis.
2. Nisrine was affected emotionally by the crisis and the challenges in finding a job.
3. The economic crisis led to Nisrine having to support her siblings and help her father financially.
4. Nisrine was able to find a job in her field of interior design shortly after graduating.
5. Nisrine expresses pessimism that the economic situation in Lebanon will improve in the future.

## Multiple Choice

1. When did Nisrine graduate from university, coinciding with the onset of the economic crisis?

    a. July 2017    b. June 2018    c. July 2019    d. June 2020

2. What was Nisrine's attitude towards work during the crisis?

    a. She was willing to work any job to help her family.

    b. She refused to work outside her field.

    c. She decided to leave the country as soon as possible.

    d. *None of the above*

3. How did the economic crisis affect children in Lebanon according to Nisrine?

    a. It had little to no impact on them.

    b. They became burdened with financial concerns.

    c. Their parents were not able to send them to school.

    d. *None of the above*

## Matching

| | |
|---|---|
| بِشكِل كْتير كْبير | a little bit |
| كأنّو | as before |
| ما إلي | as if |
| مِنّي | due to |
| إجا عَ بالو | even now |
| كِرمال هيْك | I don't have |
| شْوَيّ | I'm not |
| ولّا | in a major way |
| بِسبب | or |
| أَوْقات | over time |
| لهلّأ | so, thus |
| مع الإيّام | sometimes |
| مِتِل قَبِل | to come into one's mind |

## Text

| | | |
|---|---|---|
| مرْحبا! حابّة إحْكي عن الأزْمِة الإقْتِصادية اللي صارِت عِنّا بِلِبْنان. | 1 | Hello, I want to talk about the economic crisis that happened here in Lebanon. |
| لِإنّو هَيْدي الأزْمِة أثّرِت بِكِلّ لِبْنان، بِالْفقير وبِالْغني وبِالْكبير وبِالصّغير. | 2 | Because this crisis affected everyone in Lebanon: the poor and the rich, the old and the young. |
| كِلّ بيْت بِلِبْنان عاش أوْضاع كْتير صعْبِة بِهَيْدي الأزْمِة. | 3 | Every household in Lebanon experienced very difficult conditions during this crisis. |
| هَيْدي الأزْمِة أثّرِت بِالْكِلّ وأثّرِت فيني أنا بِشكِل كْتير كْبير. | 4 | This crisis affected everyone and had a major impact on me. |
| لِإنّو أنا بِسِنِة اللي تْخرّجِت فيا، أنا تْخرّجِت بِشهِر سبْعة، ألْفين وتِسعْطعْش، كان بِوَقْتا عِنْدي أمل خمْسين بِالْميّة إنّي لاقي شِغِل بِبلدي لِبْنان. | 5 | Because the year I graduated, which was in July 2019, I had a 50% hope of finding a job in my country, Lebanon. |
| أنا درسِت interior design، هنْدسِة ديكور. | 6 | I studied interior design. |

| | |
|---|---|
| 7 | I had a little hope that I could find a job, not have to go abroad, not leave Lebanon, and could help my family in these difficult times. |
| 8 | About three months after I graduated from university, the revolution began, and the economic crisis worsened. |
| 9 | The exchange rate of the dollar started to rise, and the situation began to get very, very difficult for us. |
| 10 | At that time, I went through very difficult moments, experienced many hard days, and felt as if I had no role in this society. |
| 11 | I felt worthless, unable to offer anything to my country, unable to contribute anything to my family. |
| 12 | Our situation was very difficult that year. |
| 13 | I was willing to work any job just to help my family with expenses, to support my siblings, to help my father. |
| 14 | My father was going through very tough times. |
| 15 | I remember we had to deprive ourselves of many things. |
| 16 | We really, really deprived ourselves of everything. |
| 17 | Before the crisis, we could afford anything we wanted in terms of food. |
| 18 | After the crisis started, even basic necessities became hard to obtain. |
| 19 | So, those days we lived through were difficult. |
| 20 | And I lost hope of finding a job in this country. |
| 21 | Many people lost their jobs, many large companies closed, and the situation in the country became very difficult. |
| 22 | Everyone's situation changed drastically, almost 180 degrees. |

كان عِنْدي أمل بسيط إنّو إقْدر لاقي شِغِل وما سافِر وما إتْرُك لبْنان، وإقْدر ساعِد أهْلي بهدوْل الأوْضاع الصّعْبة.

بعْد تْلات شْهور تقْريباً من تخرُّجي مِن الجامْعة وبلّشِت الثَّوْرة، بلّشِت الأزْمة الإقْتِصادية تِتْفاقم.

بلّش سِعْر صرْف الدّولار يِغْلى، بلّشِت الأوْضاع كْتير كْتير تِصْعب عْلَيْنا.

أنا بوَقْتا عِشِت حالي كْتير صعْبة، مرِّت عْلَيّ إيّام صعْبة كْتير وحسّ كأنّو أنا دوْري ما إلي دوْر بهَيْدا المجْتمع.

حِسّ حالي بلا قيمِة، مِنّي قادْرة قدِّم شي لبلدي، مِنّي قادْرة قدِّم شي لأهْلي.

وَضعْنا نحْنا إشْتِغِل أيّ شي بسّ كِرْمال ساعِد أهْلي بالْمصْروف، ساعِد إخْواتي، ساعِد بيّي.

بيّي مرّ بإيّام كْتير صعْبة.

بِتْذكّر إنّو كْتير نحرمْنا.

كْتير كْتير نحرمْنا... مِن كلّ شي.

أكِل كِنّا مثلاً قبل الأزْمة قادرين نْجيب كِلّ شي بْيِجي عَ بالْنا.

بعْد ما بلّشِت الأزْمة يَعْني، صار الأساسيّات اللي نحْنا بْحاجة إلْن صعْب إنّو نْجيبْن.

كِرْمال هيْك هَيْدي الإيّام اللي مرقْنا... مرقْنا فيا كانت صعْبة.

وأنا كِنِت فاقْدة الأمل إنّي لاقي شِغِل بهالْبلد.

وكْتير عالم... وكْتير عالم تركوا شِغْلُن، شِرْكات كْتير كْبيرة سكّرِت وصار البلد وَضْعوا كْتير صعْب.

تْغيّر وضْع الكلّ ميّة وتْمانين درجة تقْريباً.

| | |
|---|---|
| 23 | هَيْدي الأزْمِة أثّرِت بالْكِلّ، بِكِلّ لِبْناني مَوْجود بِهَيْدا البلد، إن كان كْبير وَلّا كان صْغير، إن كان فقير وَلّا غني. أثّرِت بالْكِلّ. |
| | This crisis affected everyone, all of Lebanon, whether old or young, poor or rich. It affected everyone. |
| 24 | خْصوصي الوْلاد، الوْلاد صاروا يِعْتلوا همّ، يِطْلْبوا مصاري مِن أهْلُن إذا بدُّن يْروحوا يِشْتروا شي لإلُن. |
| | Especially children. Children became burdened, asking their parents for money if they wanted to buy something for themselves. |
| 25 | هِنّي وْلاد كِرْمال إنّو ياكْلوا. |
| | They, as children, need it for basic things like food. |
| 26 | هَيْدي الأزْمِة كْتير غيّرِتْنا، كْتير غيّرِت نِحْنا كلِبْنانية، |
| | This crisis changed us a lot, changed us Lebanese a lot, |
| 27 | وبعدْنا لهلّأ يَعْني عم نْعاني شْوَيّ مِن هَيْدي الأزْمِة بِسبب الغلا وأوْقات ما مِنْلاقي كِلّ شي بدْنا ياه. |
| | and we are still suffering a bit from this crisis due to the high prices and sometimes not finding what we need. |
| 28 | وأوْقات مُمْكِن لهلّأ يِمْكِن يِجي عَ بالْنا شي وما نِقْدر نِشْتريه. |
| | And sometimes, even now, we might want something but are unable to buy it. |
| 29 | بسّ انشاالله مع الإيّام بْيِرْجع الوَضِع مِتِل قبل وأحْسن، وبْيِتْحسّن وَضِع لِبْنان وبِتْحسّن حَياتْنا، |
| | But hopefully, with time, the situation will return to how it was before, or even better, and Lebanon's situation will improve, and our lives will improve. |
| 30 | ومْنِقْدر نِشْتري كِلّ شي بدْنا ياه، ومِنْلاقي الشِّغِل اللي نِحْنا مْنِحْلم فيه. |
| | And we will be able to buy everything we want and find the jobs we dream of. |

---

**Answers**

**Main Idea:** d **True or False:** 1. F[2-3, 23] 2. T[10-11] 3. T[13-14] 4. F[20] 5. F[29] **Multiple Choice:** 1. c[5] 2. a[13-14] 3. b[24-25] **Matching:** إجا عَ بالو to come into one's mind / بِشكِل كْتير كْبير in a major way / كأنّو as if / ما إلي I don't have / منّي I'm not / بِسبب due to / أوْقات sometimes / وَلّا or / شْوَيّ a little bit / كِرْمال هيْك so, thus / مِتِل قبل as before / مع الإيّام over time / لهلّأ even now

# 27 Waleed: Electricity in Lebanon

## Keywords

| | |
|---|---|
| طاقة energy | متجدّد renewable |
| كهربا elecricity | مولّد generator |
| بألواح الطّاقة الشّمسية solar panels | |

## Main Idea

a. The transition in Lebanon from traditional state-provided electricity to self-sufficient, renewable energy sources due to economic and political crises.
b. A detailed history of electricity infrastructure development in Lebanon.
c. Waleed's personal experiences and challenges with electricity in his daily life.
d. A critique of the Lebanese government's failure to provide reliable electricity to its citizens.

## True or False

1. Waleed's daughter was learning about renewable energy for the first time in her geography lesson.
2. Before the economic crisis, Lebanon had consistent 24-hour electricity supply.
3. The Lebanese people have not found any alternatives to state-provided electricity.
4. Solar energy is a traditional and long-standing source of power in Lebanese villages.
5. Wind energy is also being used as a new source of electricity in Lebanon.

## Multiple Choice

1. What was the primary source of electricity in Lebanon before the economic crisis?

    a. Solar panels   b. Wind turbines   c. State-operated power plants   d. *None of the above*

2. What factors have driven Lebanese people to seek alternative energy sources?

    a. Interest in modern technology
    b. Political corruption and economic crisis
    c. Environmental concerns
    d. *All of the above*

3. How does Waleed describe the Lebanese people's response to their challenges with electricity?

   a. As being passive and dependent on the state

   b. As innovative and resilient in finding alternatives

   c. As relying solely on international aid

   d. *None of the above*

## Matching

|  |  |
|---|---|
| تِحْديداً | additionally |
| أيْه | as it used to be |
| خِلال | as long as |
| مِتِل قبِل | during |
| ما... إلّا | especially |
| ما | firstly |
| عِنّا | instead of |
| أوّلاً | may, might |
| خاصةً | not |
| يمْكِن | only |
| بدل | specifically |
| بِالإضافة لهَيْدي | we have |
| طالما | yes |

## Text

|  |  |  |
|---|---|---|
| سلام، كيفْكُن رِفْقاتي؟ وَليد معكُن. | 1 | Hello, how are you, my friends? This is Waleed. |
| حبيباتي، اليوْم بِنْتي كان عِنْدا درْس بِالجُغْرافْيا. | 2 | My dears, today my daughter had a geography lesson. |
| إجِت سألتْني: "بابا، اليوْم الميس حِكِيتْنا عن الطّاقة المُتجدِّدة، ليْه في طاقة جْديدة وطاقة قديمة." | 3 | She came and asked me, "Dad, today the teacher talked to us about renewable energy. Why is there both new and old energy?" |
| شرحْتِلّا شو المقْصود بِالطّاقة المُتجدِّدة، بسّ معا حقّ بِسْؤالا. | 4 | I explained to her what renewable energy means, but she had a valid question. |
| في طاقة قديمة وطاقة جْديدة، تحْديداً بِلبْنان. | 5 | There is old and new energy, specifically in Lebanon. |

| | |
|---|---|
| 6 | أيّه في طاقة قديمة وفي طاقة جْديدة. الطّاقة القديمة هيِّ الكهْربا اللي مْناخِدا مِن الدَّوْلة، يَعْني هيِّ كهْربةْ الدَّوْلة. |
| 7 | الدَّوْلة بْتِبْني معامِل كهْربا. |
| 8 | بْلِبْنان في معامِل بْتِشْتِغِل على الفْيول في معامِل بْتِشْتِغِل على الطّاقة الحْرارية. |
| 9 | وطول عُمْرا، هَيْدي هيِّ معْمل جْعيتا، معْمل... عفْواً، معْمل الجِّيّة، معْمل الزّوق ومعْمل الزَّهْراني. |
| 10 | بسّ خِلال الحرْب، كِنّا نْعاني مِن أزْمة اللي أزْمةْ إنْقِطاع بالتّيار الكهْرُبائي لأسْباب مُخْتلِفة. |
| 11 | بسّ لخِلْصِت الحرب، بِفترْةْ التِّسْعينات رجْعِت الكهْربا تِجي أرْبعة وعِشْرين ساعة بْلِبْنان، يَعْني بعْد ما كانِت تِجي أحْياناً بالْأشْهُر. |
| 12 | ما نْشوف الكهْربا، بِأوّل الْألْفيْن، بعْد نِهاية الحرب بِسنةْ التِّسْعين، لـ... لحُدود الْألْفيْن وخمْسة. |
| 13 | كِنّا عايْشين بِنعيم مِن الكهْربا، تِجي الكهْربا أرْبعة وعِشْرين ساعة ونْسينا شو يَعْني 'قطْعِت كهْربا'. |
| 14 | ولكِن مِنذُ بِدايةْ الْأزْمة الْإقْتِصادية بْلِبْنان، رِجْعِت الْأزْمات الكهْربا بِشكْل سيِّئ. |
| 15 | يَعْني رْجِعْنا مِتِل قبِل، رْجِعْنا مِتِل إيّام الحرب. |
| 16 | ما نْشوف الكهْربا إلّا ساعْتيْن بِالْأرْبعة وعِشْرين ساعة، نتيجِةْ فساد سياسي، فساد مالي وأسْباب أُخْرى. |
| 17 | بسّ هوْن صار في عنّا طاقة جْديدة بْلِبْنان. شو هيِّ؟ ما أخدِت شكِل واحد صارِت عم تاخُد أشْكال مُخْتلِفة. |
| 18 | الطّاقة الجْديدة اللي عنّا بْلِبْنان هوِّ اللُّبْناني نتيجةْ الحرب اللي عاش فيها وغياب الدَّوْلة. |

| | |
|---|---|
| 6 | Yes, there is old and new energy. The old energy is the electricity we get from the state, meaning the state's electricity. |
| 7 | The state builds power plants. |
| 8 | In Lebanon, there are plants that operate on fuel and others on thermal energy. |
| 9 | For a long time, these have been the Jeita plant, the... sorry, the Jiyeh plant, the Zouk plant, and the Zahrani plant. |
| 10 | But during the war, we suffered from different reasons for power outages. |
| 11 | After the war, in the 1990s, electricity returned to being available 24 hours in Lebanon, unlike when it sometimes wouldn't come for months. |
| 12 | We didn't see electricity, in the early 2000s, after the end of the war in the nineties, until... until around 2005. |
| 13 | We lived in a kind of paradise with electricity available 24 hours, and we forgot what it meant for the power to be cut. |
| 14 | But since the beginning of the economic crisis in Lebanon, power issues returned severely. |
| 15 | We went back to how it was before, like during the war. |
| 16 | We only see electricity for two hours every 24 due to political corruption, financial corruption, and other reasons. |
| 17 | But now there's new energy in Lebanon. What is it? It hasn't taken one form but has evolved in different ways. |
| 18 | The new energy in Lebanon is the Lebanese themselves, a result of the war they lived through and the absence of the state. |

| |  |  |
|---|---|---|
| 19 | بطّل يمكن ما في شعْب بالْعالم لا يعْتمد على الدّوْلة لتأْمين إحْتياجاتو اليوْمية وإحْتياجاتو الأساسية قدّ الشّعْب اللّبْناني، اللي عْتمد بدائل مخْتلفة لتأْمين الكهْربا. | It's become impossible to find a nation in the world that doesn't rely on the state to secure its daily and basic needs as much as the Lebanese people, who have relied on various alternatives to secure electricity. |
| 20 | أوّلا، كان إعْتماد موتيرات الكهْربا الكبيرة اللي بتْنْتج كميّات كبيرة من الطّاقة من الكهْربا. | Firstly, there was reliance on large generators that produce large amounts of electricity. |
| 21 | فا عمد بعْض الأشْخاص إلى شراء هيْدي المولّدات الكبيرة وتثْبيتا بالأحْياء وبيْع الكهْربا للشّقق والشّركات. | So, some people intended to buy these large generators and install them in neighborhoods, selling electricity to apartments and companies. |
| 22 | ولكن كمان نتيجةْ إنّو هيْدي المولّدات ما فيها تعْطي كهْربا لأرْبعة وعشْرين ساعة، ونتيجةْ الغلاء اللي البعْض كان يعْمد لتسْعير الخمْسة أمْبير بميّة دولّار وميّة وعشْرين دولّار وميّة وتلاتين دولّار، كمان حاول اللّبْناني... وخاصة بالضّيع والمناطق اللي بعيدة عن بيْروت، حاول اللّبْناني إنّو يْفتّش عن مصادر جْديدة لإنْتاج الكهْربا. | But also as a result of these generators not being able to provide electricity 24 hours, and due to the high costs some charged (like 100, 120, 130 dollars for 5 amperes), Lebanese tried... especially in villages and areas far from Beirut, Lebanese tried to look for new sources of electricity production. |
| 23 | فا هوْن يمْكن ظهر عنّا أنْواع طاقة جْديدة على اللّبْناني فا صار في عنّا... | So, at this point, we may have seen the emergence of new types of energy for the Lebanese, so now we have... |
| 24 | هلّا هيّ يمْكن ما تْكون جْديدة على الأشْخاص العايْشين برّاةْ لبْنان، ولكن على اللّبْناني هيّ جْديدة. | Now, these might not be new to people living outside Lebanon, but for the Lebanese, they are new. |
| 25 | ظهر عنّا طاقةْ الألْواح الشّمْسية اللي صرْنا مثلًا لمّا تطّلع على الضّيع البْعيدة عن بيْروت. | Solar panel energy has emerged among us, which we, for example, see when you look at the distant villages from Beirut. |
| 26 | تْلاقي أسْطح البْيوت اللي كانت تتْزيّن بالزّريعة والمونة، مع مخْتلف أنْواعا صارت تطّلع على سقْفا قرْميد مْغطّى بألْواح الطّاقة الشّمْسية. | You'll find the rooftops that used to be adorned with plants and provisions, with their various types, have now become covered with solar panels on their terracotta-tiled roofs. |
| 27 | يعْني بدل القرْميد الأحْمر صارت المباني البْيوت مْغطّاة بألْواح الطّاقة الشّمْسية، | That is, instead of the traditional red tiles, buildings and houses are now covered with solar panels, |
| 28 | بالإضافة لهيْدي صار في عنّا ألْواح... أوْ عواميد بتشْتغل على توْليد الطّاقة من الرّياح... من الرّياح. | In addition to this, we now have panels... or poles that operate on generating power from the wind... from the wind. |

| | |
|---|---|
| 29 | طالما في نفس باللِّبْناني، طالما هُوِّ عم يِسْعى لِأِنّو يْحسِّن وَضْعو المعيشي، طالما هُوِّ يِبْحث عن بدائِل لِلْحَياة وبدائِل لِلْإِسْتِمْرار بِالْحَياةْ. |
| | As long as the Lebanese have breath, they strive to improve their living conditions and find alternatives to continue living. |
| 30 | جدّ اللِّبْناني هُوِّ عِبارة عن طائِر فينيق، دائِماً يِبْحث عن الأمل. |
| | Really, the Lebanese are like the phoenix, always searching for hope. |

---

## Answers

**Main Idea:** a **True or False:** 1. T[2-3] 2. T[13] 3. F[19-20] 4. F[25-26] 5. T[28] **Multiple Choice:** 1. c[6-8] 2. b[16] 3. b[29] **Matching:** تحْديداً specifically / أيْه yes / خِلال during / مِتِل قبِل as it used to be / إلّا ما ... only / ما not / بِالإضافة لهَيْدي additionally / بدل instead of / يِمْكِن may, might / خاصةً especially / أوّلاً firstly / عنّا we have / طالما as long as

121 | Lebanese Arabic Voices

# 28 Rita: Religion in Lebanon

## Keywords

ديانة = دين religion    طائْفة (طَوايِف) sect    صُعوبة difficulty

## Main Idea

a. Rita describes her personal religious beliefs and how they differ from the general Lebanese population.
b. Rita focuses on the negative aspects of religious sectarianism in Lebanon, blaming it for many of the country's problems.
c. Rita discusses the complexity of religion in Lebanon, explaining its impact on politics, education, and social life.
d. Rita gives a detailed comparison of religious practices between Lebanon and the United States.

## True or False

1. Rita mentions that Lebanon has a significant number of religious sects, making it a country rich in diversity.
2. Rita describes her personal experiences with religious diversity in Lebanon as a barrier to social interaction.
3. Rita mentions what relgion she belongs to.
4. According to Rita, socially, people of different religions in Lebanon rarely interact with each other.
5. In Lebanon, religious affiliations play a crucial role in the political structure, including the designation of key government positions.

## Multiple Choice

1. What is Rita's view on the relationship between religion and politics in Lebanon?

    a. Religion influences politics only during elections.

    b. Politics has no influence on religious practices in Lebanon.

    c. Religion plays a critical and intertwined role in politics.

    d. *None of the above*

2. According to Rita, how does the religious diversity in Lebanon affect the education sector?

    a. Schools are segregated based on religion.
    b. They take breaks for both Muslim and Christian holidays.
    c. Religious teachings dominate the curriculum.
    d. Religion is completely excluded from schools.

3. What does Rita say about the living arrangements of different religious communities in Lebanon?

   a. There are designated cities for each religious sect.

   b. Inter-religious interactions are discouraged.

   c. Christians and Muslims live in completely separate neighborhoods.

   d. Christians and Muslims live side by side and interact socially.

## Matching

|  |  |
|---|---|
| لَيْش | at the same time |
| تَـ | especially |
| بِذات الوَقِت | even |
| خْصوصي | himself, itself |
| بَيْنما | in order to, so that |
| بِحدّ ذاتو | next to each other |
| تبع | regarding, related to |
| وَقْتا اللي | so |
| إلُن | they have |
| حدّ بَعْضُن | when |
| بقى | while |
| حتّى | why |

## Text

|  |  |
|---|---|
| بدّي إفْتح مَوْضوع الدّين بِلِبْنان يَلّي هُوِّ مَوْضوع حِسّاس شْوَيّ. | 1. I want to open a discussion about religion in Lebanon, which is a somewhat sensitive topic. |
| وأغْلبيّة اللِّبْنانيّين أمّا فكّروا فيه أوْ مأثّرين فيه بِطريقة أوْ بْأُخْرى. | 2. Most Lebanese either have thought about it or are affected by it in one way or another. |
| لَيْش هالمَوْضوع مْهِمّ هالْقدّ؟ لِأنّو بِلِبْنان في تَمْنطَعْشر طايْفة بْبلد كْتير صْغير. | 3. Why is this topic so important? Because in Lebanon, there are eighteen sects in a very small country. |
| تأعْطيكُن فِكْرة عن صِغْرو، بسّ كون عم بِشْرح عن حجم لِبْنان لأصْحابي الأميرْكان، | 4. To give you an idea of its small size, when explaining the size of Lebanon to my American friends, |

**123 | Lebanese Arabic Voices**

|  |  |  |
|---|---|---|
| 5 | بْقلُّن إنّو حجْمو مِن حجِم رود آيْلاند، يَلّي هيِّ أصْغر ولاية أميرْكية. | I tell them it's about the size of Rhode Island, the smallest state in the US. |
| 6 | تْخايَلوا بلد هالْقدّ صْغير في هالْقدّ طَوايِف مِخْتلِفة. | Imagine a country so small with so many different sects. |
| 7 | هَيْدا الشّي بِذات الوَقِت بيجيب غِنا للبْنان لأنّو بإخْتِلافْنا أكيد غِنا، غِنا وإخْتِلاف بْوِجْهِة النّظر، بتْطلُّعْنا للدّني، بإيمانّا. | This, at the same time, brings richness to Lebanon because with our differences, there is certainly richness, richness and diversity in perspectives, in how we view the world, in our beliefs. |
| 8 | هَيْدا الشّي بْيَعْطي غِنا، بسّ بِذات الوَقِت أكيد كمان بيجيب بعْض الصُّعوبات. | This brings richness, but at the same time, it certainly also brings some difficulties. |
| 9 | خْصوصي إنّو الدّين بِلبْنان بيأثِّر عَ عِدّة... عَ عِدّة مجالات يَعْني. | Especially since religion in Lebanon affects... several areas. |
| 10 | بيأثِّر عَ المجال السّياسي، بيأثِّر عَ المجال الإجْتِماعي، بيأثِّر عَ المجال التّعْليمي. | It affects the political field, it impacts the social field, and it influences the educational field. |
| 11 | ورح خبِّرْكُن اليوْم شْويّ عن بعْض هَيْدي التّأْثيرات. | Today, I'll tell you a bit about some of these influences. |
| 12 | بالْمجال السّياسي، بِلبْنان مِش مِتِل مطارِح بالْعالم بيْقسْموا بين الدّين وبين الدّوْلِة. | In the political realm, Lebanon is not like other places where there's a separation between religion and state. |
| 13 | مثلاً بأميرْكا، في تفْرِقة بين الدّين والسّياسي. | For example, in America, there is a separation between religion and politics. |
| 14 | بيْنما بِلبْنان هَوْدي الإشْيا مرْبوطين كْتير بِبعْضُن. | While in Lebanon, these two are very much intertwined. |
| 15 | مثلاً الرّئيس الجُمْهورية اللّبْناني لازِم يْكون مسيحي ماروني. | For instance, the President of the Republic must be a Maronite Christian. |
| 16 | وَزير رئيس الوِزارة لازِم يْكون مِسْلِم سِنّي. | The Prime Minister must be a Sunni Muslim. |
| 17 | رئيس البرْلمان لازِم يْكون مِسْلِم شيعي. | The Speaker of Parliament must be a Shia Muslim. |
| 18 | حتّى البرْلمان بِحدّ ذاتو المقاعِد يَلّي فيه مْقسّمين حسب الطّوايِف. | Even parliament itself, its seats are divided according to sects. |
| 19 | وقْتَت اللي عِمْلوا هَيْدي القوانين تبع تقْسيم المقاعِد البرْلمانية، | When they made these laws regarding the division of parliamentary seats, |
| 20 | كان في أكيد أسْباب عديدة، بسّ واحِد مِنّا كان يتْأكّدوا إنّو الطّوايِف مْمثّلة بْشكِل مظْبوط بالبرْلمان حسب نِسْبة بِـ... بالبلد. | there were certainly several reasons, but one of them was to ensure that the sects were properly represented in the parliament according to their proportion in the country. |

| | |
|---|---|
| 21 | However, this certainly also brings difficulties because when certain parties win a majority in the parliament, |
| | بسّ أكيد هَيْدا الشّي كمان بيجيب معو صُعوبات لأنّو وَقْتا اللي أحْزاب مُعيّنة بْتِرْبح أغْلبية بالبرْلَمان، |
| 22 | it might make the segments of society that belong to these parties feel like they have more influence than the other sects. | 
| | يمْكن هَيْدا الشّي يْخلّي الفِئات بالمُجْتمع يَلّي... يَلّي بْتِتْبع هالأَحْزاب تْحِسّ إنّو صار عنْدا نُفوذ أكْبر من الطّوايف الأخْرى. |
| 23 | This can cause friction between the different sects in society. |
| | وهَيْدا الشّي أكيد بيسبّب حزازيّات بيْن الطّوايف بالمُجْتمع. |
| 24 | If we look, for example, at the education sector, at the schools, schools in Lebanon have many holidays throughout the year because they take breaks with both Muslims and Christians. |
| | إذا مْنِطْلع مثلاً بْقِطاع التّعْليم، بالمدارس، المدارس بلِبْنان بْتِفرّص إيّام كْتيرة بالسّنة لأنّو بتفرّص مع المُسْلمين ومع المسيحيّين. |
| 25 | In countries where there isn't a strong link between religion and other state matters like education or politics, they might not observe every religious holiday like we do in Lebanon. |
| | يَعْني يمْكن مثلاً دُوَل يَلّي ما عِنْدُن هالرّبط بين الدّين وال... بقيّة المواضيع بالدّوْلة مِتِل التّعْليم مِتِل السّياسة يمْكن ما بيفرّصوا عَ كلّ عيد ديني مِتِل ما مِنْفرّص بلِبْنان. |
| 26 | But certainly, the positive aspect of this matter is that we have schools with students from all sects and religions, |
| | بسّ أكيد الشّي الإيجابي بهَيْدا المَوْضوع إنّو عنّا مدارس فيا تلاميذ من كافّة الطّوايف والأدْيان، |
| 27 | which certainly enriches our students and makes our children aware from an early age of the diversity of opinions and beliefs, which is important. |
| | يَلّي هُوّ أكيد بْيغْني تلاميذْنا وبيخلّي أطْفالْنا يوعوا من عُمر مْبكّر عَ إخْتِلاف الآراء وإخْتِلاف الإيمان، يَلّي هُوّ شي مْهمّ. |
| 28 | Thirdly, socially, in Lebanon, we have cities where Christians and Muslims live side by side as neighbors. |
| | تالِت شي إجْتماعيّاً، بلِبْنان في عنّا مُدُن بلِبْنان فيا مسيحيّين ومُسْلمين قاعْدين حدّ بعْضُن جيران. |
| 29 | They often visit each other, eating at each other's homes on certain days. |
| | إلُن زمان كْتير بيروحوا بْيِجوا عِند بعْضُن، بْياكْلوا عِند بعْضُن. |
| 30 | Sometimes, we have churches and mosques next to each other, because in the cities where there are both Muslims and Christians, |
| | في إيّام عنّا كنايس وجَوامع حدّ بعْضُن لأنّو المُدُن يَلّي فيا إسْلام ومسيحيّين، |
| 31 | they all want to pray, so there are definitely places of worship in these cities or villages. |
| | كلُّن بدُّن يْصلّوا بقى أكيد في عِنْدُن معابد بهَيْدي المُدُن أوْ الضِّيع. |
| 32 | And in Lebanon, socially, once we set politics aside, people from different religions get along, as I mentioned, visiting each other. |
| | وبلِبْنان إجْتِماعيّاً، بسّ نْحُطّ السّياسة عَ جنب، النّاس من ديانات مخْتِلْفة بْيِتْفْقوا مِتِل ما ذكرِت بيروحوا وبْيِجوا عِند بعْضُن. |
| 33 | There is even a kind of openness, I mean. |
| | حتّى في... في نوْع من الإنْفِتاح يَعْني. |

| |  |  |
|---|---|---|
| 34 | أنا شخْصِياً مسيحية، بسّ مْنعْرِف... شايْفين يَعْني عَ مدى سْنين ناس مِسلْمين حاطّين مثلاً شجْرةْ ميلاد عَ عيد الميلاد، أوْ حتّى مسيحيّين بيروحوا بْيُفْطِروا مع إخْوانّا المُسْلِمين خِلال شهر رمضان. | I'm a Christian myself, but we know... we have seen, for example, over the years, Muslims putting up Christmas trees during Christmas, or even Christians going to have Iftar with our Muslim brothers during Ramadan. |
| 35 | هَيْدي هيْك فِكْرة... يَعْني مُلخّص صْغير عن الدِّيانةِ بِلِبْنان. | This is a thought... a brief overview of religion in Lebanon. |
| 36 | انشاالله كمان هَيْدا الشّي يْخلّيكُن إنّو تْروحوا تعِمْلوا أبْحاتْكم الخاصّة وتْشوفوا كيف الدِّيانة بْتأثِّر أكْترَ عَ لِبْنان. | Hopefully, this encourages you to do your own research and see how religion further influences Lebanon. |

---

**Answers**

**Main Idea:** c **True or False:** 1. T³⁻⁷ 2. F⁷ 3. T³⁴ 4. F²⁸⁻³⁴ 5. T¹⁵⁻¹⁸ **Multiple Choice:** 1. c¹²⁻¹⁸ 2. b²⁴⁻²⁵ 3. d²⁸⁻³¹ **Matching:** ليْش why / تَـ in order to, so that / بِذات الوَقِت at the same time / خْصوصي especially / بَيْنما while / بِحدّ ذاتو himself, itself / تبع regarding, related to / وَقْتا اللي when / إلُن they have / حدّ بعْضُن next to each other / حتّى even / بقى so

# 29 Mohammad: Corruption and Favoritism in Lebanon

## Keywords

فساد corruption    محْسوبية favoritism    قرف mess, disgusting state

## Main Idea

a. Mohammad suggests that corruption and favoritism in Lebanon are minor issues that have been exaggerated by the media.
b. Mohammad explains how corruption was once pervasive but has improved considerably after the revolution.
c. Mohammad outlines how corruption and favoritism are pervasive issues in Lebanon.
d. Mohammad criticizes the Lebanese people for their lack of initiative in addressing the rampant corruption of officials.

## True or False

1. According to Mohammad, Lebanon's small size and population make it very difficult to manage.
2. Politicians in Lebanon are accused by Mohammad of exploiting public resources for personal gain.
3. Mohammad suggests that the Lebanese people are actively resisting the cycle of corruption and favoritism.
4. The electricity situation in Lebanon used to be reliable, with 24/7 availability before it was manipulated for profit.
5. Recently, a valuable natural resource was discovered in Lebanon.

## Multiple Choice

1. What example does Mohammad use to illustrate corruption in Lebanon?

    a. The inefficiency of the transportation system

    b. The mismanagement of electricity and the use of generators

    c. The lack of educational opportunities

    d. *All of the above*

2. What effect of favoritism in employment does Mohammad mention?

    a. That it increases division between religious sects

    b. That it makes it difficult for university graduates to find work

    c. That it results in hiring unqualified individuals

    d. *All of the above*

3. Mohammad's view on the newly discovered gas in Lebanon's sea is:

   a. Concerned that it will be exploited by corrupt politicians

   b. Optimistic about its potential to improve the economy

   c. Indifferent, believing it will not affect the country

   d. *None of the above*

## Matching

| | |
|---|---|
| لا... وَلا | another |
| كِرْمال | despite all this |
| رُغْم هَيْدا كِلّو | he/it is not... nor |
| مين | here |
| ما | I hope |
| هوْن/هوْني | in order to, so that |
| تاني | neither... nor |
| مِنّو... وَلا | not |
| بال شي | who |
| ياريْت | without anything |

## Text

|  |  |  |
|---|---|---|
| لُبْنان بلد كْتير صْغير، وعدد سُكّانو مُعْتدِل يَعْني، لا هالْقدّ كْبير وَلا هالْقدّ صْغير، | 1 | Lebanon is a very small country, and its population is moderate, meaning it's neither too large nor too small. |
| يَعْني ما بدّو هالشِّغِل العِمْلاق لحتّى يِظْبُط، بسّ في مِشِكْلِة كْتير كْبيرِة بِلُبْنان، هِيِّ الفساد والمحْسوبيّات. | 2 | So, it doesn't need gigantic efforts to be managed, but there's a big problem in Lebanon, which is corruption and favoritism. |
| يَعْني الفساد هُوَّ اللي حارِق البلد كِلّو، اللي شالو. | 3 | Corruption is what's burning the whole country, what's paralyzing it. |
| كِلّ ما يْلاقوا شي جْديد ويكْتِشْفوا شي جْديد ويحاوْلوا يِشْتِغْلوا على شي يْحسّن البلد ويْظبْطوه، | 4 | Every time they find something new and try to improve and fix the country, |
| بيطْلعوا السِّياسية بْيسرْقوا وبينهْبوا. | 5 | politicians come in, steal, and plunder. |
| ويْاخْدوا أرْباحُن ويفوتوا بِكْتير طوْشات، بسّ كِرْمال يْطلْعوا مصاري. | 6 | They take their profits and get into a lot of disputes, just for the sake of making money. |

| | | |
|---|---|---|
| 7 | And the people, despite all this, keep chasing them to give them a bit of that money; they throw it at them. | والشّعِبْ رُغْمْ هَيْدا كِلّو بيضلّوا لاحْقُن لحتّى يَعْطوا شْوَيّة مِنْ هَوْل المَصاري، يْكِبّولو هِنّي. |
| 8 | So, we are caught in a huge vicious circle, a cycle of corruption and favoritism and the mess in this country. | فا مِنْفوت بِدوّامِة كْتير كْبيرة اللي هِيّ دوّامِة الفَساد ودوّامِة المَحْسوبيّات والقِرَف اللي بْهَيْدا البَلَد. |
| 9 | For instance, for electricity, someone came up with the idea—I don't know who this "fine" person is. | يَعْني الكَهْرَبا في حَدا طَلَّع فِيا للْفِكْرة، مِش عارِف مين هُوِّ هَيْدا إبْن الحَلال. |
| 10 | Electricity in this country still doesn't come 24/7, despite it used to be available 24/7 before. | الكَهْرَبا بَعْدا لهَلّا بْهَيْدا البَلَد ما بْتِجي أَرْبَعة وعِشْرين على أَرْبَعة عِشْرين، رُغْم إنّو كانِت تِجي قَبْل أَرْبَعة وعِشْرين على أَرْبَعة عِشْرين. |
| 11 | But someone discovered that there's more profit and more power in controlling people if the electricity is cut. | بَسّ في حَدا كْتَشَف إنّو فيا رِبِح أَكْتَر وفيا قُوّة تِتْحَكَّم بالْعالَم أَكْتَر، إذا كانِت الكَهْرَبا مَقْطوعة. |
| 12 | So now, for example, in an area that has electricity 24/7, they fix the situation there, | فا هَلّا مَثَلاً في مِنْطَقة مْضَوّاية أَرْبَعة على أَرْبَعة عِشْرين، مْظَبّطين الوَضِع هِنّي، |
| 13 | Someone interferes in that area, and he doesn't want the electricity to come, so it gets cut. | بِـ... بْيِجي حَدا بيدِزّ عْلَيا لهَيْدي المِنْطَقة، بيصير مَعاش بَدّو الكَهْرَبا تِجي، بْتِقْطَع الكَهْرَبا. |
| 14 | Then the same person, the politician, brings people, sets up generators, lights up the area to benefit from it, charging money every month. | بيقوم نَفْسو هَيْدا الشَّخِص اللي هُوِّ السِّياسي، بيجيب ناس، بْحُطّ مْواتير إلو وبيضَوّي المِنْطَقة لحَتّى يِسْتَفيد مِنّا، ماديّاً كِلّ شَهر. |
| 15 | He ends up having a mafia, because obviously a mafia is providing the generators. | يْصير هُوِّ عِنْدو مافيا لِأنّو تَعَوْل المَوتَرات طَبْعاً مافيا. |
| 16 | He has a mafia, and at the same time, he's making money and has control over that area. | بيكون عِنْدو مافيا، وبنَفْس الوَقِت عَم يِقْبَض مَصاري، وعِنْدو تَحَكُّم بْهَيْدي المِنْطَقة. |
| 17 | So, this is the simplest example of the corruption we are experiencing here. | فا هَيْدا أَبْسَط مَثَل على الفَساد اللي عَم نْعيشو هَوْن. |
| 18 | Another example is favoritism, meaning how someone, if they want a job… it's not like abroad, where they need just a nudge or someone to speak a word for them. | مِثال تاني هُوِّ المَحْسوبيّات، يَعْني كيف الواحَد إذا بَدّو يْفوت على شِغِل، مِش مِتِل بَرّا مَثَلاً، بَدّو هَيْك بَسّ نَكْزة أَوْ إنّو حَدا يِحْكيلو كِلْمة أَوْ شي. |
| 19 | No, here, just a phone call exchanges favors. | لأ، هَوْني بَسّ بيدِقّ تِليفون تْبييض طناجِر بين بَعِض. |
| 20 | "I did this for you before; you did that for me; now let my son get this job." | "أَنا عْمِلْتِلَّك هَيْك قَبْل، إنْتَ عْمِلْتِلي هَيْك قَبْل، يَلّا فَوِّتْلي إبْني على هَيْدي الشَّغْلة." |

| | | |
|---|---|---|
| بيْفوت عليَا، بالدُّواير الحُكوميّة، بالمَدارِس، بالأشْغال، بالقِطاع العامّ. | 21 | He gets in—in government departments, in schools, in jobs, in the public sector. |
| أيّ شي مِبْني على الفساد بهَيّدا البلد والمحْسوبيّات، يَعْني ما... مِش فِهْمان حتّى الشِّغِل بيكون هوّ مِنّو قدّو ولا إنّو عِنْدو كفاءة لحتّى يْفوت عليْه، | 22 | Everything is built on corruption and favoritism in this country, meaning even if it's not clear that he's qualified for the job or if he's competent to take it. |
| بسّ خلص بالمحْسوبية إنّو "يلَّا فوّتْلي إبْني"، وهيْك وبيفوت إبْنو وبيْمْشي حالو مِش عارِف كيف. | 23 | but just through favoritism, "Come on, let my son in for me," and so his son gets in and manages somehow, not knowing how. |
| هَيْدي المِشكْلِة المِنْواجِهة هوْن. | 24 | This is the problem we are facing here. |
| هلّأ من فترة كْتشفوا إنّو في غاز بالبحر عنّا بلبْنان، فا بلّشوا السّياسية دغْري يْسنّوا سْنانُن وحاطّين يَعْني آمال هنّي إنّي يْبلّشوا حفِر وبيْبلّشوا يْطلّعوا الغاز لحتّى إنّو يظْبط شويّ الإقْتِصاد. | 25 | Recently, they discovered gas in our sea in Lebanon, so politicians immediately started sharpening their teeth, hoping to start drilling and extracting gas to fix the economy a bit. |
| فا أنا عم بِدْعي إنّو هَيدا الشّي ما يْصير لأنّو إذا صار كلّ المصاري حتِنْقرط. | 26 | I'm praying that this doesn't happen because if it does, all the money will just get screwed. |
| وكلّ المصاري حَياخدوها هنّي، ونِحْنا حنقْعُد بلا شي فا ياريْت يْضلّ الغاز بالبحِر وما يِدْقروا هنّي. | 27 | They will take all the money, and we will end up with nothing. So, I hope the gas stays in the sea and they don't touch it. |

---

**Answers**

**Main Idea:** c **True or False:** 1. F[1] 2. T[4-6] 3. F[7-8] 4. T[10-11] 5. T[25] **Multiple Choice:** 1. b[10-16] 2. c 3. a[25-27]

**Matching:** ولا... لا neither... nor / كِرْمال in order to, so that / رُغْم هَيْدا كِلّو despite all this / مين who / منّو... ولا he/it is not... nor / بلا شي without anything / هوْن/هوْني here / تاني another / ولا... ما not / ياريْت I hope

# 30 Sandy: Employment in Lebanon

## Keywords

ثَوْرة revolution   فساد corruption   فلّ to leave   قِطاع sector

## Main Idea

a. Sandy discusses the thriving tourism and technology sectors in Lebanon, which have remained unaffected by the economic crisis and continue to provide numerous jobs for the youth.
b. Sandy outlines the government's new initiatives to combat unemployment, falsely promising immediate relief to the economic downturn.
c. Sandy describes the severe impact of economic, social, and humanitarian disasters on Lebanon's employment, leading to high unemployment rates and emigration among the youth, while highlighting the challenges faced by those who remain.
d. Sandy focuses on the improvements in Lebanon's banking sector and how these have positively influenced job stability and growth in the country.

## True or False

1. The revolution was ignited by economic and social issues, including a proposed fee on WhatsApp usage.
2. The Lebanese youth are finding ample job opportunities within the country, preventing the need for emigration.
3. According to Sandy, the unemployment rate in Lebanon has doubled since 2019
4. The Beirut port explosion in 2020 had a devastating impact on the country.
5. According to Sandy, the Lebanese government has effectively managed the crises and provided adequate support to its people.

## Multiple Choice

1. What triggered this most recent revolution in Lebanon according to Sandy?
   a. A natural disaster
   b. Religious sectarianism
   c. A proposed fee on WhatsApp usage
   d. *None of the above*

2. Which sectors does Sandy identify as still functioning in Lebanon?
   a. Agriculture and manufacturing
   b. Tourism, tech, and media
   c. Education and healthcare
   d. *None of the above*

3. Sandy's personal work solution amidst Lebanon's crises is:

   a. Working in the tourism sector
   c. Joining the government to effect change
   b. Emigrating for better opportunities
   d. *None of the above*

## Matching

| | |
|---|---|
| مِن وَرا | (he/it) is not |
| لَيْش | all that... |
| فجْأة | anyway; in any case |
| كِلّ حدا | as |
| كِلّ شي | because of |
| عَ كِلّ حال | everyone |
| مظْبوط | everything |
| مِنّو | honestly |
| بِالْمُقابِل | like |
| هلّأ | like me |
| مِتِل ما | no one |
| ما في مين | now |
| كِلّ اللي | on the other hand |
| مِتِل | precisely |
| إنْ كان... أوْ | suddenly |
| مِتْلي | through |
| عبِر | whether... or |
| صراحة | why |

# Text

| | |
|---|---|
| 1 | Hello, today I want to talk about a social issue, if we can call it that, |
| | مَرْحَبا، اليوْم بدّي إحْكي عن مِشْكِلِة إجْتِماعية إذا فينا نْقول، |
| 2 | which has been affecting the country for a while because of all the disasters, whether they are economic, social, or humanitarian, that have occurred in Lebanon from 2019 to the present. |
| | إلا فترْة ضارْبة البلد مِن وَرا كِلّ المصايِب، إن كانِت الإقْتِصادية أوْ الإجْتِماعية أوْ الإنْسانية يَلّي صارِت بِلِبْنان مِن الألْفيْن وتْسعْطعِشْ للْيوْم. |
| 3 | I think the whole world knows and has heard about the revolution that took place in 2019. |
| | بِعْتِقِد كِلّ العالم، عِرِف وسِمِع بالثَّوْرة اللي صارِت بالألْفيْن وتْسِعْطعِشْ. |
| 4 | If I were to explain why it happened, it's because of the WhatsApp tariff. |
| | إذا بدّي إحْكي ليْش صارِت، هِيّ مِن وَرا تعْرِفِة الواتْساب. |
| 5 | The government, specifically the Minister of Communications, suddenly decided to either increase, or not increase but impose a fee on WhatsApp usage. |
| | يَلّي قرَّرِت الحُكومِة وَقْتا وزير الإتِّصالات فجْأة إنّو يْعلّي أوْ مِش يْعلّي حتّى، تْصير تعْرِفِة الواتْساب مدْفوعة. |
| 6 | This meant that anyone wanting to download or subscribe to WhatsApp would be forced to pay. |
| | يَعْني كِلّ حدا بدّو يِشْتِرِك أوْ يْنزِّل تُطْبيق واتْساب يْصير مجبور يِدْفع. |
| 7 | This ignited the revolution. On top of everything, all the corruption and the failed institutions, they were forcing us to pay for WhatsApp, which is essentially a free service. |
| | هيْك بلّشِت الثَّوْرة، إنّو فوْق كِلّ شي وكِلّ الفساد وكِلّ المؤسَّسات الفارْطة، عم تِجبْرونا نِدْفع حقّ الواتْساب، يَلّي هُوّ أصْلًا خِدْمة بِبلاش. |
| 8 | The news broke out, and it grew, and we all took to the streets together. All of Lebanon gathered, and we protested. |
| | هيْك بلّشِت الخبريِة، وكِبرِت ونْزِلْنا على الشَّوارِع كِلّنا سَوى. كِلّ لِبْنان جْتمع وعْمِلْنا مُظاهرات. |
| 9 | The corruption in the banks began to show more and more, and they were stealing people's savings, of all the depositors. |
| | وبلّش الفساد يْبيِّنْ أكْتر وأكْتر بالبْنوكة ونْسرقوا مُصرِيّات العالم، كِلّ المودِعين. |
| 10 | Then, we started to see the younger generation, whether girls or boys, under thirty years of age, being forced to emigrate and leave the country because there were no more jobs here. |
| | وهوْن بلّشْنا نْشوف الصِّغار أوْ الشِّباب، إن كانوا صبايا أوْ شْباب، ما بِيْتْجاوز عُمْرُن الثَّلاثين سنِة، عم بِيْتْهجَّروا ويْفِلّوا مِن البلد، لأنّو ما بقى في أشْغال هوْن. |
| 11 | I was one of them. I had a stable job, and then, overnight, they laid me off from work. |
| | أنا كِنِت واحْدة مِنُّن. كان عِنْدي وَظيفِة ثابْتِة وبِلَيْلِة ما فِيّا ضَوْ قمر فلّوني مِن الشِّغِل. |
| 12 | So it began, and then came the Beirut explosion, the Beirut port explosion in 2020, which completely destroyed the country and crippled it... completely crippled it. |
| | هيْك بلّشِت وبعْديْن إجا إنْفِجار بيْروت، إنْفِجار المرْفأ بِبيْروت بالألْفيْن وعِشْرين، يَلّي دمَّر البلد كِلّو وشلّو... شلّو عالآخِر. |

|  |  |  |
|---|---|---|
| 13 | اللّي كانوا باقيين فلّوا، الأدْمِغة كِلّا فلِّت. ما بقي حدن. | Those who remained left. All the brains left. No one stayed. |
| 14 | بقي يَلّي مِتْلي مْآمن ببلدو وما بدّو يتركو للْعالم يَلّي مِش مْنيحة وللْفاسْدين. | Those who did stay, like me, believe in their country and don't want to leave it to the bad people and the corrupt. |
| 15 | إذا كلّنا فلّينا مين بْيبْقى؟ عَ كِلّ حال مِش هَيْدا هُوّ المَوْضوع اللي عم نحْكي فيه. | If we all leave, who will stay? Anyway, that's not the topic we're discussing here. |
| 16 | بدّنا نحْكي إنّو مع كلّ هالمْشاكِل يَلّي صارت بالبلد، طبيعي إنّو الأدْمِغة والعالم الشّاطْرة والمثْقّفة والمتعلّمة إنّا تْهاجر وتْفِلّ وهيْك مظْبوط. | We need to talk about how, with all these problems that have occurred in the country, it's natural for the intelligent, cultured, and educated people to emigrate and leave, which is precisely what's happening. |
| 17 | ومن الألْفين وتسعْطعش للْيوْم، إذا بدّنا نحْكي عن مؤشّر البطالة بلِنان، زاد ضُعْف يَلّي كان بالألْفين وتمنْطعش. | From 2019 to today, if we want to talk about the unemployment rate in Lebanon, it has doubled from what it was in 2019. |
| 18 | يَعني إذا كان مؤشّر البطالة بلِنان تْلطّعْش لخمسْطعْش بالميّة، اليوْم صار تسْعة وعشْرين بالميّة. | That is, if the unemployment rate in Lebanon was between 13 to 15 percent, today it has reached 29 percent. |
| 19 | يَعْني هَيْدا رقْم منّو هيّن. | This is not a trivial number. |
| 20 | وبالمُقابل، الدّوْلة منّا قادِر... منّا قادْرة تعْمُل شي، الدّوْلة منّا قادْرة تعْمُل شي لِشعْبا، لأنّا فارْطة. | On the other hand, the state is incapable... unable to do anything... the state is unable to do anything for its people because it is collapsing. |
| 21 | حُكومة، حُكومة تصْريف أعْمال، رئيس جُمْورية ما في. | The government is a caretaker government, and there's no president. |
| 22 | إلْنا أشْهُر، إذا مِش سِنة بالْفراغ. أكْتر من سِنة، شهْر الماضي صاروا سنة بالفراغ. | We have been in a state of vacuum for months, if not a year. It's been more than a year; last month marked a year of this vacuum. |
| 23 | المشاكل عامّة البلد. هلّأ في الحرب الإسرائيلية الفلسطينية كمان، عم بتْأثّر على كِلّ الأشْغال بالمنْطقة. | The problems have spread all over the country. Now, with the Israeli-Palestinian War as well, it's impacting all the work in the region. |
| 24 | وبعْدُن مِتل ما بيْقولوا، الأدْمِغة عم بيْسافروا وعم بيْهاجروا. | And as they say, the brains are leaving, emigrating. |
| 25 | الوَضع سيّئ جدّاً وما في مين تْناديلو، ما في مين تسْتغيث فيه أوْ تِطْلُب المُساعدة منّو. | The situation is very bad, and there's no one you can call, no one to cry for help to or ask for assistance from. |

|  |  |  |
|---|---|---|
| 26 | All we are asking for is something like a miracle, that God shows mercy on us and the people of this entire region | كِلّ اللي مْنِطْلبوا هُوِّ مِتِل مُعْجِزة، إنّا تْصير الله يِطْلطف عَلَيْنا وعَ الشّعْب بهالْمِنْطقة كِلّا، |
| 27 | so that we can stand on our feet and live a normal life with the basic necessities, whether it's electricity, water, or employment. | لنْصير قادْرين نْقوم بحالْنا ونْعيش حَياةٍ طبيعية بأَقَلّ مُتطلّبات الحَياة، إن كان كهرَبا أَوْ ماي أَوْ شِغِل. |
| 28 | Perhaps the only sector that is functioning is tourism, | يمْكِن ما في إلّا القِطاع السّياحي هُوِّ يَلّي ماشي، |
| 29 | which is the one bringing in money to the country, whether it's restaurants, nightclubs, or hotels. Honestly, this is what's working in the country. | هُوِّ يَلّي بِفَوِّت مصاري عَ هالْبلد، إن كان مطاعِم، كْلوبْز للسّهر أوْتيلات. هَيْدا هُوِّ اللي ماشي بالبلد صراحة. |
| 30 | If I were to talk about another sector that is functioning and able to provide jobs for the people and the youth who are graduating, it would probably be everything related to online, tech, and media, and all the work that can be done online. | إذا بدّي إحْكي عن قِطاع تاني ماشي وقادِر إنّو يْلبّي ويَعْطي وظائف للشّعب ولهالشّباب اللي عم تِتْخرّج، هُوِّ يِمْكِن كِلّ شي خصّو بالأَوْنْلاين وبالتّيك وبالْميدْيا وكِلّ الشِّغِل يَلّي بْيِنعمل أَوْنْلاين. |
| 31 | Like me. I work through Upwork and other platforms that allow us to earn some money, though not everyone can benefit from it. | مَتَلي أنا. بِشْتِغِل عبر Upwork وهَوْل المنصّات يَلّي عم بتْخلّينا نْطلّع شْوَيّة مصاري وحتّى مش الكِلّ بْيِقْدر يِسْتفيد. |
| 32 | Those who don't have a fresh dollar account in the bank can't do anything. | اللّي ما عِندو حْساب بِالْبَنك فْريش بالدّولار ما بْيِقْدر يَعْمل شي. |
| 33 | So, honestly, we need God's help and His intervention because we really need it. | فا الله يْساعِدْنا صراحة ويْسْتغيث فينا، لأنّو نِحْنا بحاجة لإلو. |

---

### Answers

**Main Idea:** c  **True or False:** 1. T³⁻⁷ 2. F¹⁰ 3. T¹⁸ 4. T¹² 5. F²⁰⁻²²  **Multiple Choice:** 1. c⁵ 2. b²⁸⁻³⁰ 3. d³¹
**Matching:** everything / كِلّ شي everyone / كِلّ حدا suddenly فجْأة / why ليْش / because of مِن وَرا / on the other hand بِالْمُقابِل / (he/it) is not مِنّو / precisely مظْبوط / anyway; in any case عَ كِلّ حال / whether... or / إن كان... أَوْ / like / مِتِل / all that... / كِلّ اللي / no one / ما في مين / as / مِتِل ما / now / هلّأ / like me / مِتْلي / through / عبر / honestly صراحة

# Free Topics

## 31 Charbel: The Oud

### Keywords

| عود oud | شرْقي oriental, eastern | آلة instrument |

### Main Idea

a. Charbel's lifelong professional career as an oud player and his contributions to modernizing the instrument.
b. The history of the oud in Lebanon and its evolution from traditional to contemporary music styles.
c. Charbel's casual interest in the oud as a hobby and his struggles to master it.
d. The oud as an integral part of Charbel's identity and the importance of perseverance in learning.

### True or False

1. Charbel has only been playing the oud for a few years.
2. Charbel learned to play the oud exclusively at the Lebanese Conservatory.
3. Charbel describes the oud as similar to the guitar but oriental and originally Persian.
4. Charbel was inspired by his uncle, who used to play the oud.
5. Charbel believes the oud's sound is influenced by the type of wood used in its construction.

### Multiple Choice

1. Why did Charbel initially start learning the oud?

    a. He was forced by his family.

    b. He had a deep interest in oriental singing and music.

    c. It was a mandatory course at his school.

    d. He wanted to become a professional musician.

2. According to Charbel, what is a key aspect of learning the oud?

    a. The importance of hand positioning and technique

    b. Memorizing chords and notes

    c. Learning how to read music

    d. Immersing oneself in Lebanese culture in order to appreciate the cultural significance

3. What message does Charbel convey about learning new skills or hobbies?

   a. It is only suitable for young people.

   b. Professional training is necessary for mastering a new skill.

   c. It is never too late to start learning something new.

   d. It is best to focus on one hobby at a time.

## Matching

|  |  |
|---|---|
| شي | about, around, some |
| لحالي | as |
| مِتِل ما | different |
| يَعْني | in order to |
| مِن أنا وصْغير | more |
| غيْر | on my own |
| أكْتر | something |
| سَوى | that is; I mean |
| لَـ | the more... the more |
| كِلّ ما.. كِلّ ما | there isn't/aren't |
| حيّلا شي | together |
| ما في | when I was young |

## Text

| | |
|---|---|
| بِعْزُف عود وصرْلي تِقْريباً شي تِسِع عشْر سْنين. | 1. I have been playing the oud for about nineteen years. |
| درسْتا بِالْكوْنْسِرْفاتْوار اللّبْناني. | 2. I studied it at the Lebanese Conservatory. |
| حسّيْت هيْك شْوَيّ عَ بالي إدْرُس موسيقى، سوْ قِلِت شو بدّي أعْمُل حتّى بلّشِت تْعلّمِت الغِنى الشّرْقي. | 3. I kinda felt like I wanted to study music, so I thought, 'What should I do?' and then I started learning oriental singing. |
| قِلِت أنا بدّي إتْعلّم موسيقى سوْ كان بِالْكوْنْسِرْفاتْوار بيعلّموك مع الغِنى الشّرْقي العود. | 4. I thought, "I want to learn music," and at the Conservatory, they teach you the oud along with oriental singing. |

| | | |
|---|---|---|
| 5 | سوْ دِرِسْت شي... تقْريباً شي أرْبع سْنين، بسّ بعْدين وَقَّفِت وكفَّيْت أنا مع... مع إسْتاذ لحالي، درِسْت عود لحالي. | So, I studied for about... roughly four years, but then I stopped and continued with... with a teacher on my own. I studied the oud by myself. |
| 6 | كْتير حبّيْنا الآلة، هيِّ آلة شرْقية. | I really loved the instrument, which is an oriental instrument. |
| 7 | عود هُوِّ مِتِل ما سْمِعْتوا بالأوّل، مِتِل الغيتار بسّ هيِّ شرْقية. هيِّ أصْلا... أصْلا فارسي. | The oud, as you might have heard at the beginning, is like the guitar, but it's oriental; it's originally Persian. |
| 8 | قديمة كْتير الآلة، مِن أقْدم الآلات الموسيقية بالْعالم. | It's a very ancient instrument, one of the oldest musical instruments in the world. |
| 9 | لِبْنان تْميَّز قديماً كان بالْعود يَعْني يلّي بدّو يْألِّف أغاني يلّي بدّو يْلحِّن أغاني كلّو كان يِسْتعْمِل العود، المَواويل العتابا الأغاني الحِلْوة القديمة كلّا عَ العود. | Lebanon was historically known for the oud, meaning those who wanted to compose or arrange songs used the oud, Mawawil, Ataba, and all the beautiful old songs were played on the oud. |
| 10 | هيْك بِتْحسِّسك بالْحِنية، بِتْحسِّسك بالـ... بِلِبْنان بِتْحسِّسك... يَعْني أنا تْعلَّقِت فيا هالآلة مِن أنا وصْغير وما كِنِت عارِف. | It makes you feel tender, it makes you feel Lebanese, it makes you feel... I mean, I got attached to this instrument when I was young without realizing it. |
| 11 | هُوِّ خالي كان يْدِقّ عَ العود وكِنِت إسْمعو أنا وَقِت إطْلع عَ الضّيْعة إسْمع خالي عم بيدِقّ على هالآلة الحِلْوة. | My uncle used to play the oud, and I would listen to him when I went to the village, listening to my uncle play this beautiful instrument. |
| 12 | بسّ أنا ما كِنِت عامِل حْساب إنّو أنا بدّي إتْعلّما سوْ وِصْلِت الإيّام وتْعلّمْتا لهيْدي الآلة وكْتشفِت هالـ... الـ... قدّي واسْعة هالْمجال. | But I never thought I would learn it, so as time went by, I learned this instrument and discovered how vast this field is. |
| 13 | يَعْني بين بدّك تْنقّي أيِّ آلة بْتعْطيك صوْت هَيْدا صوْت الحِنية، تعْطيك صوْت القوِّة، تعْطيك صوْت الشّرْقي أكْتر. | Meaning, depending on the instrument you choose, it gives you a sound of tenderness, a sound of strength, a sound that is more oriental. |
| 14 | بِتْفرُق أنْواع الخشب بين خشب أرز، خشب ورِد، كِلّ يَعْني... وكِلّ صانِع بْيَعْمُل آلة عود يَعْني غيْر كـ... يَعْني غيْر... غيْرعُن التانْية، غيْر صوْت غيْر... | It makes a difference, the types of wood, between cedar wood, rosewood, each means... and each maker creates a different oud instrument, I mean different... I mean different from the other, a different sound, different... |
| 15 | وإنْت هوْن بِتْصير تِكْتِشِف إنّو هَيْدي... بدّك هَيْدي الآلة لأنّو إنْتَ بِتْحِنّ لهَيْدي الآلة أكْتر. | And you discover that you want this particular instrument because you are more drawn to it. |
| 16 | سوْ هيْك شْويّ مْجال حِلو. | So, it's quite an interesting field. |

| | | |
|---|---|---|
| 17 | And I liked the idea that for a hobby, for me, for instance, I feel like playing, or with friends sitting around in the evenings, we all sing together, have fun, boisterous fun, clap, all because of the oud. | وأنا حبّيْت الفِكْرة إنّو for a hobby لإلي إنّو أنا مثلاً بِقْعُد عَ بالي دِقّ عَ بالي مع الأصْحاب قاعْدين سِهْرانين نْغَنّي كلّنا سَوى نِنْبِسِط نْهيِّص ونْزقِّف كِلّو مِن وَرا العود. |
| 18 | I'm very happy that I learned and didn't give up, kept going. | وكْتير مبْسوط إنّو تْعلَّمِت وإنّو ما سْتَسْلَمِت ضلّيْت ماشي فِيا. |
| 19 | It was difficult at first because it's not easy; | كانِت صعْبِة بالأوّل لأنّو منّا هيِّنة، |
| 20 | it's not like the guitar, where you memorize chords, or like the piano, where you have the keyboard in front of you to press. | مِش مِتِل الغيتار بْتِحْفظ أكْوِرات أوْ مِتِل البْيانو قدّامك الكيبورد لتْدِقّ عليْه. |
| 21 | No, you need a technique to position your hand correctly, to separate your feeling from the oud's feeling, | هيِّ لأْ بدّك تكْنيك تلْقط إيدك، بدّك تْجرِّب تِفْصُل بيْن إحْساسك وإحْساس العود، |
| 22 | but in the end, the more you persevere, the more you can learn, the more you love it, the more you are motivated, even if you start... | وبسّ بالنِّهايِة الواحد كِلّ ما بيثابِر أكْتر كِلّ ما بْيِقْدر يِتْعلّم أكْتر كِلّ ما... كِلّ ما بيحِبّ الشِّغْلِة كِلّ ما بيكون مْحمَّسْلا أكْتر حتّى لوْ بلّش عن... |
| 23 | I mean, I take it as a lesson that it's never too late in life. Now, I can start learning something new if God gives me the life to do so; nothing is too late. | يَعْني أنا هيْدي باخِدا عِبْرة إنّو إنْت ما في... ما في too late بالحياةِ، سوْ إنْتَ هلّأْ... فيِّ أنا بلّش حيَّلا شي ومعي وَقِت، إذا الله عطاني العُمر إنّو إتْعلَّم، so nothing is too late. |
| 24 | I encourage everyone who has a hobby and wants to learn it because, in the end, you have time now. | وبْحِبّ شجِّع الكِلّ اللي يحِبّ وعِنْدو هِوايِة وعَ بالو يِتْعلّما... يِتْعلّما لأنّو ما في شي يَعْني منّا هلّأْ النِّهايِة معك وَقِت. |
| 25 | And if you practice and have the will to do it, you will reach the result you want. | وإذا بْتِعْمُل practice ويْكون إنْتَ عِنْدك الإرادِة تعْمِلا بْتوصل للنْتيجة اللي بدّك ياها. |
| 26 | And this is also a performance of a song by Fairouz on the oud. Fairouz is a music icon in Lebanon. | وهيْدي كمان دقّ غِنيِّة بالعود لفيْروز هيِّ فيْروز مِن آيْكونْ بالْموسيقى بِلِبْنان. |

## Answers

**Main Idea:** d **True or False:** 1. F[1] 2. F[5] 3. T[7] 4. T[11] 5. T[14] **Multiple Choice:** 1. b[3-4] 2. a[21] 3. c[23]

**Matching:** مِن أنا وصْغير when I was young / غيْر different / أكْتر more / سَوى together / لَـ in order to / كِلّ ما... كِلّ ما the more... the more / ما في there isn't/aren't / حيَّلا شي something / شي about, around, some / لحالي on my own / مِتِل ما as / يَعْني that is; I mean

# 32 Nisrine: My Job

## Keywords

مُعَلِّمة teacher    تَعْليم teaching    رسالة calling, vocation; message

## Main Idea

a. Nisrine describes her journey and experiences as a teacher.
b. Nisrine critiques the education system in Lebanon.
c. Nisrine focuses on the challenges she faces as a teacher.
d. Nisrine explains why she now prefers teaching over interior design.

## True or False

1. Nisrine initially planned to become a teacher while studying at university.
2. Nisrine has been teaching at the same school for several years.
3. Nisrine's students express a desire to follow in her footsteps as teachers.
4. Nisrine acknowledges that she is beginning to experience feelings of exhaustion in her role as a teacher.
5. Nisrine feels a deep personal connection to the school where she teaches.

## Multiple Choice

1. What subjects does Nisrine currently teach?

    a. French and math
    b. History and geography
    c. Art and design
    d. Math and science

2. Why did Nisrine start teaching initially?

    a. It was her lifelong dream.
    b. Due to the economic situation and not finding a job in her field.
    c. She always preferred teaching over interior design.
    d. *None of the above*

3. What is a key message Nisrine focuses on teaching her students?

    a. Humanity, principles, and values
    b. Advanced academic subjects
    c. Professional skills for future jobs
    d. *None of the above*

# Matching

| | |
|---|---|
| لإلي | before anything else |
| مع إنّو | by the way |
| بسّ | close to |
| بْعيد عن | even though |
| وَقْتا اللي | far from |
| عَ فِكْرة | for me |
| هالشّي | like me |
| قريب مِن | so that, in order to |
| قبل كلّ شي | this |
| حتّى | when (2x) |
| مِتْلي | |

# Text

| | | |
|---|---|---|
| مرْحبا، حبّيْت إحْكي بالـ free topic عن شِغْلي. | 1 | Hello, I'd like to talk about my job for the free topic. |
| أنا بِشْتِغِل مْعلّمِة، بْعلِّم عنّا بِمدْرْسِة بالضّيْعة. | 2 | I work as a teacher, teaching at a school in the village. |
| بْعلِّم مات والسْيانْس، بْعلِّم صْفوف أوّل وتاني وتالِت. | 3 | I teach math and science for the first, second, and third grades. |
| هَيْدي تاني سِنِة لإلي بالتّعْليم. | 4 | This is my second year in teaching. |
| هَيْديك السّنِة كِنت علّم مادِة الـ française لِصْفوف الرّابِع والخامِس والسّادِس. | 5 | Last year, I taught French to fourth, fifth, and sixth-graders. |
| كْتشفِت إنّي أنا كْتير بْحِبّ هَيْدا الـ... هَيْدا الدّوْمان، هَيْدا الإخْتِصاص بالتّعْليم. | 6 | I discovered that I really love this field, this specialization in teaching. |
| وبِتذكّر وَقِت أنا كِنت صْغيرِة كِنت إحْلم بسّ إكْبر صير مْعلّمِة. | 7 | I remember when I was young, I always dreamed of becoming a teacher when I grew up. |
| مع إنّو أنا إخْتِصاصي غيْر وبْعيد كْتير عن التّعْليم. | 8 | Even though my major is completely different and far from teaching. |
| أنا تْخصّصِت بالجّامْعة هنْدسِة ديكوْر. | 9 | I specialized in interior design at university. |

| | | |
|---|---|---|
| وبِسَبَب وَضِع البَلَد والمَشاكِل والأزْمة اللي صارِت، وما لاقيْت شِغِل بِإخْتِصاصي، وضْطرّيْت إنّي إشْتِغِل أيّ شي. | 10 | But due to the country's situation, the problems and the crisis that occurred, and not finding a job in my field, I was forced to take any job. |
| ووَقْتا اللي قدَّمِت بِهَيْدي المَدْرسِة، الحَمْدلله مِشي حالي وقِبْلوني. | 11 | When I applied to this school, thankfully, things went well, and they accepted me. |
| و... عَ فِكْرة، هَيْدي المَدْرسة اللي أنا بْعلِّم فيا، هيّ مدْرسْتي أنا وَقْتا كِنْت صْغيرة، يَعْني مدْرسة طْفولْتي. | 12 | And... by the way, the school where I teach is the same one I attended as a child, so it's my childhood school. |
| وكْتير هالشّي بيأثِّر فيني. | 13 | This really affects me a lot. |
| كْتير بِنْبِسِط، كْتير بْحِبّ وَقْتا بْروح عَ مَدْرسْتي. | 14 | I'm very happy, and I love going to my school. |
| بِتْذكّر كِلّ الذِّكْريات اللي أنا كِنْت عايْشِتا قبِل. | 15 | I remember all the memories I had there. |
| بِتْذكّر رِفْقاتي، بِتْذكّر مْعلّمات اللي علّموني فيا. | 16 | I remember my friends and the teachers who taught me. |
| بِتْذكّر كِلّ الإيّام الحِلْوة، كِلّ اللّحْظات والنّجاحات اللي كِنْت أنا حقّقا بِهَيْدي المَدْرسة. | 17 | I remember all the nice days, all the moments, and the achievements I made in this school. |
| بْحِبّ كْتير شِغْلي. بْحِبّ كْتير هَيْدي المَدْرسة. بْحِبّ كْتير إنّي عم علّم وْلاد صْغار. | 18 | I really love my job, I love this school, and I really enjoy teaching young children. |
| أنا بِطبيعْتي طْفولية. | 19 | I am childlike by nature. |
| كْتير قريبة مِن الوْلاد، كْتير بْحِبّ الوْلاد، والوْلاد الحَمْدلله كْتير بِحبّوني وبيِنْبِسْطوا فيني وَقْتا اللي أنا فوت لعِنْدُن. | 20 | I'm close to the children. I love them, and thankfully, they really like me and are happy when I come to them. |
| وأنا بِنْبِسِط فيُن. | 21 | And I'm happy with them. |
| الحَمْدلله، كْتير مبْسوطة بِهَيْدا... بِهَيْدا الشِّغِل. | 22 | Thank God, I'm very happy with this job. |
| الوْلاد كْتير كْتير حِلْوين. | 23 | The children are so, so very sweet. |
| والتّعْليم كْتير بْحِبّو والتّعْليم هوّ رِسالة. | 24 | And I love teaching. Teaching is a calling. |
| وأنا كْتير بِشْكُر ربّي إنّو أنا كون قادْرة أنا قدِّم هَيْدي الرّسالة للوْلاد. | 25 | And I'm very grateful to God that I can deliver this message to the children. |
| أنا عم ساهم إنّي طوِّر هَيْدا المُجْتمَع، إنّي إبْني مُجْتمع إنّي أنا أثِّر بالوْلاد. | 26 | I am contributing to developing this society and building a community where I have an impact on the children. |

| | |
|---|---|
| 27 | I teach them--before anything else, before lessons and the subjects I teach--I teach them humanity, I teach them principles, and I teach them the values we were raised with when we were young, |
| 28 | so that they can be in the... in society in the coming years, capable of bearing responsibilities, capable of building a beautiful and advanced society. |
| 29 | I love that I am delivering a message to the younger generation, who are influenced by me because of their love for me. |
| 30 | They want to be like me. |
| 31 | I always hear from... my students saying: 'Teacher, when I grow up, I want to be a teacher just like you.' |
| 32 | I really love this. It deeply affects me, and I am delighted to hear such things. |
| 33 | I love that I am influencing them in a very beautiful and very positive way, |
| 34 | and that I am delivering a message, helping this community to develop and become better and, God willing, the best. |

علِّمُن... علِّمُن قبل كلّ شي، قبل الدُّروس وقبل الموادّ اللي عم بعْطيُن، علِّمُن الإنْسانية علِّمُن المبادِئ علِّمُن القِيَم اللي نِحْنا تْربّينا عْلَيُن وَقْتا كِنّا صْغار،

حتّى يْكونوا هِنّي بالـ... بالمُجْتمع بعْد سْنين يْكونوا قادْرين إنّو هِنّي يتْحمّلوا مسْؤوليّات، يكونوا قادْرين إنّو يبْنوا مُجْتمع حِلو ومتْطوِّر.

بْحِبّ إنّي أنا عم قدِّم رِسالة لجيل صْغير عم يتْأثّروا فيني مِن حُبُّن لإلي.

بيْحِبّوا إنّو يْكونوا مِتْلي.

دايماً بِسْمع من... تْلاميذي إنّو: أنا يا مدام، بسّ إكْبر بدّي صير مْعلِّمة مِتْلِك.

وهَيْدا الشّي كْتير كْتير أنا بْحِبّو كْتير. بيْأثّر فيني كْتير، وبنْبِسط بهَيْدا الحكي.

بْحِبّ إنّو أنا عم أثِّر فيُن بطريقة كْتير حِلْوة وكْتير إيجابية،

وإنّو أنا عم قدِّم رِسالة، وعم ساعِد هَيْدا المُجْتمع إنّو يتْطوّر ويْصير أحْسن أفْضل انْشاالله.

---

**Answers**

**Main Idea:** a **True or False:** 1. F[8-9] 2. F[4] 3. T[31] 4. F[22, 32-33] 5. T[12-14] **Multiple Choice:** 1. d[3] 2. b[10-11] 3. b[27-28] **Matching:** عَ فِكْرة by the way / وَقْتا اللي when / بْعيد عن far from / بسّ even though / مع إنّو even though / لإلي for me / حتّى so that, in order to / قبل كلّ شي before anything else / قريب مِن close to / هالشّي this / مِتْلي like me

# 33 Waleed: My Military Service

## Keywords

خِدْمِة العلم military service    تجْرِبة experience    هدف purpose

## Main Idea

a. Waleed discusses the rigorous combat training he underwent during his military service.
b. Waleed focuses on the hardships and challenges of military life.
c. Waleed tells us about an unfortunate event that happened during his military service.
d. Waleed reflects on his military service as a period of personal growth and learning.

## True or False

1. Waleed had met and interacted with people from all Lebanese sects and regions prior to his military service.
2. During his service, Waleed only interacted with people from his own sectarian and regional background.
3. During his military service, Waleed served in Arman in Northern Lebanon.
4. Waleed served in the military in a role that utilized his university degree in Chemistry.
5. The military service in Lebanon is still a mandatory requirement for all young men.

## Multiple Choice

1. Why was mandatory military service introduced in Lebanon according to Waleed?
    a. To foster unity and citizenship among youth
    b. To train youth in advanced combat skills
    c. As a response to external threats
    d. To rebuild the country post-war

2. Waleed's military service experience led him to:
    a. Dislike the military establishment
    b. Regret his time in service
    c. Appreciate the diversity of Lebanon
    d. Develop hardline political views

3. Which aspects did Waleed experience during his military service?
    a. Strengthening his sense of citizenship
    b. Meeting people from diverse Lebanese backgrounds
    c. Utilizing his Chemistry degree in service
    d. *All of the above*

## Matching

| | |
|---|---|
| بعْد فتْرة | after |
| فقط | after some time |
| إلو | because of |
| بل | but rather |
| عنْدُن | he/it has |
| كاد | in order to, so that |
| بِسبب | just, only |
| منْشان | there is/are |
| كنّا | they have |
| في | to almost [do] |
| مِن بعْد | we were |
| شو | what |

## Text

1. كيفْكُن أصْدِقائي؟ معْكُن وَليد.

   How are you, my friends? Waleed here.

2. اليوْم، حبّيْت أحْكيكُن عن تجْرِبِة كْتير حِلْوِة عِشْتا بْحَياتي.

   Today, I wanted to tell you about a really nice experience I had in my life.

3. يِمْكِن باللّحْظة اللي أنا كِنت عايش... عم بمْرُق فيها لهالتّجْرِبة، كِنت معْتِبرا إنّو هَيْدي مِن أسْوأ الفترات اللي بْتمْرُق فيّا،

   Perhaps at the moment when I was experiencing... you were going through it, you considered it to be one of the worst periods you had gone through.

4. ولكِن بعْديْن بعْد فترة بِتْصير تِفْهم وبِتْصير تْحلِّل شو الأشْيا اللي كِنت عم تمْرُق فيها.

   But later, after some time, you start to understand and analyze the things you were going through.

5. هَيْدي التّجْرِبة هيِّ الخِدْمة العسْكرية.

   This experience was the military service.

6. بلِبْنان، بعْد الحرْب الأهْلية ما خْلِصت طُلع قانون بيْفرُض على الشّباب اللّبْناني اللي فوْق التّمنْطعْشر سِنة إنّن يخِدْمو خِدْمة عسكرية إلْزامية لمُدّة سِنة بالجيْش اللّبْناني.

   In Lebanon, after the civil war ended, a law was enacted requiring all Lebanese men over the age of 18 to serve in the Lebanese army for a year.

| | | |
|---|---|---|
| 7 | The purpose of this experience wasn't just to train us in combat or to train the Lebanese youth in fighting or attacking or that... or just this, | الهدف مِن هَيدي التّجربة وَقْتا ما كان إنّو لتدْريبْنا على القِتال لتدْريب الشّباب اللّبْناني على القِتال على الهُجوم أَوْ على هالـ... أَوْ على هَيدا الشّي فقط، |
| 8 | but it also had another purpose: to strengthen the sense of citizenship among the youth. | بل كان إلو هدف تاني لتعْزيز المُواطِنية عِند الشّباب. |
| 9 | Due to the Lebanese war, communication lines between people... between the Lebanese people, especially the youth, were severed. | بِسبب الحرْب اللّبْنانية تْقطّعِت الخُطوط التّواصُل بيْن الشّعْب... بيْن الشّعْب اللّبْناني، وتِحْديداً بيْن الشّباب. |
| 10 | For example, a young Lebanese person's friends were only those from the same sectarian background. | يَعْني مثلاً الشّابّ اللّبْناني بفِتْرة مِن عُمرو كانوا أَصْدِقائو هنّي فقط اللي عِنْدُن نفس اللّوْن الطائفي. |
| 11 | Like, if they lived in the western part of the region, their friends were mostly Muslims, while those in the eastern part had mostly Christian friends. | يَعْني مثلاً هُوّ ويْن عايش بالمِنْطِقة الغرْبية، فا أَصْدِقائو أكْتر كِلُّن إسْلام، بيْنما الشّابّ العايش بالمِنْطِقة الشّرْقية أصْدِقائو كِلُّن مسيحِيّين. |
| 12 | The goal was... and nobody, for example, had friends from another sect, | كان الهدف... وما كان في حدا مثلاً عِنْدو أَصْدِقاء مِن الطّائِفة التّانية، |
| 13 | because social relationships or mutual visits between different sects were almost non-existent due to the war and because of the feelings of hatred that existed. | لأنّو العلاقات الإِجْتِماعية أَوْ الزِّيارات المُتبادلة بيْن الطّوائِف المِخْتِلْفة كانِت تْكاد تْكون مقطوعة بِسبب الحرِب وبِسبب المشاعر الكراهية اللي كانت موْجودة. |
| 14 | So, the aim of the military service was to break this barrier among the Lebanese youth | فا الهدف مِن خِدْمةْ العلم كان هُوّ كسِر هَيدا الحاجِز عِند الشّباب اللّبْناني |
| 15 | and give them the opportunity to meet, live, and share experiences with each other, to 'break bread' together, so to speak. | وإعْطائْنا الفُرْصة إنّو يْنوْجدوا بمكان يِقْدروا يِتْعرّفوا على بعْضُن ويِقْدروا يْعيشوا مع بعْضُن ويِقْدروا ياكْلوا مِتِل ما بْيْقولوا خِبِز ومِلح مع بعْضُن. |
| 16 | So, the solution was military service. | فا كان الحلّ هُوّ خِدْمةْ العلم . |
| 17 | In military service, I met young men from all over Lebanon. | بخِدْمةْ العلم تْعرّفِت على شباب مِن كِلّ لِبْنان. |
| 18 | There were even some who lived abroad. | وحتّى كان في شباب عايْشين برّاةْ لِبْنان. |
| 19 | However, because they are Lebanese and mandatory military service is required, they came to Lebanon to complete their military service... or fulfill it. | ولكِنْ لأنُّن لِبْنانية وإجْباري يَعْملوا خِدْمةْ العلم فا إجوا على لِبْنان لـ... مِنشان يْقضّوا خِدْمةْ العلم... أَوْ يْنفْذوها. |

| | |
|---|---|
| 20 | تْعَرَّفِت على شباب مِن شْمال لِبْنان، مِن البِقاع، مِن الجْنوب مِن... صُدْقاً، مِن بْشرّي، مِن زْغرْتا، مِن طْرابْلُس، مِن راشيّا الوادي، حتّى مِن ضْيَع مِن أميون ما كِنت إسْمع فيا، |
| 21 | وتْعَرَّفِت على اللّهْجات اللِّبْنانية اللي كِنّا بسّ هيْك نِسْمعا بْنِسْمع الشَّخْص اللي بيْقلِّد عم بيْقولا، |
| 22 | حتّى كان في معْنا شباب أرْمن كمان. |
| 23 | خِلال هَيْدي الفَتْرة أنا... كِنت بعِرْمان بمِنْطِقة إسْما عِرْمان بشْمال لِبْنان. |
| 24 | كانِت أوّل مرّة أنا بْزور هَيْدي المنْطِقة، بتْعرّف علَيْها. |
| 25 | كان المعسْكر بْيوقع مُقابل البحر، وبفتْرةْ الشِّتا يَعْني أنا طْلِعِت بلّشِت الخِدْمة بشهْر واحد ألْفيْن وتْنيْن لشهْر واحد ألْفيْن وتْلاتِة. |
| 26 | عَوّدونا على نوْع مِن الرّوتين... مِن الرّوتين اليَوْمي اللي إلو فايْدة، |
| 27 | مثلاً نوْم السّاعة عشرة الفايْقة السّاعة أرْبعة بتْقوم بْتحلُق دقْنك، بتْلبِّس تْياب الرّياضة بْتوقف بالنْظام، بالمجْموعة اللي إنْتَ فيها، بإنْتِظار الشَّخْص المَسْؤول عن ضابط ليَقوموا وتْبلِّش الرّياضة الصّباحية، |
| 28 | مِن الحركات التِّحْمامِة للسْتْراتْشينْغ للهرْوَلِة للرّكِض بالمعسْكر لحدّ... |
| 29 | مْنرْجع بعْدين مْنِجي مْنغيِّر تْيابْنا مْنِلبُّس تْياب البدْلة العسكرية ومِنْطْلع على التّرْويقة على السّاعة سْتّة، |
| 30 | نِتْروَّق أكل صُحّي بِناسب الوَقِت والطّقس. |
| 31 | بتِرْجع بْتنْزل بْتِتْوَزّع المهام. في عِنْدك مجْموعة بْتِتْوَكّل بتِنْظيف المعسْكر، |
| 32 | عِنْدك مجْموعة بْتِتْوَكّل بمُرافقِة العناصر الأقلّ رُتْبِة لتِنْظيف المكان. |

| | |
|---|---|
| 20 | I met people from North Lebanon, the Bekaa, the South, from... honestly, Bsharri, Zgharta, Tripoli, Rashaya Al Wadi, and even from villages in Amyoun that I had never heard of before. |
| 21 | I got to know the different Lebanese dialects, which we only used to hear impersonated by others. |
| 22 | There were also Armenian youth with us. |
| 23 | During that period, I was in a place called Araman in northern Lebanon. |
| 24 | It was the first time I visited and got to know this area. |
| 25 | The camp was located facing the sea, and during the winter, I started my service in January 2002 and [continued] until January 2003. |
| 26 | They got us used to a kind of routine... a daily routine that was beneficial. |
| 27 | For instance, going to bed at ten o'clock, waking up at four in the morning, getting up to shave, wearing sports clothes, standing in formation with the group you're in, waiting for the officer in charge to come so we could start the morning exercise. |
| 28 | This included warm-up movements, stretching, jogging, and running around the camp until... |
| 29 | Then later, we would come back to change our clothes, put on our military uniforms, and then go for breakfast at 6 am. |
| 30 | We would have a healthy meal suitable for the time and the weather. |
| 31 | Then you go out and get assigned different tasks. You have a group responsible for cleaning the camp, |
| 32 | and you have a group tasked with accompanying lower-ranked personnel to assist in cleaning the area. |

| | | |
|---|---|---|
| 33 | مِن بَعْد إنْتِهاء دَوْرةِ التّنْشِأة اللي بْتِتعرّف فيها على بَعْض العُلوم يَعْني عُلوم غَيْر مُتقدِّمة عُلوم بَسيطة إلا علاقة بالحَياةْ العَسْكرية، | After completing the basic training phase, where you learn various sciences—not advanced ones, but simple knowledge related to military life, |
| 34 | بْترْجع مِن بَعْد الشّهْرين حسب إخْتِصاصك إنْتَ شو دارِس بالجّامْعة بْوَزْعوك على مراكِز عسْكرية تِقْدر تْساعِد العسْكر اللي يْديروا هَيْدي المناصِب. | after the initial two months, depending on your university major, they assign you to military centers where you can assist the soldiers managing those positions. |
| 35 | وأنا بِطبيعةِ... الشّهادةِ... شهادْتي الجّامعية اللي هِيِّ كيمْيا، شْتغلِت بمطرحين، | Because of my... my university degree in Chemistry, I worked in two places: |
| 36 | أوّل مطرح هُوّ مُخْتبر إلو علاقة بمُراقبةِ الجودة، وتاني محلّ هُوّ صَيْدلية عَسْكرية بْساعد بْوَصِف أوْ بْساعِد بِصرْف أدْوية للْعَسْكر وعائلاتُن. | The first place was a laboratory related to quality control, and the second place was a military pharmacy where I assisted in prescribing or dispensing medications to soldiers and their families. |
| 37 | تجْرِبة حِلوةِ. للأسف لْغِت هَيْدي التّجْرِبة بلِبْنان وبْظُنّ لازِم يْعيدوا إحْياء هَيْدي التّجْرِبة بِمفاهيم جْديدة وبْطريقة عَصْرية أكْتر. | It was a wonderful experience. Unfortunately, this experience has been discontinued in Lebanon, and I think it should be revived with new concepts and in a more modern way. |

---

**Answers**

**Main Idea:** d **True or False:** 1. F[10-12] 2. F[17-21] 3. T[23] 4. T[35-36] 5. F[37] **Multiple Choice:** 1. a[7-8] 2. c[14-22] 3. d[7-8, 17-22, 35-36] **Matching:** بَعْد فَترة after some time / فقط just, only / إلو he/it has / بل but rather / عِنْدُن they have / كاد to almost [do] / بِسبب because of / مِنْشان in order to, so that / كِنّا we were / شو what / مِن بَعْد after / في there is/are

# 34 Rita: Lebanese Abroad

## Keywords

| | |
|---|---|
| مَوْضوع topic, subject | برّاةْ لِبْنان outside of Lebanon |
| مجال field | جُذور roots |

## Main Idea

a. Rita focuses on the challenges faced by Lebanese immigrants in adapting to new cultures.
b. Rita talks about the economic contributions of Lebanese expatriates to Lebanon.
c. Rita explores the global presence of Lebanese people and their notable achievements in various fields.
d. Rita talks about her personal experiences as a Lebanese expatriate.

## True or False

1. According to Rita, Lebanese people are concentrated in just a few countries around the world.
2. According to Rita, Lebanese people abroad have had little impact on fields such as politics and literature.
3. Among the notable figures with Lebanese heritage mentioned by Rita are Ralph Nader, Carlos Slim, and Gibran Khalil Gibran.
4. Rita has long been aware of all Lebanese individuals who have gained prominence in various fields globally.
5. Rita mentions Amal Clooney as a source of pride for the Lebanese community due to her legal work in human rights.

## Multiple Choice

1. Which sector did Rita not mention Lebanese people having significant success in?

    a. Politics    b. Literature    c. Technology    d. Beauty

2. Which US Secretary of Defense of Lebanese heritage does Rita mention?

    a. Colin Powell    c. James Mattis

    b. Mark Esper    d. Robert Gates

3. Which artistic field does Rita highlight as having surprising Lebanese influence?

    a. Film and music        c. Fashion design

    b. Painting and sculpture    d. Culinary arts

## Matching

| | |
|---|---|
| وِيْن | about it |
| مِش | among which |
| عَ | like |
| وِيْن ما كان | much, a lot |
| مِتِل | not |
| ما فينا | someone; person |
| مِن بَيْنا | there is/are |
| عنّو | to |
| رح | we can't |
| يَلّي | where |
| في | wherever |
| كْتير | who, which, that |
| حدا | will |

## Text

| | | |
|---|---|---|
| بدّي إحْكي شْوَيّ عن مَوْضوع اللِّبْنانِيّين اللي ساكْنين برّاةْ لِبْنان. | 1 | I want to talk about Lebanese people living outside Lebanon. |
| حسب مِن وِيْن بِتْجيبوا معْلوماتْكُن ومصادِرْكُن، أكيد الأرْقام بْتِتْغيّر شْوَيّ. | 2 | Depending on where you get your information and sources, the numbers might vary. |
| بسّ بِحسب بعْض المصادِر، في تْمْنْطعْشر مِلْيوْن لِبْناني حَوالى العالم، وخمْس وسبْعين بِالْمِيّة مِنُّن ساكْنين برّاةْ لِبْنان. | 3 | But according to some sources, there are eighteen million Lebanese around the world, and seventy-five percent of them live outside Lebanon. |
| يَعْني، تْلات رْباع اللِّبْنانِيّين بِالْعالم مِش ساكْنين بِلِبْنان. | 4 | That means three-quarters of Lebanese worldwide do not live in Lebanon. |
| يِمْكِن مِن هيْك مِنْحِسّ إنّو بسّ نْكون مْسافْرين عَ شي بلد، كِلِّ ما تْطلّعْنا مِنْلاقي لِبْناني، لأنّو مِنْتِشْرين وِيْن ما كان. | 5 | Maybe that's why we feel like we encounter Lebanese people everywhere we go; because we are spread all over. |

| | | |
|---|---|---|
| 6 | Certainly, there are regions in the world with more Lebanese than others. | أكيد، في مناطِق بِالْعالم فيا لِبْنانِيّين أكْتر مِن غَيْرا. |
| 7 | For example, in Latin America, there are many Lebanese. | مثلاً أميرْكا اللّاتينية، كْتير فيا لِبْنانِيّين. |
| 8 | In some US states like Michigan and Massachusetts, there are also many Lebanese. | بعْض الوِلايات بأميرْكا، مِتِل ميشيغِن وماساتْشوسِتْس، كْتير فيْن لِبْنانِيّين. |
| 9 | And, of course, in other places around the world. | ومَطارِح غَيْرا أكيد بِالْعالم. |
| 10 | There's one topic we can't not talk about when talking about Lebanese people abroad. | في مَوْضوع ما فينا ما نِحْكي عنّو بسّ نِحْكي عن اللِّبْنانِيّين برّاةْ لِبْنان. |
| 11 | Those are the achievements Lebanese have made in various fields. | يَلّي هُوّ الإنْجازات اللي أحْرزوه اللِّبْنانِيّين بِمجالات عديدة. |
| 12 | They've achieved great success in many fields, including politics, literature, beauty, wealth, acting, business, | حقّقوا نجاحات كْتير كْبيرة بِمجالات عديدة مِن بَيْنا السِّياسة، الأدب، الجمال، الغِنى، التّمْثيل، الأعْمال. |
| 13 | I mean, in any field one talks about, one finds some prominent Lebanese in it outside of Lebanon. | يَعْني كِلّ مجال واحد بْيِحْكي عنّو بِيلاقي حدا لِبْناني بارِز فيه برّاةْ لِبْنان. |
| 14 | You might know some of the names I'll mention, but some names will surely surprise you. | يِمْكِن بعْض الأسامي اللي رح إذْكِرا بْتِعِرْفُوا بسّ أكيد في أسامي رح تْفاجِئْكُن. |
| 15 | For instance, in politics, did you know that Ralph Nader, who ran for the US presidency several times, has Lebanese roots? | مثلاً إذا مْنِحْكي سِياسِيّاً، هل كِنْتوا عارْفين إنّو رالْف نادِر، يَلّي هُوّ تْرشّح عَ رِئاسِةْ الجُمْهورية الأميرْكية كذا مرّة هُوّ مِن جُذور لِبْنانية؟ |
| 16 | Or Mark Esper, who was the US Secretary of Defense under Trump, also has Lebanese heritage? | أوْ مثلاً مارْك أسْبِر، يَلّي كان وَزير الدِّفاع الأميرْكي تحْت تْرامْب، إنّو كمان عِنْدو جُذور لِبْنانية؟ |
| 17 | I was particularly surprised by Mark Esper, as I wasn't aware of this at all. | أنا كْتير صدمْني مارْك أسْبِر لأنّو ما كِنت عارْفة بِهَيْدا المَوْضوع أبداً. |
| 18 | Even we Lebanese are sometimes surprised by names, not knowing they have any Lebanese roots, but it turns out they have Lebanese roots. | حتّى نِحْنا اللِّبْنانِيّين إيّام مْنِنْصِدِم مِن أسامي، ما مِنْكون عارْفين عِنْدا ولا جِذِر لِبْناني، بْيِطْلع عِنْدُن جُذور لِبْنانية. |
| 19 | In the business sector, there are many Lebanese whose names are globally prominent, like Carlos Slim and many others. | بِقِطاع الأعْمال في كْتير كمان لِبْنانِيّين، أسامينْ يَعْني بِرزِت عالمِيّاً، مِتِل مثلاً كارْلوس سْليم، وغَيْرو كْتير مِن رِجال الأعْمال. |

| | | |
|---|---|---|
| 20 | In literature, surely you've heard of Gibran Khalil Gibran, who spent much of his life and creativity presenting books like "The Prophet," one of the most sold books worldwide. | إذا مِنْطلّع بِمجال الأدب، أكيد سامْعين بِجُبْران خليل جُبْران، يلّي قدّم كْتير مِن حَياتو ومِن إبْداعو للْعالم بِكْتُب مِتِل كْتاب النّبي، يلّي هُوِّ مِن أكْتر الكُتُب يلّي مِنْباعة نِسْخات مِنّا عالميّاً. |
| 21 | In beauty, you've probably heard of Rima Fakih, who won Miss USA in 2010 and has a Lebanese background. | إذا مِنْطلّع بِمجال الجمال مثلاً، أكيد سامْعين بِريما فقيه، يلّي رِبْحِت Miss USA بِالْألْفين وعشْرة يلّي هِيِّ أصْلا لِبْناني. |
| 22 | If we look at other fields, you will find many in science, and as I mentioned, in other fields, | إذا مِنْطلّع بِمجالات أُخْرى، كْتيرة بِتْلاقوا بِالْعُلوم، مِتِل ما ذكرت بِمجالات أُخْرى، |
| 23 | but maybe the most surprising field when I start mentioning names is the artistic field, whether that's in acting or in singing. | بسّ يِمْكِن أكْتر مجال رح يْفاجِئْكُن، بسّ بلِّش إذْكُر أسامي هُوِّ الْمجال الفنّي، إن كان بِالتّمْثيل، إن كان بِالْغِنّي. |
| 24 | Did you know, for instance, that Vince Vaughn, an American actor, has Lebanese roots? | هل مثلاً كِنْتوا عارْفين إنّو فينْس فوْن، الْمُمثِّل الأميرْكاني، عِنْدو جُذور لِبْنانية؟ |
| 25 | Or Keanu Reeves, an American actor, has American, uh... Lebanese roots? | أوْ كِيانو ريفْز، مُمثِّل أميرْكي، عِنْدو جُذور أميرْكية... لِبْنانية؟ |
| 26 | Shakira, Salma Hayek, and Zoë Saldana all have Lebanese heritage. | شاكيرا، سلْمى حايِك، زوي سالْدانا، كِلُّن هَوْدي عِنْدُن جُذور لِبْنانية. |
| 27 | Or maybe you have heard of Danny Thomas, who founded St. Jude, the large hospital specializing in treating children suffering from cancer, who is also of Lebanese origin. | أمّا يِمْكِن سامْعين بِداني توماس، يلّي هُوِّ أسّس سانْت جود الْمِسْتشْفى الكْبيرة يلّي بِتْخصّص بِعِلاج الأطْفال يلّي بيعانوا مِن السّرطان، كمان أصْلو لِبْناني. |
| 28 | But perhaps the one I am happiest that is of Lebanese origin is Amal Clooney, the international lawyer who has worked on many major human rights cases and really achieved great success. | بسّ يِمْكِن أكْتر حدا أنا بِنْبِسِط إنّو أصْلو لِبْناني هُوِّ أمال كْلوني، الْمُحامِية العالمِية اللي شْتغلِت على كْتير قضايا كْبيرة لِحقوق الإنْسان وأحْرزِت عنْجدّ نجاحات كْتير كْبيرة. |
| 29 | As Lebanese, we are very proud of Lebanese or those of Lebanese descent who have achieved great things, like the ones I've mentioned. | نِحْنا كلِبْنانيّين، كْتير مِنْفْتِخِر بِناس لِبْنانيّين أوْ مِن جُذور لِبْنانية، حقّقِت نجاحات كُبْرى، مِتِل يلّي ذكرْتُن، |

| | | |
|---|---|---|
| 30 | I hope hearing about these individuals today encourages you to research and discover other prominent figures with Lebanese roots. | وانْشااللّه يْكون سمعْكُن لهالإشْيا اليوْم شجّعْكُن إنْتو كمان تْروحوا تعمْلوا أبْحاث وتْشوفوا مين غيْر هوْل الأسامي عِنْدُن جُذور لبْنانية . |
| 31 | You might be as surprised by the results as I was. | يمْكِن تِتْفاجئوا مِن النّتايج مِتِل ما أنا تْفاجأت. |

---

## Answers

**Main Idea:** c **True or False:** 1. F[6-9] 2. F[11-14] 3. T[15, 19-20] 4. F[17-18] 5. T[28] **Multiple Choice:** 1. c[12-13, 21] 2. b[16] 3. a[24-26] **Matching:** وين where / مِش not / عَ to / وين ما كان wherever / مِتِل like / ما فينا we can't / في there is/are / كْتير much, a lot / يَلّي who, which, that / رح will / عنّو about it / مِن بَيْنا among which / حدا someone; person

# 35 Mohammad: Personal Growth

## Keywords

إنْطِوائي introverted    طوّر to develop    شتْغِل عَ حالو to work on oneself

## Main Idea

a. Mohammad describes his journey from dealing with depression and introversion to enhancing his social life and overall outlook.
b. Mohammad tells us about his battle with addiction and how finding a supportive community helped him recover.
c. Mohammad details his struggle with procrastination and how adopting time management strategies transformed his productivity and personal satisfaction.
d. Mohammad shares his experience overcoming anger management issues through mindfulness and meditation.

## True or False

1. Mohammad has always been outgoing and sociable throughout his life.
2. Mohammad describes his online interactions through PlayStation as being positive toward his development.
3. Mohammad expresses that nothing lasts forever, including sadness, and encourages positive thinking about the future.
4. Mohammad now considers himself to be extremely sociable and outgoing.
5. Mohammad emphasizes the importance of positive thinking in overcoming his challenges.

## Multiple Choice

1. At what age did Mohammad start experiencing depression and autism symptoms?

    a. Around ten years old
    b. In his late teens
    c. At twenty-two years old
    d. As a young adult

3. What prevented Mohammad from attempting suicide?

    a. The fear of social stigma
    b. The belief that suicide leads to eternal damnation
    c. Medication that improved his mental health
    d. The support from his online friends

3. How does Mohammad currently view his social life?

    a. He still avoids going out completely.

    b. He goes out, has many friends, and appears more normal.

    c. He only interacts with people online.

    d. He is constantly surrounded by people.

## Matching

|  |  |
|---|---|
| بِدون ما | [impersonal] one |
| حتّى لمّا | away from |
| مْنيح | because of |
| مِن وَرا | even though I |
| مْبعّد عن | even when |
| مع إنّي | everything that |
| كِرْمال | for |
| لمُدِّة كْتير طَويلة | for a very long time |
| شو ما كان | thing |
| شي | well |
| شو | what |
| كِلّ اللي | whatever |
| الواحد | without __ing |

## Text

| |  |  |
|---|---|---|
| 1 | بِيمْرُق عَ راس الإنْسان كْتير إشْيا، وكِلّ يوْم وكِلّ شهِر وكِلّ سِنة بْيِتْطوّر ويِتْحسّن، وبيصير يَعْني بيطوّر مِن حالو بِدون ما يْحِسّ. | A lot goes through a person's mind, and every day, month, and year, they develop and improve, and they evolve without even realizing it. |
| 2 | وحتّى لمّا يْكون عم بِشْتِغِل عَ حالو بيلاقي نتيجة، يَعْني حتّى بْيوْم بيلاقي نتيجة إذا شْتغل عَ حالو مْنيح. | Even when working on themselves, they find results, meaning even in a day, if they work well on themselves, they find a result. |
| 3 | أنا حْإحْكيلْكُن اليوْم كيف طوّرِت نفْسي مِن تقْريباً خمْس سْنين لهلّأ. | Today, I'll tell you how I improved myself from about five years ago until now. |

| | | |
|---|---|---|
| 4 | أنا إنْسان إنْطِوائي وخجول، يَعْني عِشِت طوْل حَياتي إنّي ما بْحِبّ العالم مِن وَرا إشْيا كْتيرة. | I am an introverted and shy person, meaning I've spent my life not liking people because of many things. |
| 5 | مِن وَرا تنَمُّر، مِن وَرا صدَمات، مِن ورا مشاكِل نفْسية. | Because of bullying, traumas, psychological problems. |
| 6 | فا وْصِلِت مع المَواضيع إنّي أوْصل لتوحُّد وإكْتِئاب بعُمْر كْتير صْغير، يَعْني يِمْكِن كان عُمْري شي عشر سْنين. | So, I reached a point where I was experiencing autism and depression at a very young age, maybe when I was about ten years old. |
| 7 | كِنِت ضلُّني قاعِد بِالْبيْت عَ الـPlaystation ومْبعّد عن العالم. | I used to just sit at home on the PlayStation and away from the world. |
| 8 | مع إنّي إنْطِوائي وخجول، كِنِت إتْعرّف عَ عالم كْتير على الـPlaystation يَعْني أوْنلاين. | Even though I was introverted and shy, I met a lot of people on PlayStation, I mean online. |
| 9 | نِقْعُد نِلْعب ونِتْسلَّى ونِضْحك ويَعْني عايش حياة تاني كِنِت. | We would play, have fun, laugh, and I was living a different life. |
| 10 | بسّ بْضلُّني بْعيد عن العالم، ما كان بدّي هالشّي. | But I was still away from the world, and I didn't want that. |
| 11 | فا قِلِت بْحاوِل إشْتِغِل عَ حالي. ضلّت ساحْبة معي الإكْتِئاب مِن عُمُر العشْر سْنين للتْنينْ وعِشْرين سِنة، يَعْني مِن كم سِنة هَيْدا الحكي. | So, I tried to work on myself. I kept dragging depression with me from the age of ten to twenty-two years, I mean a few years ago. |
| 12 | دايْماً كان يِخْطُر بْبالي أفْكار عن الإنْتِحار، أفْكار إنّو ما في حلول تِتْلاقى، ما في شي يِنْعمل ما في شي يَعْني يِنْعاش كِرْمالو، | I always thought about suicide, thoughts that there were no solutions, nothing to be done, meaning nothing to live for, |
| 13 | بسّ طبْعاً دايْماً كان يِصُدّْني فِكْرةْ إنّو اللي بْيِنْتِحِر بيفوت عَ النّار، إنّو نِحْنا هوْني بْإخْتِبار هَيْدا الدِّني مِنّا دايْمة لحدا. | but of course, I was always deterred by the thought that those who commit suicide will go to hell, that we are here as a test, and this life is not permanent for anyone. |
| 14 | فا كان يِمْشي مْواضيع شْويّ، وكِنِت عارِف حالي أصْلاً. | Things would go by a bit, and I knew myself. |
| 15 | إذا جرّبِت أنا شي مرّة إنْتِحِر، كِنِت ما كون عم بيحْكيكُن أنا هلّأ بْهَيْدا الـvoice. | If I had ever tried to commit suicide, I wouldn't be talking to you now in this recording. |
| 16 | المُهِمّ ضلّيتني على هالْحالة لمُدّة كْتير طَويلة وأنا داق خِلْقي مِن حالي يَعْني، فا ما حفوت بْتفاصيل كْتير وإطوّشْكُن. | Anyway, I stayed like that for a very long time, and I was fed up with myself, I mean, so I'll skip a lot of details and not bore you. |
| 17 | بسّ الخْلاصة هِيِّ إنّو ما في شي بيدوم، وحتّى الحُزِن ما بيدوم. | But the summary is that nothing lasts, and even sadness doesn't last. |

| |  |  |
|---|---|---|
| 18 | I mean, whatever you're going through, and whatever is troubling you, and whatever dark thoughts you have, like not seeing any future or anything good happening, | يَعْني شو ما كان إنْتو اللي مارّقين فيه، وشو ما كان الشّي اللي مْتعّبكُن، وشو ما كان تِفْكيركُن عتْمة ومِش شايْفين شي يَعْني، ما شايْفين مُسْتقْبل ولا شايْفين شي مْنيح حَيْصير، |
| 19 | all that is just thoughts in your mind. | هَيْدا كِلّو بسّ تِفْكير بِعقْلكُن. |
| 20 | God has planned good things for you in the future, and God willing, everything will be fine. | الله مْخلّالكُم الخيْر لقِدّام، وانْشاالله كِلّ شي حَيْكون تمام. |
| 21 | One must think positively. | الواحد لازِم يْفكّر بإيجابية. |
| 22 | They should sit alone and think, imagine themselves in the future as successful people, | يَعْني يقْعُد بَينو بين حالو هُوّ يْفكّر يِتْخيّل حالو بِالمُسْتقْبل كإنْسان ناجح، |
| 23 | and God willing, God will lead them to it if they strive for it, strive and not just sit idle and depressed, not knowing what to do. | ونشالله الله بيوَصِّل لهَيْدا الشّي إذا بْيِسْعالو... يِسْعى وما يْضلّوا قاعِد ومِكْتئِب وما عارِف شو يَعْمُل. |
| 24 | After all these things that happened to me, now I've become a, well, I won't lie to you, not a sociable person who likes people a lot. | مِن بعْد هالمَواضيع كِلّا اللي صارِت معي، هلّأ، صِرت إنْسان مِش حقلْكُم إجْتِماعي وبْحِبّ العالم كْتير وإقْعُد كذِّب عْليْكُن. |
| 25 | But I'm much better than before. I mean, I go out, come and go, appear normal, and have many friends, thankfully. | بسّ أحْسن بِكْتير مِن قبْل، يَعْني بِنْزل وبْروح بجي وبِضْهر عادي وعِنْدي كْتير رِفْقة الحمْدُلله. |
| 26 | I'm working on myself. | بِشْتِغل عَ حالي. |
| 27 | I know I have time to work on myself and to go out, play, have fun, and make an appearance. | بعْرِف عِنْدي وقْت إشْتغِل فيه عَ حالي وعِنْدي وقِت إنْزل إلْعب فيه وإتْسلّى وإضْهر. |
| 28 | So, one should never... never despair, no matter what life throws at you, turn it into something beneficial for you. | فا الواحد ما... ما يِيْأس أبداً لوْ شو ما كانِت الحَياة عطِتك سْتعْمِلا لشي لصالْحك. |

---

### Answers

**Main Idea:** a **True or False:** 1. F⁴ 2. T⁸⁻⁹ 3. T¹⁷⁻²⁰ 4. F²⁴⁻²⁵ 5. T²¹⁻²³ **Multiple Choice:** 1. a⁶ 2. b¹³ 3. b²⁵⁻²⁷

**Matching:** بِدون ما without / لمّا ___ing / حتّى even when / مْنيح well / مِن وَرا because of / مْبعّد عن away from / شو ما كان whatever / لمُدَّة كْتير طَويلة for a very long time / كِرْمال for / مع إنّي even though I / الواحد one [impersonal] / كِلّ اللي everything that / شو what / شي thing

# 36 Sandy: The Lebanese Music Scene

## Keywords

فنّ art    فِنّان artist    كَوْني since I; being as I am...

## Main Idea

a. Sandy's personal success story as a mainstream artist in Lebanon.
b. The surprising financial prosperity of the Lebanese art scene.
c. Government censorship in the Lebanese art scene.
d. The difficulties faced by alternative artists in Lebanon.

## True or False

1. Sandy's production company is supported by a large corporation or entity.
2. Sandy believes that alternative artists in Lebanon receive adequate opportunities to showcase their talents.
3. Sandy's artistic work mainly deals with commercial themes.
4. Sandy mentions the lack of services and psychological comfort in Lebanon.
5. Sandy is optimistic about the current state of support for alternative art in Lebanon.

## Multiple Choice

1. What is the primary struggle of alternative artists in Lebanon, according to Sandy?

    a. Government censorship
    b. Lack of financial and moral support
    c. Overabundance of mainstream art
    d. Lack of creativity and original ideas

2. Sandy's music is influenced by which of the following factors?

    a. Her religious background
    b. Her love of classical Lebanese music
    c. Her experiences as a single mother and living in a challenging country
    d. *All of the above*

3. Which sectors does Sandy hope to get support from for alternative artists?

    a. Government institutions only
    b. Private investors and cultural event organizers
    c. Mainstream media channels
    d. *None of the above*

# Matching

| | |
|---|---|
| مِنّو | (he/it) is not |
| وَلا | any |
| أَيّ | everyone |
| كِلّ حدن | how much |
| ياريْت | I wish; I hope |
| حدن | in spite of |
| إن كان... أَوْ | nor |
| حيّلا شي | on the other hand |
| بالْمُقابِل | someone |
| قدّيْش | something |
| بِالرّغْمِ مِن | whether... or |

# Text

1. مرْحبا، المَوْضوع يَلّي حابّة اليوْم إحْكي عنّو هُوّ مَوْضوع بِخُصّني شْويّ، لِأَنّو يِمْكِن أنا بِنْتِمي لهيْدي الفِئة مِن المُجْتمع.

   Hello! The topic I want to talk about today is a bit personal to me because I belong to this segment of society.

2. ويَلّي هِنّي كِلّ الفنّانين الموسيقيّي، المُلحّنين، كِلّ حدا خصّو بالفنّ ومش قادِر يوصل لمحلّ، لأنّو البلد عنّا ما كْتير بيْدعمو، لا مادّيّاً ولا معْنويّاً.

   It concerns all the musicians, composers, and anyone involved in the arts who can't make it big because our country doesn't provide much support, neither financially nor morally.

3. نِحْنا مِنْسمّي حالْنا الفنّ البديل، لأنّو الفنّ الرّئيسي هِنّي العالم الكْبيرة والأسامي الكْبيرة، يَلّي مْنعْرفا، يَلّي عِنْدا تمْويل وعِنْدا مين بيْدعما، وعِنْدا مين وَراها بيْدفع عنّا ويْموّلا ويْوَزّعْلا ويِنْتِجْلا ويْسجّلا.

   We call ourselves the alternative art scene because mainstream art is dominated by big names and celebrities, those who have funding and support, people to back them, finance and distribute their work, and produce and record for them.

4. إنّما نِحْنا الصْغار الفنّانين يَلّي ما عنّا دعْم أبداً، عم مِنْكافح إلْنا سْنين.

   But we, the small-time artists who have no support at all, have been struggling for years.

5. أنا واحْدِة مِنُّن. إلي سْنين بْكافح لإقْدر أوْصل.

   I'm one of them. I've been struggling for years to make it.

|  |  |  |
|---|---|---|
| 6 | يِمْكِن أيْه عِنْدي شِرْكِة تِسْجيل وإنْتاج وتَوْزيع، بسّ كَوْني أنا ما عِنْدي جَماهير كْبيرة بَعْد كَوْني بْعَد صْغيرة. | Maybe yes, I have a recording, production, and distribution company, but since I don't have a large audience yet, I'm still considered small. |
| 7 | كَوْنو الفنّ يَللّي بْقدّمو منّو فنّ ساخِر وَلا تِجاري وَلا بيْتِعاطى أمور وَمَواضيع سْخيفِة وقُصَص ما إلا صِلة بالْواقِع أوْ باللّي عم نْعيشو اليَوْم. | Since the art that I present is not commercial or trivial, nor does it deal with silly matters or stories that have no connection to reality or what we are experiencing today. |
| 8 | كَوْني بِنْت عُمْري أرْبَعة وتْلاتين سِنِة، عايْشِة فتْرة ما بَعْد الحرْب اللّبْنانية وأكيد عِنْدي تداعِيات ومشاكِل نفْسية. | As a 34-year-old woman who has lived through the post-Lebanese war era, I certainly have psychological repercussions and problems. |
| 9 | كَوْني كَمان إمّ عَزْبا وكَوْن البلد يَللّي أنا عايْشِة فيه منّو مقدّمْلي أيّ... أيّ خدمات أوْ أيّ راحة نفْسية. | Being a single mother and living in a country that does not provide any services or psychological comfort. |
| 10 | أكيد هَيْدا الشّي كِلّو حَيْنِعكِس بالْموسيقى يَللّي عم جرّب أعْمَلا، كَوْني أنا بْغنّي، بْلحّن وبِكْتُب الموسيقى تبعي. | Of course, all of this is reflected in the music I am trying to create, as I sing, compose, and write my own music. |
| 11 | أيْه عِنْدي شِرْكِة إنْتاج، بسّ هالشّرْكِة الإنْتاج تابْعة لْشَخْص أوْ شَخْصين عم يِدْفعوا ويدْعموا مِن مُصْرِيّاتُن هِنّي، يَللّي عم بيْطلْعُوا كَمان مِن شِغِلْن ومِن تعبُن ومِن شقاهُن. | Yes, I do have a production company, but this production company is supported by one or two individuals who are funding and supporting it with their own resources, which also come from their hard work and effort. |
| 12 | بِتْمنّى تْكون هَيْدي صرْخة لِكِلّ حدا بيآمِن بالْفنّ البديل وبيآمِن بِكِلّ شَخْص عم يْجرّب يَعْطي مِن قلْبو، إن كان بالْموسيقى وَلا بالرّسْم وَلا بالرّقْص وَلا بالكِتيبة وَلا بالإنْتاج الموسيقي وَلا بأيّ فِئة بِتْخِصّ الفنّ البديل. | I hope this is a cry out to everyone who believes in alternative art and supports every person who tries to give from their heart, whether it's in music, painting, dancing, writing, music production, or any aspect of alternative art. |
| 13 | عم بِتْجرِّب تعْطي وما عم تِقْدر تْلاقي الدّعْم أوْ أيّ مْساعِدة بالْمُقابِل. | We are trying to give but can't find the support or assistance in return. |
| 14 | هَيْدي صرْخة مِنّي ومِن كِلّ حدن عم بيعيش نفس المرْحلة مِتْلي. | This is a cry from me and from everyone who is experiencing the same phase as I am. |
| 15 | ياريْت مِنْقْدر ناخُد فُرْصة أكْبر، حدن يِقْدر يِجي ويدْعمْنا إن كان مادّيّاً أوْ معْنَوِيّاً، أوْ يِمْكِن يَعْطينا الفُرْصة إنّو نْفرْجي حالْنا، | I wish we could get a bigger opportunity, that someone could come and support us either financially or morally, or maybe give us a chance to show ourselves, |

| | |
|---|---|
| 16 | to go abroad and be able to record in big studios and have the opportunity to show off. |
| | نِطْلع لبرّا نِقْدر نْسجِّل بِسْتوديوات كْبيرة، نِقْدر نْفرْجي. |
| 17 | We're not just asking for financial support or money. |
| | مِش عم نِطْلُب الدّعْم المادّي أوْ المصاري بسّ. |
| 18 | Of course, it helps, but also, if someone could come to us and say, |
| | لأ هوْلي أكيد بْيْفيدوا بسّ كمان إذا إجا حدا قلْنا: |
| 19 | "We're having an exhibition, a music concert, or, I don't know, a festival, and we would like you to come perform or display Lebanese talents," |
| | "والله نحْنا عنّا معْرض عنّا حفل موسيقي عنّا ما بعْرف مهْرجان وحابّين إنْكُن تجوا تِرقْصوا أوْ نْفرْجي المواهِب اللّبْنانية"، |
| 20 | it's something that could really benefit us. |
| | حيّلا شي بْيِقْدر يْفيدْنا. |
| 21 | I hope this can be a cry for those who can't raise their voice, to deliver this voice and show and try to reflect what we have. |
| | ياريْت تْكون هيْدي صرْخة لَيَلّي ما عم بْيِقْدر يطلِّع صوْتو، يْوَصِّل هيْدا الصوْت ويْفرْجي ويْجرِّب يِعْكِس نحْنا شو عنّا. |
| 22 | On the other hand, it reflects our situation and how incapable this country is of helping us, even providing a mere one percent of what we are giving to this country. |
| | وبِالْمُقابِل شو الوضع يلّي عنّا وقدّيْش هيْدي الدّوْلة عاجْزة عَ إنّا تْساعدْنا وتعْطينا عَ القليلة واحد بِالْميّة مِن يلّي نحْنا عم نعْطي لهالْبلد. |
| 23 | Despite everything, we remain steadfast and stay because we believe in it. |
| | بِالرّغِم مِن كلّ شي صامْدين وباقْيين، لأنّو مِنّآمِن فيه. |

---

Answers

**Main Idea:** d **True or False:** 1. F[11] 2. F[15-16] 3. F[7] 4. T[9] 5. F[12-13, 22] **Multiple Choice:** 1. b[2-4] 2. c[8-10] 3. b[19] **Matching:** منّو (he/it) is not / ولا nor / أيّ any / كلّ حدن everyone / ياريْت I wish; I hope / حدن someone / قدّيْش how much / بِالْمُقابِل on the other hand / حيّلا شي something / إن كان... أوْ whether... or / بِالرّغِم مِن in spite of

# lingualism

*Visit our website for information on current and upcoming titles, free excerpts, and language learning resources.*

# www.lingualism.com

www.ingramcontent.com/pod-product-compliance
Lightning Source LLC
Chambersburg PA
CBHW081429070526
44586CB00020B/2531